ROUGH WATER

STORIES OF SURVIVAL FROM THE SEA

EDITED BY CLINT WILLIS
FOREWORD BY TONY BULLIMORE

WEST LOTHIAN
COUNCIL
LIBRARY SERVICES

£2

D0417659

MAINSTREAM
PUBLISHING

EDINBURGH AND LONDON

910.45

copyright © 1999 by Clint Willis
Introductions copyright © 1999 by Clint Willis
All rights reserved

First published in Great Britain in 1999 by
MAINSTREAM PUBLISHING COMPANY (EDINBURGH) LTD
7 Albany Street
Edinburgh EH1 3UG

ISBN 1 84018 263 6

First published in the United States by
Balliett & Fitzgerald Inc.
66 West Broadway, Suite 602
New York, NY 10007
and
Thunder's Mouth Press
841 Broadway, 4th Floor
New York, NY 10003

No part of this book may be reproduced or transmitted in any form or
by any means without written permission from the publisher, except
by a reviewer who wishes to quote brief passages in connection with a
review written for insertion in a newspaper, magazine or broadcast

A catalogue record for this book is available from the British Library

Book design: Sue Canavan
Frontispiece photo: storm waves © Peter McGowan/Stock Newport
Printed and bound in Great Britain by Biddles Ltd

contents

For
Charles Perry Willis
a Navy man, a gentleman, and a good reader

and

Elizabeth Faison Cooper Willis
a New Orleans girl, a good singer, and a good sport

Foreword

L ike many of those who have written the incredible stories you are
about to read, I have sailed the oceans of the world, competing in
some of the great races, and have experienced the awesome
destructive ferocity of the sea.

I have been to the Southern Ocean and been swilled around like
dirty laundry in the devil's washing-machine by the relentless pounding of wave after wave. I have also experienced, during some of the
most dramatic moments afloat, nature at its most stunningly beautiful.
It's incredible that many accounts of survival against the odds also
include vivid descriptions of fish, birds, stars, colourful skies and isolated landscapes that few people ever get to see. There's a great feeling
of privilege in battling with the seas and being rewarded with unique
sights and experiences. It's also salutary that adventurers facing their
doom when something goes wrong become lyrical about their loved
ones left behind on dry land. Most of us can only ever put to sea

because we have the support of special people back on *terra firma*.

I have great empathy with every story told here, but some are more personal to me than others. I was with Steve Callahan when he came back from his incredible ordeal, for example. Just imagine seventy-six days adrift in an inflatable boat the length of your own body with nothing to eat but raw fish. Surviving that length of time takes a very special person.

I wonder if Steve would ever have gone to sea again had I not asked him to sail my yacht *City of Birmingham* from Newport, Rhode Island, to Quebec ready for her next race. I had just completed the OSTAR (Observer Single-Handed Transatlantic Race) and was delighted when Steve and his wife Kathy eagerly accepted my invitation to make the delivery. Whatever your ordeal, and his was one of the most extreme ever survived, the sea usually remains an impossible magnet to resist.

Sir Robin Knox-Johnston is undoubtedly one of the greatest mariners of my generation. He was the first person to sail single-handed non-stop around the world, and the dramas he recounts aboard *Suhaili* make compulsive reading. Suffering knockdowns and serious equipment failure, he seems to have kept himself going whatever the conditions with plenty of coffee, and in the end completed one of mankind's greatest ever adventures.

It's tragic but, I suppose, inevitable that sometimes the sea will claim its victims for good. The romanticised and fictionalised stories about the sinking of the *Titanic* pale when you read the chillingly factual account told by a young man who was in a lifeboat that had to glide gently away from his drowning shipmates. From more recent times, I guarantee you will be haunted by the story of five young Americans adrift in a life raft after their yacht was lost in a sudden storm. Imagine the anguish of the remaining four when one of their number went mad through drinking sea water and slipped to his death from the back of the boat.

All the stories here are a reminder that the sea will always yield cracking yarns. Whether you are a romatic dreamer or serious seafarer, whether you venture out to sea yourself or look and wonder at the crashing waves from a holiday clifftop, you will appreciate the mixture of superhuman endeavour and good fortune that enabled these sailors to live to tell their tales.

I love the ocean and have been pitting my wits against it for thirty years. I've had some pretty close calls but ultimately we mariners survive because we have a deep respect for the sea and know that we can never tame it. When I next set sail I know that it will challenge me, it'll throw everything it can at me and it will try again to crush me with its power, but I have to be out there with it. Even though I know what it's like and have stared death in the face on more than one occasion, there's nothing like coming back and recounting your adventure and hearing other people's. When I was rescued by the Australian Navy from the hostile, icy waters of the Southern Ocean, everyone wanted to hear my story, but I'm just as keen to hear and read other peoples fantastic yarns. And so it is with this book. Each story is different but they are all a great testimony to the indomitable human spirit of adventure that will never be quelled, even by the cruel sea.

— *Tony Bullimore*

Introduction

I have cherished a healthy fear of the sea since I was three years old, when my brother and sister warned me that crabs would pinch my toes if I waded even a few feet into the shallows of the Gulf of Mexico. It turns out that crabs are the least of it.

So much happens to people who go to sea. A friend took his little boy and girl wading—not swimming, just wading—in Mexico thirty years ago. The undertow caught the children and my friend swam after them. They clung to him, and his strength was almost gone before a village fishing boat loomed up in the fog and rescued all three. A neighbor took his two sons out in a fishing skiff without life jackets; a storm blew up and the boat flipped and one boy drowned. My father once turned a corner in a battleship and came upon a room filled almost to overflowing with bodies of the dead; the ship was taking part in one of the island invasions of the Pacific War. Another friend bent in ankle-deep surf on a Hawaiian island to examine things growing on an enormous piece of driftwood; a ripple in the tide shifted the log so that it rolled onto his leg. He required a rescue and medical attention at a remote clinic. "Ah," said the doctor, when my friend staggered in with his wounds and his story. "The cruel sea."

The sea is not cruel, but it sometimes is without mercy. Once you leave the shore, you leave behind a certain freedom; you must play by the sea's rules. Explorer Ernest Shackleton and his men, exhausted from their trials in Antarctica, and within sight of shore where they hope to find safety and warmth, cannot land: The sea will not permit it. Search-and-rescue pilots wish to save two sailors whose boat is sinking in a huge storm off New Zealand; the waves are too big for them. An amateur yachtsman makes a series of simple mistakes in judgment and seamanship in the Azores, and his family's life changes. A young man sits in a lifeboat and hears the cries of other people dying in the water; there is nothing to be done. Five incompetent—or perhaps just incautious—young sailors lose their boat, and sharks eat two of them; a third dies from blood poisoning.

Many of the characters, real and invented (two of the sixteen pieces included here are fiction), who populate this anthology do manage to wring a kind of mercy from the sea. They discover that, godlike, the sea sometimes helps those who help themselves. Steven Callahan builds a still and a speargun to stay alive on his raft for seventy-six days; he remains cheerfully reflective through much of his ordeal. Robin Knox-Johnston, utterly alone among the enormous seas of the Roaring Forties, endures a knock down—his boat rolls so that the mast and sail enter the water—and scrambles on deck in the dark to make what repairs he can. The rest must wait for morning, so he dives below to cook porridge; that and a mug of coffee and a cigarette leave him feeling, in his words, "quite happy" (his mood holds until he spills a bottle of brandy— two weeks' supply). After surviving an almost unspeakably bloody engagement between an American warship and a British warship, young Samuel Leech of the Royal Navy holds his Swedish messmate down while a doctor cuts off the man's leg; Leech then moves on to comfort a boy whose friend has been killed.

Some people in this book go to sea as travelers or to fight. Others go for commerce, still others for sport or adventure or exploration. Most find what they're looking for; some find more. A man I know spent four years at sea half a century ago; he says no two sunsets during all of that time were alike. Perhaps you could say the same of sunsets on land—but at sea one may be more likely to notice the differences, along with much else.

The literature of the sea is vast, but not nearly so vast as the sea itself. The sea seems truly boundless in the stories included here; the men and women are sharply bounded by their emotions and their knowledge. The thought is hardly original, but it's worth repeating every so often: We are astonishingly small and weak, ridiculously puny, in relation to the waters of the Earth.

That's a terrifying reality when the sea has you in its grip, out of sight of land, far from the help you must have or die. Of course, most of us are aware of the sea's power and our own frailty only as an idea— when, say, we take a sailboat out into a sheltered harbor with a friend who knows what he's doing. Or even when we walk or drive to the beach and wade a few inches into the water.

I see the sea every day, and I'm still afraid of it. But that's fine; it feels natural. Racked up in bed with these stories, listening for the foghorn off Cape Elizabeth, it's good to know for certain that I'm on land for the moment and that the sea, while not cruel, is nevertheless stronger than I'll ever be.

—*Clint Willis*

from Shackleton's Boat Journey
by F. A. Worsley

When their ship was crushed by ice during a 1914 voyage to Antarctica, a party of 28 men fended off death by starvation and exposure for more than five months. Expedition leader Sir Ernest Shackleton, with ship's captain F. A. Worsley (b. 1872; d. 1943) and four other men, went for help. The six men crossed 800 miles of the world's roughest water in a small boat, sighting remote South Georgia Island after 14 days. Then their luck almost ran out.

Our eleventh day was splendid—a day's grace. Moderate southeast breezes. Blue sky and passing clouds. The sea was moderate, and the great long westerly swell went shouldering lazily across us. We only shipped an occasional small sea, and, again hanging out our gear, got it into a pleasantly moderate state of dampness. We felt very uppish indeed that night, when we crawled into our sleeping bags and thought with pity of our unfortunate pals on Elephant Island, though they were probably pitying us at that moment.

The day before I had taken observations of the sun, cuddling the mast with one arm and swinging fore and aft round the mast, sextant and all. This day I found the best way was, sitting on the deck, to jam one foot between the mast and halyards, the other against the shroud, and catch the sun when the boat leaped her highest on the crest of a sea, allowing the "height of eye" accordingly. Position 55°31'S, 44°43'W, run N36°E fifty-two miles; total 496.

From my navigation book: "In assisting with the 'Primus' I burn my fingers on the aluminium rest for the cooker. My subsequent antics with the crumpled up thing that now bears a faint resemblance to a lady's hat that I am endeavouring to trim, sends everyone into yells of laughter, in which, after a while, I cannot help joining too." This was quite the heartiest laugh we had on the passage, helped, no doubt, by the two good days we had enjoyed. We had one other good laugh, but I cannot now remember what it was about.

The twelfth day a southeast breeze blew strong on the starboard beam. It was clear weather, but overcast and squally, with a lumpy sea and southwest swell. We shipped seas. Everything was wet through again.

Our plug tobacco had gradually disintegrated and washed apart into its original leaves, which were carried by the water under and to and fro through the ballast. Sometimes, with the aid of reindeer hair, they choked the pump. Sea-sodden pieces were salvaged by the seamen, and, while Crean and I were operating the "Primus," laid on the crumpled rest previously mentioned to be dried or scorched.

After meals the leaves that had not found their way into the hoosh were torn up, shredded and laboriously rolled with toilet paper into a cigarette. Macarty or Vincent then performed prodigies of drawing at it, and when at a dull glow handed it, as a special treat, to Sir Ernest, who, not liking to hurt anyone's feelings, took it gingerly, puffed away for a minute and, when the donor's back was turned, slyly handed it to Crean, who puffed valiantly for a while. It was often too strong even for him, and so by degrees found its way back to the maker, who finished it with gusto.

From the ceaseless cold and soaking we suffered much bodily inconvenience. The constant chafing of wet clothes had also made our thighs sore and inflamed. One thing we were spared, that was small lodgers—too wet and cold for them.

That day was the *James Caird*'s biggest twenty-four hours' run, N50°E ninety-six miles; but being by dead reckoning it may have been a little less or a little more. Wallis Island, at the west end of

South Georgia, bore N80°E 155 miles. It sounded quite close to us. Our position was 54°30'S, 42°36'W.

The thirteenth day was also clear but overcast, with a north by west gale and a heavy, lumpy sea that increased so much after noon that we were forced to heave to with the reefed jib on the mainmast. Since leaving Elephant Island I had only been able to get the sun four times, two of these being mere snaps or guesses through slight rifts in the clouds.

Our hands had become awful objects to look upon. Crean's and mine, in addition to being almost black with grime, blubber, and soot, were ornamented with recent frostbites, also burns from the "Primus." Each successive frostbite on a finger was marked by a ring where the skin had peeled up to, so that we could count our frostbites by the rings, after the method of a woodman telling the age of a tree.

From the day after leaving Elephant Island we had been accompanied at intervals by albatross, the stateliest bird in flight in the world, and mollyhawks, a smaller species of albatross. These birds, peculiar to the Southern Ocean, are only seen as far south as the edge of the pack ice. Their northern limit is 30°S, though I once saw both a few miles within the tropics to the south of St. Helena, following the cool current. The albatross is sometimes divided into two species, the Wandering and the Royal, the latter slightly larger, though it is possibly only an older bird of the same species. Their usual spread of wings from tip to tip is about eleven feet. I have measured a Royal fourteen feet across, and there is one in the Adelaide Museum that is given as sixteen feet! This gives them the largest span of wing of any bird in the world.

Awkward on the land, ludicrous when struggling to rise from a smooth sea, the albatross is most graceful and stately on the wing. He sweeps before the gale with a mighty rush, then, turning sharply, lets the wind strike his underside, soars almost perpendicularly, and again turns with the wind, coming down in a long, symmetrical swoop, carelessly lifting a few inches to clear the top of a breaking sea, while conforming his flight to the surface of the ridges and hollows. He is a noble sight when the white cross of his back, shoulders, neck, and rump shows startlingly against the heavy black of an advancing squall.

Never seeming to rest, week after week, he follows the sailing ship; day after day he followed our boat. His poetic motion fascinated us; the ease with which he swept the miles aside filled us with envy. He could, with a southwest gale, have made our whole journey in ten hours.

In some of the few fine watches we had, Crean made noises at the helm that, we surmised, represented "The Wearin' o' the Green." Another series of sounds, however, completely baffled us.

I sang—Macarty thought it was a recitation—that classic:

> She licked him, she kicked him,
> She wouldn't let him be;
> She welted him, and belted him,
> Until he couldn't see.

> But Macarty wasn't hearty;
> Now she's got a different party.
> She might have licked Macarty,
> But she can't lick me.

The last part triumphantly to Macarty, but I doubt if he believed it. Then I sang "We're Bound for the Rio Grande." No one complained. It's astonishing how long-suffering people become on a trip like this.

The fourteenth day. After being hove to for twelve hours, we again carried on for the land. It was blowing a moderate north-northwest gale with a high northerly sea. Clear till dawn, it then clouded over with fog banks.

Making the land, it was most important to get "sights" for position, but the conditions for observing the sun were most unfavourable. It was misty, the boat was jumping like a flea, shipping seas fore and aft, and there was no "limb" to the sun, so I had to observe the centre by guesswork. Astronomically, the limb is the edge of sun or moon. If blurred by cloud or fog, it cannot be accurately "brought down" to the horizon. The centre is the spot required, so when the limb is too blurred you bring the centre of the bright spot behind the clouds down to the horizon. By practice, and taking a series of "sights," you can obtain an average that has no bigger error than one minute of arc.

At 9:45 a.m. the sun's limb was clear, but it was so misty that I kept low in the boat to bring the horizon closer, and so a little clearer. The lateness of the hour, and the misty horizon, made a poor observation for longitude. At noon the sun's limb was blurred by a thick haze, so I observed the centre for latitude. Error in latitude throws the longitude out, more so when the latter is observed, as now, too near noon. I told Sir Ernest that I could not be sure of our position to ten miles, so he would not agree to my trying to weather the northwest end of South Georgia, for fear of missing it. We then steered a little more easterly, to make a landfall on the west coast.*

In some respects our condition had become worse. The last two days we had only brackish water from the stove-in "breaker" to drink. This seemed to add to our thirst. We dipped it through the bunghole, with the six-inch by one-inch tube provided for the purpose, and strained it with a piece of medicated gauze, to free it of sediment, dirt, and reindeer hair. One gill a man a day was all that could be spared. The hot milk at night was stopped and hoosh was only made twice daily.

I think the others all suffered badly from thirst; for some reason it did not trouble me so much, though I would have liked a few hot toddies or a jug of cocoa. The situation had grown critical. If we had been driven off the land, or had not seen any ice, we should have been done for, unless we could have killed sea birds for their blood.

When short of water, keeping men wet with sea water compensates to a large extent. This, I think, applies to a normal or hot climate, where, the pores being open, the skin can "drink." We were wet all the time, but it did not appear to reduce our thirst, probably because the cold closed our pores.

Just before dark, eighty miles offshore, we saw a piece of kelp. We joyfully hailed it as a sign of nearness to the land, though it may have

---

* The whaling stations of South Georgia were located on the northeast coast. Shackleton decided to make for the uninhabited southwest coast rather than risk missing the island entirely because of poor visibility, the prevailing westerlies, and the ten-mile error factor.

been borne by the current from the Shag Rocks—the mythical Aurora Islands to the westward.

All night we steered east-northeast, with a strong north-northwest breeze, recklessly burning inches of our precious candle. The seas came fast and merrily over us as usual, but we had a happy feeling that our worst troubles were over; we were nearly there.

At dawn on the fifteenth day, May 8, we saw some pieces of seaweed. Cape pigeons, albatross, mollyhawks, and the bobtailed birds grew numerous.

I looked anxiously for the sun. My navigation had been, perforce, so extraordinarily crude that a good landfall could hardly be looked for. The sky was overcast, and the weather misty and foggy, with a few clear intervals. Cross swells, and a heavy, confused, lumpy sea, made us wetter than usual, but a subdued joy and a species of quiet excitement held us, for we were making the land, and even hoped by dark to be on good solid earth once more, with beautiful clean water gurgling down our parched throats. We talked of how soon we should be at the whaling stations, with clean, dry clothes, and clean, dry beds to sleep in. Poor fools! We didn't know.

Fifteen miles offshore we saw the first shag. The sight of these birds is a guarantee that you are within fifteen miles of the land, as they hardly ever venture farther out.

By noon the fog had cleared, but heavy, ragged, low clouds were driving hard across from west-northwest, and still we had not sighted land.

Misty squalls at times obscured the view. Several patches of kelp were seen; and then, half an hour past noon, Macarty raised the cheerful cry, "Land ho!" There, right ahead, through a rift in the flying scud, our glad but salt-blurred eyes saw a towering black crag, with a lacework of snow around its flanks. One glimpse, and it was hidden again. We looked at each other with cheerful, foolish grins. The thoughts uppermost were: "We've done it. We'll get a drink tonight. In a week we'll get them off Elephant Island."

The land, Cape Demidov, the northern headland of King Haakon Sound, was ten miles distant when sighted. Wonderful to say, the landfall was quite correct, though we were a little astern through imperfect rating of my chronometer at Elephant Island.

We had been exactly fourteen days on the passage from land to land.

An hour later the coast was visible to port and starboard. A desolate, forbidding coast, but that did not trouble us much.

As we drew inshore we passed close north of an area of huge "blind" rollers on an uncharted shoal. Norsemen call them "blinders." Ahead of us, and to the south, sudden great spouts of white and terrific roaring combers showed where the battle raged between the wild westerly swell and uncharted reefs off the coast.

By 3 p.m. we could see small patches of green and areas of yellow-brown tussock showing through the snow on Cape Demidov.

Sir Ernest considered it too dangerous to stand on when I told him King Haakon Sound was right ahead and Wilson Harbour to the north. The former lies open to the west, and it would have been madness to land, in the dark, with a heavy sea, on a beach we had never seen and which had never been properly charted.

Wilson Harbour would have been good, but it was to wind'ard, and against the heavy sea we could not make it.

After a fierce, stormy-looking sunset the wind hauled to west-south-west and blew a hard gale with rain, snow, sleet, and hail to give a bitter edge to our disappointment.

We stood off on the starboard tack till midnight, then hove to, eighteen miles offshore.

The heavy westerly swell increased. All night the *Caird* fell about in a very dangerous, lumpy, and confused sea, that seemed to run in on us from all directions, so that we sometimes shipped two seas over from opposite sides at the same time.

All night, even when hove to, with the reefed jib on the main, we had to bale and pump at very frequent intervals. It seemed to me that she was leaking badly besides shipping seas overall.

At daybreak on May 9 we were wallowing in a terribly heavy cross sea, with a mountainous westerly swell setting us in on the coast before the furious westerly gale then raging. We felt none too easy in our minds, for we knew the current was aiding the wind and sea in forcing us towards destruction.

All day we were stormed at in turns by rain, hail, sleet, and snow, and half the time our view was obscured by thick, driving, misty squalls that whipped the sea into lines of yeasty foam.

By noon the gale had risen to hurricane force, hauled to southwest, and was driving us, harder than ever, straight for that ironbound coast. We thought but did not say those words, so fateful to the seaman, "a lee shore."

Each time we were lifted high on a towering swell we anxiously searched the horizon to leeward for the break of an unknown reef or the dreaded coast. "Sea room, sea room, or a change of wind," was our mental prayer.

Dead reckoning was of slight use to give us our position in this hurricane, for the currents and tides on this coast, though fast and dangerous, are still unrecorded. All we knew was we were setting onshore.

We remained hove to till 2 p.m., when through a sudden rift in the storm-driven clouds we saw two high, jagged crags and a line of precipitous cliffs and glacier fronts on our lee quarter. We were being literally blown onshore—in the most dangerous and unknown part of the coast—the stretch between King Haakon Sound and Annenkov Island.

As we drove inshore it seemed that only three or four of the giant deep-sea swells separated us from the cliffs of destruction—coast of death.

If we could have appreciated it, a magnificent, awe-inspiring scene lay before us.

The sky all torn, flying scud—the sea to wind'ard like surf on a shallow coast—one great roaring line of breaking seas behind another, till lost in spume, spindrift, and the fierce squalls that were feeding the seas. Mist from their flying tops cut off by the wind filled the great hollows between the swells. The ocean was everywhere covered by a gauzy tracery of foam with lines of yeasty froth, save where boiling white masses of breaking seas had left their mark on an acre of the surface.

On each sea the boat swept upward till she heeled before the droning fury of the hurricane, then fell staggering into the hollow, almost becalmed. Each sea, as it swept us closer in, galloped madly, with increasing fury, for the opposing cliffs, glaciers, and rocky points. It seemed but a few moments till it was thundering on the coast beneath icy uplands, great snow-clad peaks, and cloud-piercing crags.

It was the most awe-inspiring and dangerous position any of us had ever been in. It looked as though we were doomed—past the skill of man to save.

With infinite difficulty and danger of being washed overboard we got the reefed jib off the main, set it for'ard, set reefed lug and mizen, and with these large handkerchiefs endeavoured to claw offshore, praying to Heaven that the mast would stand it.

She gathered way, then crash! she struck an onrushing sea that swept her fore and aft even to the mastheads. While all baled and pumped for dear life, she seemed to stop, then again charged a galloping wall, of water, slam! like striking a stone wall with such force that the bow planks opened and lines of water spurted in from every seam, as she halted, trembling, and then leaped forward again. The strains, shocks, and blows were tremendous, threatening every minute to start her planking, while the bow seams opened and closed on every sea. Good boat! but how she stood it was a miracle of God's mercy.

While one steered, three worked the pump, one baled with the two-gallon hoosh pot, and the sixth stood by to relieve one of the others. Half the time he assisted with the small baler, and when opportunity offered, passed out a small lump of hoosh or some sea-damped lumps of sugar. Every hour we changed round to reduce fatigue.

As we looked at that hellish rock-bound coast, with its roaring breakers, we wondered, impersonally, at which spot our end was to come.

The thoughts of the others I did not know—mine were regret for having brought my diary and annoyance that no one would ever know we had got so far. At intervals we lied, saying, "I think she'll clear it."

For three hours, our thirst almost forgotten, we looked Death square in the eye. It was not so much terrifying as chilling, especially in conjunction with the ceaseless rush of breaking seas over us.

Just then the land parallel to our course, and onto which we were being driven, receded slightly to the eastward, giving us a little more sea room.

Then just as it seemed we might draw clear, a new danger threatened. The mountain peak of Annenkov Island loomed menacingly close on the lee bow. We headed to wind'ard of it, but leeway and the heavy sea appeared to be carrying us on to its western point. We could have kept away and gone to leeward of it, but we dared not, with darkness coming on; besides the danger of the coast we were clearing, an eight-mile-long reef was marked on the chart, between Annenkov and South Georgia. We caught glimpses of it and others not charted and held on to wind'ard. Our chart, imperfect at best, was almost illegible from sea stains, and so was but a doubtful guide.

Darkness settled on six men driving a boat slamming at the seas and steadily baling death overboard. The pale snow-capped peak gleamed spectrally aloft, resting on black shades of cliffs and rocks, fringed by a roaring line of foaming breakers—white horses of the hurricane, whose pounding hooves we felt, in imagination, smashing our frail craft.

We peered under the clew of the sail and said encouragingly to each other, "She'll do it," even when we felt it most impossible. The island came so close that we had to crane our necks to look up at the peak. At one time we were almost in the yeasty backwash of the surf; I believe that some eddy of the tide or current drove us clear.

Foot by foot we staggered and lurched drunkenly past the ravening black fangs of the rocky point. The moments became so tense that we feared even to speak—just held our breath or baled harder.

By 9 p.m. we knew we were safe. High, almost overhead it seemed, the great peak loomed mysteriously through the darkness. Right abeam, long pale fingers from the surf reached back—threatening but impotent—no longer did we fear them; every minute the clamorous roar on the rocky point became more faint with distance on the lee quarter.

Strangely, as soon as the worst danger was passed, the hurricane decreased rapidly. Half an hour later the wind came ahead from south-southwest.

We wore her round before the wind and stood back northwest, taking care to pass well to wind'ard of our enemy.

For nine hours we had fought at its height a hurricane so fierce that, as we heard later, a 500-ton steamer from Buenos Ayres to South Georgia had foundered in it with all hands, while we, by the grace of God, had pulled through in a twenty-two-foot boat. I doubt if any of us had ever experienced a fiercer blow than that from noon to 9 p.m.

After the boat was freed of water, the watch could handle her and keep her afloat. At midnight three men crawled below for three and a half hours' sleep. The other three got their sleep in the morning watch before sunrise. Now we had time to realize how bad our thirst was. The water finished, our mouths and tongues were so dry and swollen that we could only chew a few morsels of food.

At daybreak, all reefs shaken out, the *Caird* was doing her best to get us to a drink and the shelter of the nearest good bay to the north, before another gale came on. The wind backed to northwest and was falling, so we had to make for King Haakon Sound, the entrance to which lay nine miles ahead.

The sun shone at intervals on the snow-clad land, and indigo blue majestic rollers that topped up on the shoals, spouted white beacon warnings on the reefs, and hurled their loud shouting cohorts on the black spears of the rocky headlands. The ebb and flow of their strife could be heard five miles offshore.

Quoting from my navigation book: "All very thirsty and badly in need of sleep. Some of our people, in fact, seem just about played out. Macarty, Vincent, Crean, and I take turns at the two oars, sitting up on the deck trying to pull into the bay."

Breakfast was a sorry jest. We chewed, and with difficulty swallowed, a lump of hoosh the size of a hen's egg. Crean, crawling from his sleeping bag under the thwart, struck it with his shoulder. The pin that held the mast clamp in place must have worked upwards during the hurricane, till the point alone held. The slight shock from Crean's shoulder knocked it out. The clamp swung open, and the mast started to fall aft, but Macarty caught it and clamped and secured it with the pin. Happening then it was a trifling incident, but the pin had probably held in that precarious position all night. Had it fallen out in the hurricane, the mast would have snapped like a carrot, and no power on earth could have saved us. Providence had certainly held us in the hollow of his hand.

Soon after breakfast we passed between two headlands six miles apart, and by noon could see north of us two large glaciers which promised floating ice. For a while we steered towards this bay, but seeing that there was no shelter and we could not make it before dark, the course was resumed for King Haakon Sound.

By noon the wind had shifted to east and blew strong in our teeth right out of the sound. At the same time the tide was setting us to the south'ard. We lowered the sails; Crean and I pulled with the two oars, relieved at short intervals by Vincent and Macarty, as owing to the cramped position it was impossible to pull for long. The wind was too strong for us, and finding we were setting unpleasantly close to the breakers, we again set jib, mainsail, and thrice-accursed mizen, and so beat up against the wind.

We could make no pretence of eating a midday meal. We just longed for water.

For four hours we tacked, tacked, tacked, till we were sick of it. Although our boat was overballasted, she made little or no gain to wind'ard. We again got out the oars, this time to assist the sails, and by pulling to wind'ard only, counteracted the boat's griping, and so saved the drag of the rudder across her stern. Now, by dint of hard work, we gradually drew nearer to the strange, block-shaped rocks and islets that stretch, like a boom defence, across two-thirds of the entrance. We noted that at the head of the sound was a comparatively low, easy slope or saddle leading to the interior. We speculated we could win our way by this on foot across South Georgia.

Still no floating ice to ease our thirst—the wind blew stronger. It looked as though we might, in the darkness, once more get driven out to sea.

Late in the afternoon we got up to patches and lines of kelp extending from the chain of rocky islets. Had it come to the worst, we could have moored the boat to the kelp for the night by seizing strand after strand of the long leathery, slippery plants, and, laying them together, formed a fine resilient cable. Darwin observed kelp reaching the surface in 100 fathoms. I have often seen it do so in eighty to ninety fathoms. This gives it a length of 600 feet—100 feet longer than the tallest tree in the world.

Evening drew on, and it was evident that without a change of wind we could not get our overburdened boat into the sound, and land that night. Then, through the gathering gloom, we saw to the south what looked like a cove with a possible landing behind a headland which broke the heaviest of the Southern Ocean swells.

We weathered its entrance, then turned and ran before the wind for 300 yards, closely searching the rocky shores for a possible landing. There was none. We were then abreast of the entrance to the cove, and, putting out the oars to steady her, we hauled to the wind on the port tack and passed between the rocks that stood off both headlands, leaving such a narrow passage that our oars fouled the kelp on both sides.

We then lowered the sail and pulled about sixty yards, between cliffs rising eighty feet high that flanked the tiny cove, until we came to the boulder beach at the head. It was now dark.

As we beached the boat in the surf at the southwest corner of the cove and jumped ashore, we fell down into pools of running water; kneeling, we lapped it up greedily.

Sir Ernest decided to get everything out of the boat to haul her clear of the water. He clambered about ten feet up the rocky face at the foot of the cliff on our starboard side, where I threw him a rope, which he made fast to hold the boat. In doing this, through stiffness and awkwardness from being so long cramped in the boat, he fell some way and hurt himself, but luckily sustained no serious injury. At this time the boat's stern swung against the rocks, unshipping the rudder and carrying away the lanyard that held it, so that in the darkness it was lost.

It seemed, in our exhausted condition, a terribly laborious and endless job unloading and clearing the boat of all gear. I well remember the sensations of misery and fatigue crawling along in water and darkness under the canvas covering of the boat, splashing cold and wet on hands and knees, passing stores up to Crean, who passed them to Sir Ernest. While Macarty and Vincent carried everything above reach of the waves, McNeish held the boat. This took up until 8 p.m., and we were continually falling, owing to our swollen and numbed feet and cramped feeling from lack of exercise in the boat.

Meantime Sir Ernest got the "Primus" going, and we had hot milk made from dried milk powder. This put fresh life into us, and we soon finished the work.

Then we had time for a meal. While the others cooked hoosh, I held the boat, hauling the painter taut and belaying it round a boulder. In spite of all efforts the boat bumped heavily in the surf on the boulders—we were too weakened to haul her clear—to such an extent that we expected her to be stove in every moment. We afterwards found the planks had chafed in places to the thinness of cardboard.

After a delicious feed of boiling hot hoosh cooked over the "Primus," Crean exploring returned across the eighty yards of boulders that separated us from the cliffs on the other side of the cove with the joyful news of a "cave." It is hard to realize what the word meant to us. Apart from the ineradicable schoolboy love of a cave, it sounded to us like a great dry, roomy dwelling with a steady floor, after the never-ending motion of the boat, the cold and wet, and sleeping on the ice floes. However, it proved to be merely an undercut face of the cliff, with huge fifteen-feet-long icicles hanging down in front, ready to impale an unwary visitor. When we saw it we rather damped Crean's enthusiasm; still, it served our purpose.

Stumbling, falling—our feet were numbed, yet sore, soft, and superficially frostbitten from sixteen days' soaking in cold sea water, and we had partly lost control of them—we shambled along with our sleeping bags and the least wet of our clothing. We must have looked a sorry, miserable crew. At least two were nearly "all in." Sir Ernest told me afterwards that he was convinced they would have died, had we been out in the boat another twenty-four hours. Still, we were not woebegone, but looking forward with weary joy to a sleep on stable land once more. On a sloping bed of dry shingle we laid our sodden sleeping bags and, crawling in, snuggled against each other for some degree of warmth.

This was 10 p.m. Sir Ernest took the first watch by the boat, and, with his usual unselfishness, kept three hours instead of one. Just after he had been relieved by Crean we heard a shout. Rushing and falling along the boulder beach, we found that an extra large sea surging the boat had torn out the boulder to which I had belayed the painter. Crean, hanging on, had been dragged into the surf up to his waist. We "tailed on" to the painter, and after some exertion managed to get her bows hard aground so that we could hold her. During our efforts a crosscurrent had taken the boat and us with it along the beach till we were only twenty yards from the cave. This was better. It was then 2 a.m. and there was no more sleep for us.

Three of us held the boat and, when a heavier swell rolled in, the other three hauled with us against the undertow. We made a hot drink of milk and at daybreak hoosh was served piping hot.

Then we set seriously to work to get the boat up the beach. The tide here rises only three feet, but at high water we hauled her as far up as we could, and then to lighten the boat stripped her of everything movable. We had not rope enough to rig a purchase, so we placed her two masts and the spare mast under her keel and worked her uphill. Boulders sticking up in our course hindered us, but by noon we had got her so far up that we felt easier, and had a good rest and feed. Then we got her on to a patch of shingle where, using the masts as rollers, we hauled her diagonally and zigzag up the incline, until we got her in safety on the tussocks. Had we been fit and strong, we could have got the boat up with an hour's hard work; as it was it took us from daylight to dark and exhausted us. Sir Ernest had decided that he would not risk taking the boat around South Georgia to the east coast in her cut-down condition.

After our crossing of South Georgia the *James Caird* was sent by Sir Ernest to England and landed in Liverpool. In the spring of 1920 I brought her from Liverpool to London in a truck attached to a passenger train. My friend Commander Stenhouse, captain of Shackleton's other ship the Aurora, came to assist me. Sir Ernest then lent her to the Middlesex Hospital, when students dragged her through the streets of London, collecting money for the hospital.

She was next taken to the Albert Hall, where Sir Ernest lectured for the hospital, and later I assisted him to transfer her to the roof of Selfridge's, where a small charge to see her was made for the same purpose.

In 1921, Shackleton having presented her to Mr. Rowett, she was taken to the latter's estate at Frant, where she was not improved, in her old age, by the exposure, so Mr. Rowett handed her over to Dulwich, Sir Ernest's and his old school, where she now is. [In 1967 the *James Caird* was presented to the National Maritime Museum in Greenwich.]

Looking back on this great boat journey, it seems certain that some of our men would have succumbed to the terrible protracted strain but for Shackleton. So great was his care of his people, that, to rough men, it seemed at times to have a touch of woman about it, even to the verge of fussiness.

If a man shivered more than usual, he would plunge his hand into the heart of the spare clothes bag for the least sodden pair of socks for him.

He seemed to keep a mental finger on each man's pulse. If he noted one with signs of the strain telling on him he would order hot milk and soon all would be swallowing the scalding, life-giving drink to the especial benefit of the man, all unaware, for whom it had been ordered.

At all times he inspired men with a feeling, often illogical, that, even if things got worse, he would devise some means of easing their hardships.

from Rescue in the Pacific
by Tony Farrington

In June, 1994, a hurricane-strength storm battered a small fleet of yachts taking part in a cruising regatta from New Zealand to Tonga. The event touched off the largest search-and-rescue operation of modern times in the South Pacific. Journalist and seasoned sailor Tony Farrington recounts an attempt by a giant container ship to pluck two sailors—one badly injured—off their small yacht in the storm's enormous seas.

Saturday, June 4, at 1300

Captain Jim Hebden was uneasy about the weather reports he received as the 7,246 ton roll-on, roll-off container ship *Tui Cakau III* sailed from Fiji toward Auckland. The weather had been idyllic when they departed the port of Lautoka on June 2, but as the ship steamed farther into the South Pacific, Hebden became increasingly concerned. Instincts acquired during 18 years of sailing the Pacific warned him that all was not right.

He studied the barometer and noted in the log that it was still plummeting. It had fallen from a pressure of 1,000 mb at midnight to 985.5 mb at noon. The rapid drop was alarming, an indication that they were in for trouble from the weather.

"There are no old, bold sailors," he would often remind his Fijian crew, most of whom had sailed with him for more than a decade. It was a simple philosophy. It meant he was not one to take unnecessary risks. He ordered the crew to tighten the cargo lashings and to check them every two hours. They were on a cyclone watch.

He had encountered his share of storms and cyclones in the South Pacific. One storm had thrown him out of his seat on the bridge. Another had ripped out a seat bolted down to the deck of the bridge. He'd seen lockers hurled across the deck, and cargoes slip their lashings. Experience had taught him to prepare well in advance. You could never be sure that even the combined technology of the meteorological offices in Fiji, Australia, and New Zealand was sophisticated enough to spot in advance the often beautiful, spiraling wisps of cyclone, hurricane, or storm formations.

To the west of the *Tui Cakau,* a larger cargo ship traveling from Suva to Sydney reported it was battling a 60-knot storm that had ripped out a radar mast. The ship was taking on water.

Given a choice in threatening conditions, and had he been forewarned, Jim Hebden would have elected to stay in port or run from the storm. Now, however, it was too late to take evasive action. His only comfort was that the *Tui Cakau* appeared to be on the fringe of the storm. As long as she remained there, she would avoid the worst of the weather.

Two hours later, the rain squalls stopped and the sea fought with itself, confused that the wind had suddenly dropped. Capt. Hebden spotted birds flying in the distance. Blue sky broke through the clouds. To a less-experienced sailor, it could appear the worst had passed. But Jim Hebden suspected he had, in fact, reached the outer edge of the vortex itself.

His suspicion was confirmed when the wind and waves rose once more. The *Tui Cakau* was lifted and shaken and dropped again and again by seas attacking from all angles. He checked the barograph. It had fallen another three points.

He reread the weatherfaxes. The high-pressure zone over the South Pacific was trapped between two depressions in a pincer movement, as if locked in combat. Three giant forces were contesting their strength; cold polar air reaped by the southern low in Antarctica was spinning against warm air the northern low had harvested in the tropics. This clash of invisible gladiators intensified as they moved closer, locking horns to form a swirling, roaring demon that raged across more than 20,000 square miles of Pacific Ocean. It was a rogue "bomb" storm, one that should not have been awaked at this time of the year.

"Bombs" in the subtropics may deepen faster than a weather map can reasonably show. The resulting weather may change from fair to foul faster than a boat can travel. North Atlantic bombs are well known by English sailors (for example, the Fastnet storm of August 1979). The frequency of such storms in the South Pacific has not been determined exactly but is roughly two to four times a year. In June 1983, one such bomb destroyed the *Lionheart*, and seven crew were lost as they tried to enter Whangaroa Harbour in eastern Northland (New Zealand). In June 1989, another bomb capsized the trimaran *Rose Noelle*, and her crew of four drifted at sea for five months.

Now the *Tui Cakau* III, 450 feet long and 60 feet wide, was trapped in the storm area with 60 yachts, few of which were more than 50 feet in length. In the center of the storm lay the yacht *Destiny*, tiny, vulnerable, disabled, and alone. She was the first yacht the storm had attacked.

The air force had raised the *Tui Cakau* on Channel 16, and he had immediately offered assistance. He was now unsure about the wisdom of his decision, but he would never have refused to aid another vessel in distress unless the rescue attempt clearly jeopardized his own vessel and its crew. With only 1,000 tons of cargo aboard, the ship was light. The reduced weight affected the ability of its catamaran hulls to handle the enormous seas. He was constantly forced to head off the waves. As the weather worsened, Capt. Hebden reduced speed to 3.5 knots, and he became increasingly concerned about the ship's ability to continue toward the yacht. The Orion's air crew kept regular radio contact with him, and he listened anxiously as they talked to the woman on *Destiny* every half-hour.

He couldn't pick up *Destiny*'s weak radio signal, but he knew from the one-sided conversation of the air crew that their plight was desperate. The strong, confident voice of Flt. Lt. Bruce Craies continued to offer advice and reassurance, and belied his true feelings about the odds of a successful rescue.

"Paula, are you there?" he heard Craies call. Again he could not hear the response.

He heard a voice from the plane: "Paula, this is the doctor . . . one more question, how old is Dana?"

"Copy. Forty-two. You've done everything you can, and help's on its way. I'm sure he'll be fine."

Jim Hebden was not as confident as the doctor sounded. He estimated the wind at Force 10 (up to 55 knots) and heard from the Orion crew that around *Destiny* it was blowing at more than 80 knots.

"We're still 50 miles away. At this rate it'll be two o'clock in the morning before we get to her," he told his officers.

The sea swirled under the gap between the *Tui Cakau*'s twin hulls as it raised her on each crest, rolling her precariously. Tumultuous waves attacked her sides. With each roll, the crew grabbed at handholds and steadied themselves. An officer, clutching a VHF microphone, was hurled across the bridge. Water cascaded over the bow and onto the bridge four decks above the weather deck, itself four decks above the sea.

Capt. Hebden was awed by the forces at work. Even as he stood on the bridge, almost 50 feet above water level, he still had to look up to the crest of a wave curling ahead of the ship. He studied the sea's fury. A series of waves about 40 feet high, then a monster towering over the bridge itself, possibly 100 feet high, crashed over them. The pattern was irregular but repeating. They curled up over him, their white crests blocking the sky.

"Jesus, there's another one!" he exclaimed, when yet another gigantic wave reared over the ship.

They held him fascinated. The troughs were as long as the *Tui Cakau* herself, the faces of the tumbling seas were near-vertical.

Jim Hebden and his officers had their hands full. They used all their skills to keep control of the ship. Each time they recognized an attack, they reduced power a little. The *Tui Cakau* sat there, momentarily waiting for the ocean's punch, and then, just as it hit, they gunned her forward to hold her course.

Despite their ability, they did not always win. She was frequently caught off-guard. On one occasion, two large waves wrestled each other and tumbled ahead of her. They lifted her up and rolled her over 40 degrees. The *Tui Cakau* shuddered as the cargo of wood stacked in the hold was strewn about like discarded matches. A Fijian crewmember was tossed into the air as if a carpet had been pulled from under him. The chief officer was lifted out of his chair and hurled through the air. He crashed to the floor, breaking a leg.

It was obvious now that the Orion's crew feared *Destiny* would break up. They called the *Tui Cakau* for confirmation that she could still reach the yacht. The woman on *Destiny* had reported that the sound of the mast smashing against the boat had changed. It was now less brittle, more spongy, indicating that the spreader tip may have reached the core of the fiberglass sandwich that comprised the hull.

Jim Hebden radioed back to confirm he was still trying to achieve his mission. He estimated his time of arrival at 2 a.m. But he wondered if he'd be able to find *Destiny* in the dark, storm-tossed seas. Chances were he would steam right by her or, even worse, accidentally collide with her. Even with radar he wouldn't be able to detect *Destiny* because of the screen clutter caused by the rain and spray.

The crew of the Orion reported their concerns about the increasingly low morale aboard the yacht. As the limping *Destiny* endured more pounding from the waves, screams echoed over the radio. They knew Dana was in considerable pain and immobile. The doctor aboard the Orion indicated the man could have broken a rib, and that it may have punctured a lung. He also suspected he had a broken femur.

Capt. Hebden took instructions from the doctor on how to treat Dana if he were successfully lifted aboard the *Tui Cakau*. As they battled their way toward the yacht, a sick bay was set up to accommodate *Destiny*'s crew. An oxygen bottle was taken from an oxyacetylene set, and a hose and primitive face mask were attached to supply oxygen should they need it. Capt. Hebden considered it fortunate he had, himself, been hospitalized recently and remembered how a saline drip had been attached to his arm. He checked again to make sure the *Tui Cakau*'s course would place them just north of the stricken yacht.

In the early hours of Sunday, June 5, the Orion's crew radioed that they were running low on fuel, and were heading for Nadi, Fiji. They had been airborne for 13 hours. It was tedious work. The Orion was a proven aircraft, 27 years old, a survivor of the Cold War when New Zealand, Australia, and the United States patrolled the Pacific, hunting for Soviet submarines. Its interior was sparse, and few comforts were available to the 11 crewmembers.

"This is the worst weather I've experienced in the couple of thousands of hours I've had up here," Flt. Lt. Craies told his copilot. "I've never seen it like this before."

Sqd. Ldr. Yardley agreed. He admitted to feeling queasy. Motion sickness plagued all the crew. The Orion had bucked and bounced for hours. To have to sit at the back of the aircraft, strapped into their seats, was a particularly unpleasant endurance test for the crew who worked at the bank of instruments along the side of the plane. The spotters, peering out of the bubble windows at the sea below for hours on end, also had a hard ride.

All day, Yardley had maintained radio communications with the RCC, *Destiny*, and the *Tui Cakau*, plotting the Orion's course and assessing its range and fuel reserves. To extend their flying time they had climbed to 8,000 feet, where conditions were surprisingly better than at lower altitudes. There, cruising with two of the four engines shut down to conserve fuel, they found blue skies, smooth air, and only 8 knots of wind.

Before shutting down two engines, Craies assessed the risks. The plane could not fly on a single engine. On one engine the plane would descend toward the ocean at about 500 feet a minute, giving him about 16 minutes to restart one of the others. Moisture could enter the shut-down engines, where it might turn to ice, preventing ignition or possibly damaging the engines.

The bond that the Orion's crew had developed with the American woman they had never seen made them reluctant to leave *Destiny* in the perilous conditions she still faced. It was a curiously intimate relationship, nurtured by hours of conversation across radio waves. The crew felt pity for her. She sounded strong, yet gentle; frightened but determined. They shared her terror, her hope, her desperation, her tenderness, her faith, and her frustration. To Paula, they were angels out of the blue, her only hope for survival. They flew so low, so close, they were almost beside her, at times only a couple of hundred feet away. Yet they were incapable of holding out a hand she could grasp, to pluck her out of the maelstrom. It was cruel to be so close and yet so helpless. This was the ultimate frustration.

They would never forget her pitiful cry as once more they flew low over *Destiny*: "I hear your plane. God, I wish you could lift me off."

Paula's psychological state worried Dr. Powell. She would need great physical and mental strength if things got worse. It was vital she maintain her judgment and energy to assist with the rescue. He suggested that the crew aboard the Orion try to improve her morale by keeping her constantly busy. They did so by prompting her to check batteries, tidy the boat, and watch over Dana.

As the day progressed, Dr. Powell was impressed with the impact Craies and Yardley had on her spirits. Their reassuring manner gave her hope that she would, indeed, survive this ordeal. He fed them ideas continuously on how to maintain the conversation.

Nevertheless, the incessant pounding took its toll on Paula. "Oh God!" they heard her scream with despair as the boat rolled again and again. "Oh God!"

The slight improvement in her spirits evaporated at nightfall, and she questioned whether they would be able to continue the battle for survival.

"I don't know if I can cope with this," Dr. Powell heard her confide at one stage. "Did you say the boat would be here in the morning? I'm not sure we'll last that long."

Yardley was so depressed by the remark that he could no longer talk to her, despite Dr. Powell's urgings. Craies kept up the banter in an attempt to lift her spirits.

It appeared to work when, at about 2100, she was back on the air saying: "Dana says he wants a can of Fiji Bitter. It would be good."

During previous search-and-rescue operations, Sqd. Ldr. Yardley had never closely identified with people in distress. He had always tried to remain detached, but for the past 10 hours he had been consoling, encouraging, and advising Paula, participating in her ordeal. There had been long periods of anguish that seemed to last an eternity. They had heard the hapless couple praying for survival, and pitied them as the radio caught them screaming, terrified, when the boat rolled.

Just trying to keep the plane aloft was a stressful occupation. The concentration required for the task was accentuated when they dropped a sonar locater beacon beside *Destiny* to keep track of her during the night, insurance against losing her if either the EPIRB or the boat's batteries failed. Activating the beacon should have been a simple, routine task, one that Craies had performed scores of times previously. They simply flew over the sonar beacon and pressed a button in the cockpit to start it working.

Now, flying conditions were so bad that even the simplest of jobs was difficult, and Craies found he couldn't press the button. He jokingly cursed his slow reflexes and apologized to Yardley, who peered at his screen, waiting for the electronic signal to respond. But his crew knew that all Craies's attention was needed to keep the plane on course as it bounced about, only a few hundred feet over the ocean. It was not until the third pass that he finally managed to press the button at the right time.

It was like flying in mountains, precision flying that demanded exhausting concentration and skill. It was not as if they were dealing with a stationary target. *Destiny* drifted at about 2 knots. Even with their sophisticated electronic equipment, the Orion's crew often had difficulty locating her. They could keep track of her only within a two-mile radius. With the plane slowed to its minimum flying speed of 120 mph, there was still very little time to make contact with the yacht. When they dropped down low to search for *Destiny* they could see little, even in daylight. Driving rain and sleet hit the cockpit windows, and the sky and sea merged in a gray shroud that kept visibility to a minimum.

When their fuel ran low, they radioed the RCC:

Kiwi 315: Suggest Kiwi 315 be replaced by an aircraft.

RCC: Kiwi 315, understood . . . at present investigating opportunity for Australian or American assistance. Will have to confirm. HQ are looking at getting aircraft airborne to meet your PLE [position of last exit]. Over.

Kiwi 315: RCC. Copy. Obviously aircraft must stay with *Destiny* as it may be holed at any time and has no life raft.

RCC: Copied. *Destiny* no life raft. We agree it must be continuous on-top coverage. Over.

Kiwi 315: Don't be surprised by [wind] velocity in excess of 70 knots. Sea state nine. Over.

RCC: Copied. Information we have is vessel has a life raft. Can you confirm it is either damaged or washed overboard? Over.

Kiwi 315: Life raft has come adrift from vessel and has now floated away. Over.

RCC: Will discuss possible requirement to drop life raft to vessel before last light so that it could be retired prior to, or in case, the vessel is holed in the night. Over.

Kiwi 315: I will take up that suggestion on board but believe that will be impossible because the one person who can walk does not want to get outside the vessel due to the conditions. Over.

RCC: Understood. Have nothing more for you. Will be transmitting to you updated weather information when it comes to hand from the Met. office. Over.

Kiwi 315: Standing by. Out.

At the rescue coordination center, Bill Sommer was trying to find a plane and crew to replace the departing Orion P3. The air force had another plane on standby, but finding off-duty airmen was difficult on a holiday weekend.

He knew how important it was to have another Orion in the rescue vicinity during the night to keep morale high and to guide the *Tui Cakau* III to the area.

He contacted Hawaii and Australia to ascertain whether any U.S. Coast Guard or naval ships or aircraft were in the area, or if the Australians had any craft at Fiji or Norfolk Island that could lend assistance. But the U.S. Navy no longer cruised the region, and the Australians had nothing stationed on the islands.

Finally, the New Zealand Air Force managed to scramble together another crew, and another Orion set off to replace Kiwi 315.

En route to Fiji, Kiwi 315 briefed the relieving aircraft about *Destiny*'s background, the psychological condition of her crew, Dana's suspected injuries, and the sea and wind conditions. Dr. Powell was not optimistic. He doubted Dana would remain well enough to be rescued, nor did he believe Paula could keep her spirits up through the longest, blackest, and coldest period of darkness. The possibility of the boat's breaking up was foremost in their minds.

Kiwi 315's flight to Fiji was tense. Low on fuel and with no reserves for a diversion, they were concerned with their own survival. The plane's three officers and crew were tired and grim as they finally flew over the lights of Nadi and put the Orion on the tarmac with only 1,000 pounds of fuel left in the tanks.

On the way to Fiji, Kerikeri Radio had informed them of the plight of another yacht, the *Mary T*, which was taking on water 200 miles away from *Destiny*. It sounded like another job for this weary crew.

But the aircraft's engineers, meticulously inspecting the Orion's engines as they cooled down after its stressful patrol, found oil leaking from the Number 2 engine. It was a substantial leak and would need to be repaired before they could take off again. The crew volunteered to start repairs immediately, but Flt. Lt. Craies discouraged them. After all, it was after 2 a.m. Fifteen hours in the air had taken its toll on these men. They all needed to snatch a few hours' sleep before setting off later in the morning, probably at around 1000 on Sunday, June 5.

Meanwhile, aboard *Destiny*, Paula and Dana could not fathom how they would be rescued. Dana, lying helpless in his wet foul-weather gear, wondered if he would be able to get out of the cabin and deck without passing out. Paula wasn't strong enough to carry him. The cold had tightened the muscles in his legs and hips, adding to the torture from his broken bones.

As they worried and wondered, a new voice came over the VHF radio. It, too, had a New Zealand accent that could be difficult to understand occasionally. The relief Orion had arrived. It would guide their rescue ship to them. However they were going to be rescued, they were on the last lap now. Tired as they were, a mixture of fear, excitement, and anticipation robbed them of any desire to sleep.

Sunday, June 5, about 0200

As Kiwi 315 touched down at Fiji, the *Tui Cakau* III arrived in the vicinity of the stricken yacht *Destiny*. It was one of the Pacific's darkest nights. The *Tui Cakau* rolled and heaved, her engines straining as the stern lifted out of the water.

Capt. Jim Hebden stood alone on the wing of the bridge, peering into the blackness but seeing nothing, as rain and spray stung his face.

There was no doubt they were close. The Orion that had relieved Kiwi 315 was keeping them informed and, when they heard them talking to Paula on the VHF, the air crew were encouraging her and Dana by telling them it would not be long before the rescue ship arrived. The airmen sounded confident that once the freighter arrived, rescue would be a simple formality.

Jim Hebden knew better. The rescue attempt could place the American couple in even greater peril. The ship might accidentally steam right over them in this bad visibility.

The sea conditions were so atrocious that he didn't dare to launch a tender. Holding a 7,000-ton ship alongside a 45-foot yacht in calm conditions was difficult enough. In this storm it might prove impossible, particularly as the *Tui Cakau* had a 6-foot lip protruding from her hull at water level. That lip could crush *Destiny* in an instant if she drifted underneath.

He would not normally even attempt to enter a port or go alongside a wharf in a wind blowing as hard as this, so laying the *Tui Cakau* alongside a tiny yacht was a daunting prospect. It would take only one misjudgment, or one lapse of concentration, to destroy *Destiny* completely.

When he'd received the call for assistance from Kiwi 315 15 hours earlier, the swell had been so bad that he couldn't head directly toward the yacht. Instead, he'd plotted a course that would take him north of the yacht. The new course was easier on the ship and her crew.

Had it not been for the distress call, Capt. Hebden probably would have chosen to heave-to and ride out the storm, particularly since one of his officers had broken a leg. Even on this easier course, they could make only 3 knots instead of their normal 11. Getting this far had been a long, hard, uncomfortable slog.

There was still no sign of *Destiny*. Nothing. Even the radar screen was a senseless profusion of glowing dots depicting rain, spray, and myriad huge seas.

"Can you mark her for me?" Capt. Hebden asked the Orion pilot on the VHF. "I can't see a damn thing. The sea clutter is throwing stuff all over the radar screen. Has she, by any chance, got a light?"

The air crew said she did, indeed, have a faint light that he should be able to spot when he was within range. They agreed with Capt. Hebden that it was too dangerous to attempt a rescue in the darkness.

The *Tui Cakau* would stand by for the rest of the night. If the yacht did break up before dawn, Capt. Hebden said, he'd go to their aid immediately, despite the extra complications. But, if it came to the worst, how could they possibly save the couple in the darkness? They'd surely be swept away, lost in the churning white crests of the seething ocean. If *Destiny* didn't hold together until daylight, the chances of her crew's surviving, even with the *Tui Cakau* standing by, were dismal indeed. Sunrise was still four hours away.

The *Tui Cakau's* crew still talked to the Orion P3 on a radio channel that *Destiny* couldn't hear. Nobody wanted Paula to know the difficulties confronting the rescuers.

Capt. Hebden had heard the American woman begging the Orion

crew to have them rescued as soon as possible. She feared the boat could soon disintegrate. They had no life raft and no way of surviving if *Destiny* sank.

For a long time, Capt. Hebden and his Second Mate discussed the best way to rescue the American couple. Eventually, a simple plan evolved. It was born of pure desperation. Two men would descend the side of the *Tui Cakau* and jump directly aboard the *Destiny*. They would go below and carry the injured man on deck. The woman too, if necessary. It would be extremely dangerous. It was not a task the captain could *order* anyone to carry out.

The officers and crew aboard the *Tui Cakau* were a close-knit community. Some had served with Capt. Hebden the full 18 years he'd been with Sofrana Unilines. The majority had been with him for at least 10 years. They trusted his seamanship and he, in turn, had full confidence in their strength and bravery. Most were good friends, tough men, but blessed with the gentleness and tolerance typical of the Melanesian race.

The thought of endangering any of his crew caused Jim Hebden great concern. But there was no alternative if they were to save the couple aboard *Destiny*.

He had in mind two men. The first, Joeli Susu, had been a soldier in the Fijian Army. He had served with United Nations peacekeeping missions, and his strength and fitness were legendary. He was often seen jogging around the ship's decks, holding two oxyacetylene bottles above his head. He stood 6 feet 3 inches tall and he weighed about 260 pounds. The second, Seruvuama Valagotavuivui, a mechanic, also was a fitness enthusiast. He was as big as Joeli, and just as brave.

"I'm asking for volunteers," Capt. Hebden told them. "I won't think any less of you if you don't want to do it. It'll be very dangerous. The boat will be rolling and it'll be slippery."

Both men volunteered immediately. Of course they would rescue the Americans.

Capt. Hebden was proud of them. And he knew that, had he asked any of the other men, each would have responded just as selflessly. He had great respect for the integrity and generosity of Fijians, and could imagine no better people to work with, particularly on an assignment like this.

"Oh, by the way," he said, "I think you should go down to the boat in bare feet."

That wasn't a problem for either of them. They were used to going around barefooted. They spent most of their time at home shoeless. And everybody knew that nothing gripped a slippery, wet deck better than bare skin.

After a while, the Orion flew low over the *Tui Cakau*. They all heard it. Then there was an orange glow appearing and disappearing in the sea ahead as the plane dropped the first flare in the darkness. The whole exercise surprised and reassured Capt. Hebden.

He knew there wasn't far to go now. The plane's captain had promised to drop the first flare when they were a couple of miles from *Destiny*.

The *Tui Cakau* rolled heavily as she held a course in the direction of the fading flare. The sea was still very angry. Capt. Hebden kept the ship forging ahead slowly.

Another flare appeared farther away. They were getting closer. The Orion's crew had promised to drop it about 300 yards from the yacht.

He marveled at the skill displayed by the men in the air. They were flying in winds of 80 knots, jolting though the pitch-black night a few hundred feet above the sea, dispatching flares to guide them to the yacht, a pinprick in a vast and hostile ocean. He admired their precision, their bravery.

Excitement gripped the tiny group on the bridge. One of them thought he saw a light. They all peered ahead. Capt. Hebden resumed his post out on the wing of the bridge. Nothing. The boat lumbered over the waves in the darkness. Still not a sign of anything. Somebody called: "There it is again."

This time, the light remained long enough for all to see. This time, there was no mistaking it. Capt. Hebden quickly punched a button on the satellite navigation system to record the ship's position. Now the GPS could guide them back to this spot anytime they wanted.

And now that they'd got this close, Capt. Hebden was determined not to lose the yacht's crew even if *Destiny* broke up before dawn. He suggested a contingency plan. They would fire a line across to her and have the woman haul a life raft aboard the sinking yacht. But, as he discussed it with his officers, it seemed doubtful that the woman would have enough strength; and her husband was incapacitated.

There was, in fact, little else they'd be able to do in the darkness, at least little they could logically plan in advance. If the worst came to the worst, they'd attempt some sort of rescue. No doubt about that. Meanwhile, their earnest hope was that *Destiny* would hold together a few hours longer.

Capt. Hebden encouraged the off-duty crew to snatch some sleep while he circled the *Destiny*, waiting for dawn. It wasn't easy to keep contact with the yacht in that black storm. If Capt. Hebden went outside a two-mile radius, he lost the pinprick of light that marked *Destiny*'s position. When the *Tui Cakau* came stern-on to the wind in her circling, her speed catapulted to 11 knots. When she came beam-on, the seas rolled her 40 degrees. And when she came head-on, she would rear and plunge, and slow to 3 knots.

He used the solitude to plan the rescue. He had to have his ship on a course that would bring her close alongside *Destiny* and enable her to hold her position there. It had to be the track on which the 7,000 tonner would be most stable; if she rolled down on *Destiny*, the little yacht would be crushed to splinters in seconds. Once again, he worried about the projecting 6-foot dip at *Tui Cakau*'s waterline. His main objective was to reduce the freighter's roll as much as possible. It was unfortunate he did not have a full cargo on this trip: The greater weight would have made the ship easier to control during the rescue. In her light condition, her considerable windage pushed her to leeward as soon as she lost way.

The *Tui Cakau*'s bridge and accommodation sections were forward. Containers were lashed to her weather deck amidships. Aft was a large superstructure from which the smokestack protruded. The storm-force wind pressed hard against all this top hamper, complicating the precision piloting necessary for the rescue. On the positive side, the ship had twin, variable-pitch screws, twin rudders, and bow thrusters, all of which added considerable maneuverability.

Capt. Hebden chose an approach heading of 300 degrees. It was the bearing on which the *Tui Cakau* rolled least. Unfortunately, it placed the wind and sea on the starboard quarter, and increased her speed. But he believed he could check her way and hold her against the weather, to leeward of *Destiny*, while the yacht drifted slowly down toward the ship.

Dawn arrived slowly to reveal a tumultuous ocean on which 50-foot waves broke. Islands of foam hurtled past them. At 0600 on Sunday, June 5, he raised the ship's crew; all of them, engineers, cooks, and deck-hands. He lined them up on the starboard deck, where he intended lowering the ship's life raft with the two volunteers and a stretcher down the hull side. All hands were needed to lower the raft and haul it back up again with the Americans inside.

He set up a communications relay with handheld radios. It involved cadets, the quartermaster, the radio operator, and the Second Mate keeping in touch not only with each other, but also with the Orion and *Destiny*.

"You stay in the wheelhouse," Capt. Hebden ordered the radio operator. "I don't want anyone to disturb me. Everyone just stay out of my way. And if the lady comes off the boat and wants to talk to me before I get off here, I don't want to see her. Just everybody keep the hell out of my way."

They didn't take offense at their skipper's abruptness. They had not worked together for more than 10 years without understanding why he behaved this way as he stood isolated on the starboard bridge wing. Capt. Hebden needed to be alone. He needed total concentration for the task ahead. From his position, he had a full, unobstructed view of his men on the weather deck, the life raft dangling over the side, and the crippled little *Destiny* herself, now just yards away. His vantage point enabled him to work the ship's engines, rudders, and bow thrusters while keeping an eye on the yacht.

Working in tight situations from the wing, he always felt confident. From here, he had piloted the ship into all sorts of tight corners of the

South Pacific. From here, he had an unobstructed view along the starboard side and across the deck. He poised himself over the controls.

Sunday, June 5, at 0630

Aboard *Destiny* they were not so confident. The constant drilling on the hull had continued its soft mushy sound. As the night had progressed, they'd listened to wood splintering. The spreader was inching closer to total penetration. Paula had pleaded for the ship to come alongside in the dark and get them off, or at least cut away their rigging and let their mast sink to get rid of that dangerous spreader. They didn't believe *Destiny* would survive till morning. But Capt. Hebden had been adamant that a night rescue, unless in an absolute emergency, posed unacceptable risks for all involved.

Now, in the pale light after dawn, Paula huddled in *Destiny*'s cockpit. The yacht was a wretched sight, broken and disfigured; disgustingly littered with oil, dirt, food, and trash.

A few hours earlier, she'd glimpsed the *Tui Cakau* through a porthole, steaming past in the darkness. She had disappeared in the swell, then reappeared as the massive waves lifted her. With only her lights visible, she'd looked fairly small: a little ship lost in the vastness of the black ocean.

But when Paula got a look at her in daylight, she was astounded. "Oh my God!" she exclaimed as the *Tui Cakau* loomed out of the grayness. "Oh my God! Dana, get up here! Look at the size of this vessel."

But Dana, of course, couldn't move. He called to her, but she didn't hear him.

She and Dana had not thought much about the vessel that would rescue them. Paula had deluded herself that the rescue would echo scenes from the television program *Baywatch*; a lifeguard's boat would slide alongside for her to step into. As simple as that. She'd never imagined her rescuer would be a middle-aged British sea captain piloting a ship eight stories high.

Below, Dana lay on his bunk, still tormented by pain. He could hear the *Tui Cakau*'s engines and, although he could not see the ship, he felt her presence on the sea outside. He was gripped by a strong sense of foreboding and fear.

Paula watched the container ship as she wallowed out of the murky seascape. It was still difficult to distinguish the point in the distance where the sky met the sea. The ship appeared to be bearing down on them at a tremendous pace, towering above them larger and larger the closer she got.

Dana heard the throb of the ship's engines through the howling wind. The closer she moved toward them, the louder the noise. The motors now sounded so close, he thought the ship was on top of them. His fear intensified.

Out on the wing, Capt. Hebden was apprehensive. With the wind aft, he was running toward *Destiny* faster than he had anticipated. He saw the solitary figure of the woman in the cockpit, half out of the companionway.

As the ship approached, Paula realized with dread the new problems that now confronted them. The *Tui Cakau* rolled heavily in the opposite direction to *Destiny*'s roll. It seemed impossible that the two vessels could get close enough for them to evacuate. Above her, somber black faces craned over the rails.

As the boat passed her port side, she saw Capt. Hebden far up on the bridge. Their lives were now totally in the hands of this stranger. Only his skill could save them. There were no other rescue vessels within hundreds of miles and there was no sign that the storm would abate. The stranger on the bridge had the power to pluck them from the sea, to rescue them from the hell in which they had cowered for an eternity. Or he could fail—a thought too horrible to contemplate.

Capt. Hebden had been on duty for 24 hours. Strangely, he did not feel tired. He was totally focused on his mission to save lives.

The truth was, it wasn't just his skill that counted. The sum of all the skills of all the crew of the *Tui Cakau* would decide whether the rescue attempt was successful or not. One slip, and the couple would die. One mistake at any time would have them crushed under the freighter's side. *Destiny* would shatter into hundreds of pieces. Her crew would be hurled into the sea, carried away, scuffing and tumbling in the cresting waves.

Capt. Hebden fought with the controls, thrusting them into reverse to slow the ship, using the bow thrusters to keep her nose to weather. But the wind kept pushing her down the swell. He thrust the controls into reverse on full power, with the rudders to starboard, at the same time forcing the bow thrusters on full throttle to port so that the combined force of the power would shove the ship closer to *Destiny*.

Paula stared in horror. The *Tui Cakau*'s stern lifted out of the sea. The big ship was so close, it sprayed water all over Paula. As her propellers spun at the top of a wave, her bow fell down the other side. The engines roared their protest above the shrieking of the wind and the crashing of the sea. The propellers seemed to pull *Destiny* toward the vessel's sheer cliffs of blue steel.

The *Tui Cakau* rolled and pitched and roared as Capt. Hebden fought to control her. He could see now that this approach wasn't going to work. The side of the ship crashed into *Destiny*'s bow, smashing her pulpit. *I've misjudged it*, he thought. *I've got to get out of this*. He'd have to go around and try again. He pushed ahead on full power and burst away from *Destiny*, leaving Paula staring up at the side of the ship, convinced the wake would suck her under the stern.

Well, Capt. Hebden thought as the ship rolled violently, *she's not impressed with that one, is she?* He saw Paula ducking inside the companionway.

Dana lay paralyzed in his bunk below, terrified as the noise and the ship's shadow passed over the portlight in his cabin. Then, as quickly as it appeared, it was gone.

"What happened? What happened?" Dana wanted to know as Paula appeared below. Her face was drained of color from the shock of the experience above.

"We almost got sucked under the stern and into the propeller," she said. "It was sucking us sideways. I could hear the engine and see the churning water. It, it was just awful. I don't think they can get us off."

Hopelessness and fear seeped into her soul. "Maybe we should stay on *Destiny*," she said.

Capt. Hebden had a new plan. "Look," he said to the Second Mate, "I can't hold her with the wind aft. We'll have to attempt a go from directly downwind of the yacht."

On that course, heading straight into the wind and swells toward *Destiny*, the *Tui Cakau* would pitch, raising and dropping her bow and her stern, rather than roll. It would be a much safer motion for the rescue. But, even using the full power of the bow thrusters and the engines, he wouldn't be able to keep her pointed into the wind and alongside *Destiny* for long. And it was still risky.

Nevertheless, he had to try. There wasn't much choice. It was too rough to chance sending his men across in a small boat. The only way to get the Americans off the yacht would be to place his 450-foot-long ship alongside their 45-foot yacht and hold her there long enough for his men to slip down the side, board *Destiny*, and assist her occupants to scramble up the ship's sheer, four-story-high steel hull.

While he held the *Tui Cakau* steady, eight pairs of strong Fijian hands would lower his two volunteers over the side in a life raft. A gangway net and a boarding ladder would be secured on the ship's side, just in case they had to climb up from the boat. It seemed an ambitious strategy in hurricane-force winds, but there was no alternative.

Suddenly, the conditions changed. The wind unexpectedly eased to a mere gale. Capt. Hebden reacted quickly. Here was his chance.

The ship's radio operator told Paula to prepare for another rescue attempt. She reluctantly returned to the cockpit to receive the lines they said they would shoot across to her. Dana, terrified at their prospects for survival after the shock of the first futile attempt, tried to get out of his bunk. But the pain was too much.

The *Tui Cakau* approached *Destiny* a second time, rising and plunging in the swell. Capt. Hebden braced himself against the motion, focused on the job in hand.

They're meant to live, he told himself. *The wind has dropped. They're not meant to die.*

On the weather deck below, men held the lines to the life raft. The two rescuers waited for the order to jump in and be lowered down the ship's side. Other men stood ready with a rocket, to fire a line over *Destiny*. Paula stood by to secure the line. It would hold the yacht alongside the ship long enough for them to escape.

The *Tui Cakau* inched closer. They fired the rocket. The wind caught it and it veered away from its target.

"Why did you shoot so high?" a voice shouted.

Dana heard the noise of the rocket being fired, but he had no idea what was going on outside, only that the ship seemed to be terrifyingly close. It loomed above him like an evil black shadow, darkening the portholes.

Paula braced herself on deck, awed by the huge bow bearing down on her, then sweeping past at what seemed excessive speed. The men above rained lines down on her as the *Tui Cakau* drifted closer to *Destiny*. She grabbed one and made it fast around a winch. A gangway net and a pilot ladder hung enticingly over the side.

As the *Tui Cakau* came alongside, Capt. Hebden again used all his piloting skill. He gunned the bow thruster to port and gave full thrust forward to one engine while he powered the other in reverse. He held the rudders full to starboard. With the wind and the engines working against each other the *Tui Cakau* sat alongside the little boat, acting as a breakwater.

But nothing could prevent the final jarring contact between the two vessels rolling, rising, and falling at different rates in those giant seas. The sickening "crack" of metal splitting fiberglass pierced the storm's crescendo as *Destiny* smashed into the *Tui Cakau*. It was as if she had screamed in pain. Part of the yacht's caprail tore away, and she lurched back, bouncing off the unyielding metal wall. Paula fell backward on the deck. She picked herself up and quickly jumped back into the cockpit, out of the way of the plummeting life raft. Again *Destiny* crashed and lurched sideways as she scraped along the freighter's side.

Below in his bunk, Dana was terrified. He felt like a trapped animal. He listened to the explosive sound of the engines churning the water outside as Capt. Hebden worked the controls in his battle to keep the *Tui Cakau* alongside *Destiny*. The yacht rolled and crashed against the ship, and once again the sound of splintering fiberglass echoed through the cabin.

The two vessels collided time and again, throwing Paula across the deck and jostling Dana in his bunk below. The looming steel wall beside his head terrified him. The recurring, deafening grinding made him fear the ship would crack his cabin open like the shell of an egg.

Either I'm going to stay here and die, or I'm going to stand up and get out of this square I'm in, Dana thought. With that, he lifted himself up. The pain that shot through his limbs was overshadowed by his fear and his determination to save his life.

He grabbed the overhead handholds and pulled himself along, hand over hand, dragging his useless leg through the water that splashed beneath him. Hobbling on his good leg, he pulled himself to the companionway steps. As he hung on with both arms, he wondered how he would swing his damaged limb up and out through the entrance. Then he saw Paula. She was hanging precariously on a gangway net wrapped around the ship's life raft, holding on by her hands, her feet dangling in space as the ship rose upward in the swell, taking Paula with it. His pain was so great, Dana was sure he would pass out.

As the life raft had been lowered toward her, Paula had tried to position herself to jump into it as it landed on the yacht, but she had been forced to lurch toward the companionway to avoid being crushed as it crashed to the deck.

Before she could decide what to do next, a big Fijian, the former soldier Joeli Susu, jumped out and grabbed her, Capt. Hebden's words still ringing in his ears. "Get them off. No arguments. Just get them off. The first thing you do is get the lady and throw her into the life raft. Ignore it if she wants to stay with her husband. Get them out." Susu knew he had to act swiftly to save not only their lives, but his own as well.

"I'm here to save you," he said by way of introduction. Voices from above shouted, urging her to get into the raft.

Paula clung to a bag into which she had packed a few meager possessions—passports, money, and other documents. Susu grabbed the bag and tossed it into the life raft, and before Paula could comprehend what was happening she was hurled toward the rubber craft.

I can't miss it, she thought, but at that moment the boats rolled apart. Paula missed the life raft but managed to grab the net surrounding it, and clung to it desperately. At that moment, the line holding the two vessels snapped.

"Oh no! Oh no!" Paula screamed as her left hand started to lose its grip on the wet net. She looked down at the maelstrom below as it yawned up in one last determined attempt to claim her. Without the tether the boats drifted farther apart.

Dana peered out of the companionway in horror. *She'll be crushed between the boats,* he thought.

Paula heard someone yelling at her: "Get your legs up. You've got to get your legs up the side."

She struggled to comply. Then, suddenly, large hands grabbed her. Valagotavuivui, the second Fijian volunteer, took her by the arms and the seat of her pants, and yanked her up and into the raft, which was quickly hauled up to the deck of the ship.

She staggered when she reached the deck, and they steadied her. She looked over the side for Dana, but she couldn't see him. She wanted desperately to see him. She might never see him again. She wanted to stay, but they led her away to the sick bay. She was too weak to resist.

On the wing of the bridge, Capt. Hebden had his own problems. The Chief Engineer had warned him to cut back on power; the engines were overheating under the stress of jockeying the propellers against the drive of the bow thrusters and the rudders. *Only a few minutes more,* he thought. *That's all we need.*

The crew of the *Tui Cakau* had sent more lines down to Susu to help secure *Destiny* closer to the ship again, and Valagotavuivui descended to join him.

Dana, standing in the yacht's companionway, thought: *I'm going to die here.* He recoiled as the pain stabbed him again. *I'll be killed next time the boats collide. I've got to get out of here.*

Before he could move, the two Fijians descended on him.

"Oh good, you can stand. Good. Come up and get on the ladder," one of them said.

"I can't even move. I've got to have a stretcher."

They yelled to the *Tui Cakau* in a language he did not understand. An old canvas stretcher, a relic from World War II, appeared from nowhere.

In the cabin, Dana hung from overhead handholds while the men secured the stretcher firmly around him. The pain was indescribable, searing through his damaged ribs and his shattered leg. Then they lowered him to a horizontal position and got him to the foot of the companionway steps. There they tilted him upward again and tried to carry him up the steps into the cockpit. It was a difficult task. It took all their strength and agility to haul Dana's 200-pound weight up and through the narrow passageway while the yacht jerked and bumped unpredictably against the ship. There were no secure footholds anywhere. The men fell over him and over themselves as *Destiny* tossed and rolled viciously. Time after time, they picked themselves up and dragged Dana a few feet farther before another wave smashed the two boats together and they were knocked off their feet again.

Finally, they dragged him into the cockpit. There they fastened lifting lines around the stretcher near his feet, his hips, and his head. Pain shot through his body as they tightened the lines around him.

Then the line from the ship to the foot of the stretcher tightened as the vessels rolled apart. Dana was dragged along the deck. Only *Destiny*'s port lifelines saved him from falling into the sea still trussed to the stretcher.

The Fijians dashed after him but were knocked down as the ship and the yacht rolled and smashed into each other. The men picked themselves up and pulled him from the side of the yacht before he could slip overboard and be crushed when the ship crashed against *Destiny* again.

Dana looked about him, totally confused and delirious. *Where's the land?* he wondered. The combination of pain, exhaustion, medication, shock, and hypothermia was taking its toll. Off and on, over the hours of his ordeal, he'd imagined he was in a cove surrounded by mountains, not in an angry ocean of enormous waves.

After being hoisted a little way into the air, he slammed hard against the side of the *Tui Cakau*. As the ship rolled, he swung far out and then hurtled back toward the freighter's steel sides again, striking even harder.

The hoisting stopped and he grabbed the lifting line, trying to relieve the pain it caused as it cut into his damaged ribs.

He yelled as, once again, he swung out from the ship's side. "Oh, no!" He knew what would follow. He braced himself. The stretcher rammed into the side of the freighter again. He felt a new pain shoot through his back. The ship rolled to starboard and he plunged down toward *Destiny*.

But suddenly he felt himself being lifted at full speed. He reached the ship's gunwale. People pinned him down. They held him tightly to stop him falling back into the sea that had tried so relentlessly to claim him. Then they gently lowered him onto the *Tui Cakau*'s deck as his two rescuers clambered up to the deck and safety. It had all happened with bewildering speed.

Dana looked up at the Fijians' smiling faces. He was safe, but he would never again see *Destiny*, the faithful vessel that had been his home and companion for seven years. He felt he had failed her.

On the bridge, Capt. Hebden was relieved. It was over. He'd managed to hold the ship steady long enough to get the couple off in some of the worst possible conditions for a rescue. Thank God his crew were safe as well. Miraculously, the lethal lip near the ship's waterline had not lifted out of the water above *Destiny*. Had it done so, it would have crushed her and those on board.

Above the *Tui Cakau*, the crew of the circling Orion cheered at the news of the successful rescue. But there was no time for celebration. The plane banked and set off to search for *Quartermaster*. She still had not reported her position. As they flew away, the crew of the Orion told Capt. Hebden that he might be required to assist another yacht, *Sofia*. She was 80 miles to the south.

from Adrift: Seventy-Six Days
Lost at Sea

by Steven Callahan

In 1982, Steven Callahan's sloop sank six days out from the Canary Islands. He was left adrift in a five-and-a-half foot inflatable raft with three pounds of food and eight pints of water. Callahan (born in 1952) survived 76 days on his raft, distilling water and eating raw fish that he caught with a home-made speargun. He drew upon deep emotional and intellectual reserves to find joy in his predicament.

The metal is hard and cold. After an hour of leaning over the bulwark, my elbows are in icy pain. I stand and thrust my hands deep into the wool coat the captain has brought me. "I'll bet you never thought you'd see this city again," he says, looking at me quizzically. I peruse the horizon. It is no longer flat and empty but is full of monolithic skyscrapers, gray smog. The noise of the city rises above even the rumble of reversed engines. Heavy, tattooed arms pull aboard hawsers as thick as thighs and whip them around the capstans. Slowly the ship is worked in to the dock. More and more lines are tossed and set. The water eddies around us. The behemoth is reeled in. No, I never thought I'd see New York again.

Then there is darkness and chaos. My head is struck with a club, cold, wet, and hard. The assaulter roars, rumbles, and rolls away into the night. I am on the dark side of the earth, a quarter world away from New York. The wind is up and so is the sea. *Rubber Ducky* lurches and crashes as if caught in a demolition derby. "Still here," I moan.

Each night, soft fabrics caress my skin, the smell of food fills my nostrils, and warm bodies surround me. Sometimes while wrapped in sleep I hear my conscious mind bark a warning: "Enjoy it while you can for you will soon awaken." I am used to the duality of it. Usually when I sail alone, the sounds of fluttering sails and waves, the motion of my boat rising and plunging, never leave me even as I hang in my bunk dreaming of faraway places. If a movement varies slightly or an unfamiliar noise slaps against my eardrum, I am immediately awakened. Yet last night's dream was almost too real. My life has become a composition of multilayered realities—daydreams, night dreams, and the seemingly endless physical struggle.

I keep trying to believe that all of these realities are equal. Perhaps they are, in some ultimate sense, but it becomes increasingly obvious that in the survival world my physical self and my instincts are the ringmasters that whip all of my realities into place and control their motions. My dreams and daydreams are filled with images of what my body requires and of how to escape from this physical hell. Since I have gotten the still to work and have learned how to fish more efficiently, there has been little to do but save energy, wait, and dream. Slowly, though, I find I am becoming more starved and desperate. My equipment is deteriorating.

I must work harder and longer each day to weave a world in which I can live. Survival is the play and I want the leading role. The script sounds simple enough: hang on, ration food and water, fish, and tend the still. But each little nuance of my role takes on profound significance. If I keep watch too closely, I will tire and be no good for fishing, tending the still, or other essential tasks. Yet every moment that I don't have my eyes on the horizon is a moment when a ship may pass me. If I use both stills now, I may be able to quench my thirst and keep myself in better shape for keeping watch and doing jobs, but if they both wear out I will die of thirst. My mind applauds some of my performances while my body boos, and vice versa. It is a constant struggle to keep control, self-discipline, to maintain a course of action that will best ensure survival, because I can't be sure what that course is. Is my command making the right decisions? Might immediate gratification sometimes be the best course to follow even in the long run? More often than not, all I can tell myself is, "You're doing the best you can."

I need more fish, and the constant nudging I feel through the floor of the raft tells me that the dorados are around in sufficient numbers to make fishing a reasonable expenditure of energy. After several misfires, I finally skewer a dorado by the tail, but it doesn't slow him down much. He yanks the raft all over the place while I frantically try to hold on, wishing that I could train these fish to pull me in the direction I want to go. He pulls free before I can get him aboard. Oh well, try again. I start to reset the spear gun—but the power strap is gone, now sinking through three miles of seawater! This could be real trouble.

It's my first major gear failure; but I've dealt with a lot of jury rigs before so I should be able to figure something out. It's always a challenge to try and repair an essential system with what one has at hand. In fact, I sometimes wonder if one of the major reasons for ocean racing and voyaging is to push one's self and one's boat just past the edge, watch things fail, and then somehow come up with a solution. In many ways, having a jury rig succeed is often more gratifying than making a pleasant and uneventful passage or even winning a race. Rising to the challenge is a common thread that runs through a vast wardrobe of sea stories. I've stuck back together masts, steering gear, boat hulls, and a host of smaller items. Although I don't have much to work with, repairing the spear should be relatively simple.

The important thing is to keep calm. The small details of the repair will determine its success or failure. As always, I can only afford success. Don't hurry. Make it right. You can fish tomorrow. The arrow and the gun handle are still intact. It is only the source of power that is missing. I put the arrow on the shaft of the handle in the normal manner, but I pull the arrow out through the plastic loop on the end of the handle shaft in order to lengthen the weapon as much as possible. I wind two long lashings around the arrow and shaft. I use the heavy codline, which is better than synthetic line because it shrinks when it is wetted and then dried, thereby tightening the lashings. The smooth arrow still rotates, so I add a third lashing, then I add frappings to the lashings. These are turns of the line around the lashings at right angles. When pulled tight, the frappings cinch up the lashings and should keep them from spreading out haphazardly. There are notches in the butt of the arrow, which normally fit into the trigger mechanism in the handle. Through these notches and back through the trigger housing, I pass loops of line to keep the arrow from being pulled out forward by an escaping fish.

I am aware that my repaired spear is a flimsy rig for catching dorados. Normally a diver pulls on his spear gun arrow when retrieving a fish. I must drive my lance through the fish, putting the rig in compression rather than tension. When I pull a fish out of the water, it will put a large bending load on the arrow as well. However, my new lance feels pretty sturdy, and I'm ready to try it out. Patience is going to be the secret, and strength. Power was stored in the elastic power strap; now the improvised spear has to be thrust at a moment's notice with all of the power I can muster if I'm to drive it through a thick dorado.

I lean my left elbow on the top tube of the raft to steady my aim, and I lightly rest the arrow of the spear between my fingers. I pull the gun handle high up onto my cheek with my right arm, tensed and steady, awaiting the perfect shot. I can sight down the shaft, and rocking back and forth gives me a narrow field of fire. On the water's surface is an imaginary circle about a foot in diameter into which I can shoot without moving my steadying elbow off the raft tube. If I am not well braced, my shots will become wild. The effective range of the spear has been shortened from about six feet to three or four. I must wait until a fish swims directly under my point so that it will be in range and the problem of surface refraction—which makes the fish appear to be where it is not—will be minimized. This problem is extreme at oblique angles to the water. When I shoot, I must extend my range and power as much as possible. I thrust my arm out straight and lunge as hard as I can with my whole body, trying to hold my aim. The shot must be instantaneous, because the fish are so quick and agile, but it also must be perfectly controlled. Once I lift my left, steadying arm off of the tube, it becomes hopeless. I watch the fish swimming all over the place, but I must wait for one to swim within my field of fire. I remain poised for minutes that stretch into hours at a time. I feel like I'm becoming an ancient bronze statue of a bowless archer.

The doggies' nudging has become an advantage. I push my knees deeply into the floor just behind my arrow, luring them on. Bump, and a body slithers out, a little too far to starboard. Bump, a little too far to port. Head center! Do it! Splash! Strike! Ripping strong pull, white water, a cloud of blood. He's in the air. HUGE! A spray of blood. Ow! Feels like I'm being smashed by an oar as he slides down the spear toward me. Don't let go, get him in, quick! Fury flapping, blood flying. Watch the spear tip, the *tip, fool!* On the floor, onto him, now! The huge square-headed body lies still for a moment under my knee as I press my full weight down on him. His gills are puffing in rhythm with my gasps as I try to grasp the spear on both sides of his torso and give myself a moment's rest. A hole as big as my fist has been blasted out of his body, which stretches almost all the way across the floor. Globs of clotting blood swill about in the crater created by my other knee.

Whap, whap, whap! His thunderclapping tail smashes into action. I'm knocked over backward. He's escaped. The tip, watch the tip! He flops all round the raft, making for the exit. Pain in my wrist. Pain in my face. He's winning! I fumble for the tip of the spear as it whips about. Finally I tackle the fish, throw him down onto my sleeping bag and equipment sack, and bury the spear tip in the thick fabric. Both of us are panting. I can't reach my knife. His eye clicks around, calculating— little time left, and he knows it. Whap, whap, whap—he's off again. Look out! Fire shoots up my left arm. "Get down there, down!" Whap, whap, cracking around the raft like a bullwhip. Back on the bag again. Sprawled across him, pushing with my legs to get him pinned. Gills puffing. Get the knife. Push it in. Hits something hard—the spine. Twist it. Crack. Wait. He's still panting, slowly panting, stopped panting. Rest . . . I'll not do that again.

I can't believe that the raft hasn't been ripped. I examine the spear carefully; it is only slightly bent, and the lashings held. I listen but hear no hissing leaks. The tubes still feel hard. Blood and guts are spewed everywhere, some of it mine, no doubt. I'll try to stick to the smaller females in the future. Also from now on I will carefully arrange my equipment before beginning to fish. I'll stretch out the sailcloth across as much of the bottom as possible, put my cutting board down, and spread my sleeping bag over the tubes on the starboard half of the raft above my equipment sack. I have overcome the first serious gear failure since I coaxed the solar still to work.

For hours I slice up my grand fish. First I hack it into four large chunks, plus the head and tail. Then I slice each chunk into four long pieces, one from each side of the back and one from each side of the belly. Finally I slice these into sticks which I hang on strings to dry, like dozens of fat fingers, delicious fat fingers. I write in my log that this is a strange prison in which I am slowly starved but occasionally thrown a twenty-pound filet mignon.

The first weeks of my unplanned raft voyage have gone well—as well as can be expected. I escaped the immediate peril of *Solo*'s sinking, have adjusted to my equipment and the environment, and am now actually better stocked with food and water than when I began.

So much for the positive side. The negative is only too obvious. Lack of starches, sugars, and vitamins has let my body wither. My gluteus maximus was the first to go. Where my plump ass once was, there are only hollows of flesh ridged by pelvic bones. I try to stand as often and as long as possible, but my legs have badly atrophied and hang from my hips like threads with little knots for knees. There was a time when three hands could not encircle my thighs; now two will do, and nicely at that. My chest and arms have thinned but remain fairly strong due to the exercise demanded by survival. How the body steals heat or food from one part to lend to another, how it compensates for deprivation by shutting down all but the essential systems, how it possibly can keep this wreck running in this demo-derby of flesh, is all beyond me, amazing, almost amusing. I write in my log, "No more fat on this honky!" The cuts on my knees still have not healed. Other gashes have left thick scars. Dozens of small slits on my hands, made by my knife or fish bones, never seem to mend. Scar tissue builds up around the wounds like little volcanoes, leaving raw craters inside. Though I'm meticulous about sponging up water and keeping *Ducky* dry, I've spent about half of my time wet. The salt water sores begin as small, infected boils that grow, burst open, and leave ulcers penetrating the skin. These continue to widen and deepen, as if a slow-burning acid were being dropped on the flesh. But so far my work at keeping dry has paid off. I have only a dozen or two open sores, about a quarter inch across, clustered on my hips and ankles. My cushion and sleeping bag, when dry, are encrusted with salt, which grinds into my wounds.

March 3, Day 27

It is sunrise of the twenty-seventh day since I began my voyage in *Rubber Ducky III*. I roll and tie up the canopy's entry closure so its cold, wet skin won't lash across mine. I poke my head out, turn aft, and watch the rising sun as awestruck as a child witnessing it for the first time. I note its position relative to the raft.

Creases in *Ducky*'s soft tubes open and close like toothless black mouths, munching on strings of glue and the white chalk markings of the raft inspectors. Sometimes I wonder who made these marks and what they are doing now. I hope that they are well, for they have done a good job and I am grateful. I push the pump hose into the hard white valves and begin my work, a job as thankless and never-ending as washing dishes and as tiring as a marathon. Ringed treads on the pump have worn thick callouses into my thumbs. The bellows utters a short, high-pitched whimper each time I squeeze it, like those baby dolls that cry out and weep tears. Uuh, uuh, uuh, uuh, one, two, three, four . . . uuh, uuh, uuh, uuh, fifty-seven, fifty-eight, fifty-nine, sixty. I pause, panting, feel the tube—not quite as firm as a watermelon yet—and continue. Then the bottom tube. Noontime, sunset, midnight, and morning, I squeeze the crying pump. In the early days, I had to listen to only sixty whimpers each day; now I have to squeeze over three hundred from the hateful little beast.

The still is sagging. Each morning I blow it up, empty the salt water from the distillate, and prime it. Then I get up to take a look around. Tricky. On a ship's solid deck the waves' motions are averaged out. Here my legs fall and rise with every ripple. Tiny bubbles and gurgles tickle the bottoms of my soft feet. Their callouses washed off long ago. I hang lightly on to the canopy, conscious that a hard tug may collapse it and drop me into the sea. Standing up in my vessel is a little like walking on water.

The only companions in sight are a petrel and a graceful shearwater. The petrel looks as out of place as I, fluttering like a sea chickadee, teetering on the edge of flight, heading straight for a clumsy crash. In reality he is having no trouble. I've seen petrels in shrieking winds, flapping from one gigantic wave canyon to another. They weigh only a few ounces and you'd think that they'd be blown off the face of the world. The tiny petrels, even the much larger shearwaters, will make a very meager meal, but I'll still try to grab one if it ventures close enough. Neither has any need for my dangerous company. They are only curious enough to swoop by every now and then. Their minute black eyes flit over every detail of the raft as they pass. I can watch the flight of the shearwaters for hours. They rarely flap their wings, even when it is flat calm. Then they glide in a straight line close to the surface of the water in order to use the surface effect. In heavy airs they wheel about in large arcs and then dive down so close to the waves that you can't see any space between their feather tips and the water. To me, they are the gods of grace. The shearwaters make me feel very clumsy and remind me how ill suited I am to this domain.

Robertson's book includes tables of the sun's declination, which I use to fix my direction at sunrise. I can do the same at sunset. At night I can fix my heading from both the North Star and Southern Cross. The heavens have provided me with an unbreakable, immortal, fully guaranteed compass. To measure my speed, I time the passage of seaweed between *Rubber Ducky* and the man-overboard pole. Earlier I had calculated the distance to the pole to be about seventy feet, or $1/90$ of a nautical mile. If it takes one minute for a piece of weed or other flotsam to pass between *Ducky* and the pole, I am going $^{60}/_{90}$ of a mile each hour, or $^{2}/_{3}$ of a knot, which works out to 16 miles a day. I make up a table for times from 25 to 100 seconds, $9^{1}/_{2}$ to 38 miles a day. I never do see a 38-mile day.

Since my chart shows the entire Atlantic Ocean on one sheet, my snail's-pace progress is hardly worth plotting on a daily basis, but every couple of days I plot another eighth or quarter inch. I kid myself that I only have a little ways left to travel—why, it's only about six inches on the map.

I am confident that we, that is *Ducky* and I, have reached the lanes and will soon be picked up, but we may well have drifted beyond them. I have tried the EPIRB again to no avail. The battery must be very low now. I must wait until I see positive signs of land or air traffic before I try it again. As soon as we arrived at what I thought to be the edge of the lanes, the wind strengthened. Perhaps Zephyrus wants to push us through before we can be spotted. I'm not too disappointed; it's a relief to be moving purposefully forward. There've been no sharks. There has also been only one ship in six days—pretty empty ocean highway.

Conditions are favorable for my tub. It's blowing hard enough to move us well, but not so hard that the waves are blasted apart. Unless we are hit by a rogue wave, *Ducky* will stay on her bottom. She slues down the slopes with a speedy motion that is smooth, quiet, and peaceful, seemingly frictionless. I get a vision in my head that I can't shake, one of a spaceship gliding in large curving banks through the vastness of space. In my log I sketch *Rubber Ducky* converted to a flying saucer with a wide band around her perimeter, studded with lights. I surround her with planets, stars, and fish.

Time for breakfast. I fall back on my cushion and lean up against the equipment sack. I flip my sleeping bag over my legs, awaiting the warmth of the day. The fish sticks that have been hanging for two days are semidried and slightly chewy. Dorados begin their own daily routine, bumping my rear several times before flipping off to hunt.

Eight hard-won pints of water are carefully stored in three unopened water tins, two recapped and taped tins, two distillate plastic bags, and my working water jug. The butcher shop is chock-a-block full of fish sticks. Wet fresh protein is digested with less water than cooked or dried meat, so I try to eat a lot of my catch early on. As days pass and it gets chewier, I carefully ration the meat and begin fishing again.

I've become worried about my digestive tract. Dougal Robertson points to the case of one survivor who had no bowel movement for thirty days. By the time the body is through digesting the minuscule amount of food taken in, there simply is very little to move. I feel no urge to go but worry about a hemorrhoid that has puffed out. Should my plumbing suddenly blast loose, I may be in for a rupture and hemorrhage, which would be difficult to plug up and heal. I begin modified yoga exercises—twisting, bending, arching, stretching—slowly learning how to balance and compensate for the motion of my waterbed. On the thirty-first day, the bloody bubble begins to subside and a small amount of diarrhea relieves my apprehension.

Early morning, dusk, and night are the only times that I can coerce my body to exercise. By noon the temperature has rocketed to ninety degrees or more. It might as well be nine hundred. My body has no water to sweat. The air trapped inside of the raft is humid and stagnant. Staying conscious and tending the solar stills are major struggles. My spinning head coaxes me. Must get up, look around. Slow, easy now, to your knees. I gaze into the lively blue water. O.K. Wait now, maybe a few minutes. I try to get my eyes to focus, but they stumble about in my head, smash into the sides of my skull, and bounce back. Grab the can, careful not to drop it, already lost one. I dip it down with a gurgle, raise it above me, and let the water fall, massaging my neck and tangled hair with cool relief. Again I dip the can, again and again, imagining that I'm crawling into shaded tall wet grass under a billowing willow tree.

Slowly now, lift your head. Look right. Look left. O.K. Up on one leg, now the other. Stand. "Good boy," I say aloud as I sway about in semidelirium, hoping that I will cool off and my head will clear. The wind flash-dries the drops of seawater trickling down my body, escorting tiny streams of heat away. Sometimes the ritual works. I steady up and remain erect for several minutes. Other times my head feels as if it is being crushed by a heavy weight, my vision fills with swirling bluish haze, and I collapse, using the residue of my senses to guide my fall back into the raft. Yes, I am in much better shape than I thought I'd be by this time, but at high noon I am often "beyond the point of coherent action," as Robertson so dryly puts it. If I can just keep myself together, I can make it to the islands. But how much longer can I hang on like this?

Refiguring my position time and again, I put myself about a thousand miles away. Average speed, twenty-five miles a day. Total passage time, seventy days. If only I can guide myself to Guadeloupe. I've got the raft positioned with the canopy across the wind, and the line astern is just off center to guide *Rubber Ducky III* a little bit south of west just as fast as she can waddle.

From the Canaries I wrote to my parents and friends, "Expect me in Antigua around February 24." That was seven days ago. Yet I also warned them that the trade winds hadn't filled in yet, so I might arrive as late as March 10, seven days hence. If a search is made then, I will still be out of range, way too far out to sea. If only a ship will pick me up soon, those at home won't begin to worry.

I see a shark fin zigzagging in quick pumps across *Ducky*'s bow, about a hundred feet away. It's a small fin, but I'm still glad that he shows no interest in us. Instead, he slides off to the east against the wind and current to await food that is drifting or swimming with the North Equatorial stream.

Like most predators, sharks cannot afford to be seriously hurt, because an injury or weakness can prevent them from hunting and may even invite an attack from their own kind. So most sharks bump their prey before attacking. If the prey puts up no defense, the shark will dig right in. They will eat anything; license plates and anchors have been found in their stomachs. I wonder about life rafts. I count on their bumping to give me a chance to drive them away. But I also think about *Jaws*. I have heard stories of two great white sharks caught since that film came out. Both of the real sharks were about the same size as the mechanical prop, twenty-five feet long, and weighed upward of four tons. Great whites are an unpredictable species. They are so big, ferocious, and powerful that they know no natural enemies and never worry about their prey putting up a significant defense. They give no warning of their attacks and have been known to smash boats and even attack whales.

Then there are orcas, or killer whales, known to have blown large yachts apart. I look at my little aluminum and plastic spear, weighing maybe a pound or two. The point might cause a small shark as much pain as I would feel from a mosquito bite. Even if a small shark forces a showdown at high noon, I'll be pathetically slow to the draw. I'd love the option to get out of this town.

With shivering nights and scorching days, only dusk and dawn offer a little comfort. As the sun drops to the horizon, things begin to cool off. I lounge back again as I did in the morning, flip the sleeping bag over my legs, pump up *Ducky*'s sagging limbs, and watch the sky's grand finale through my picture window. The sharp white disk peeks out now and again from behind the puffy cumulus collected at the horizon. It is past noon in Antigua. If only I had a raft that could sail at a moderate three knots, I'd be snug in harbor already. I'll make it anyway . . . if only I can summon strength I never knew I had.

As the clouds mill about and wander into the sunset, I prepare my dinner, choosing various pieces of fish for a balanced meal: a few chewy sticks, which I regard as sausages, an especially prized fatty belly steak, and a piece of backbone bacon with thin strips of brown, crunchy flesh; I crack the backbone apart and drop gelatinous nuggets of fluid from between the vertebrae onto my board. A noodle runs down the spine, and I add it to the gelatin, making a chicken soup. An invisible Jewish mama coaxes me. "Eat, eat. Go ahead, my sick darling, you must eat your chicken soup to get well." Sumptuous tenderloin steaks come from the meaty back above the organ cavity. I choose a couple of fully dried sticks for toast, since they are overcooked and crunchy. The real treats are the organs, when I have them. Biting into the stomach and intestines is like chewing on a Uniroyal tire, so I don't bother with them, but all else I consume with delight, especially the liver, roe, heart, and eyes. The eyes are amazing, spherical fluid capsules an inch in diameter. Their thin, tough coverings are quite like poly-styrene Ping-Pong balls. My teeth crush out a large squirt of fluid, a chewy dewdrop lens, and a papery thin, green-skinned cornea.

I spend an increasing amount of time thinking about food. Fantasies about an inn-restaurant become very detailed. I know how the chairs will be arranged and what the menu will offer. Steaming sherried crab overflows flaky pie shells bedded on rice pilaf and toasted almonds. Fresh muffins puff out of pans. Melted butter drools down the sides of warm, broken bread. The aroma of baking pies and brownies wafts through the air. Chilly mounds of ice cream stand firm in my mind's eye. I try to make the visions melt away, but hunger keeps me awake for hours at night. I am angry with the pain of hunger, but even as I eat it will not stop.

I save the bulk of my water ration for dessert. Since I have rebuilt my stock, I can afford to drink a half pint during the day and three-quarters of a pint at dinner, and still have a couple of ounces for the night. I slowly roll a mouthful around on my tongue until the water is absorbed rather than swallowed. When I return, ice cream will be no more pleasurable.

In these moments of peace, deprivation seems a strange sort of gift. I find food in a couple hours of fishing each day, and I seek shelter in a rubber tent. How unnecessarily complicated my past life seems. For the first time, I clearly see a vast difference between human needs and human wants. Before this voyage, I always had what I needed—food, shelter, clothing, and companionship—yet I was often dissatisfied when I didn't get everything I wanted, when people didn't meet my expectations, when a goal was thwarted, or when I couldn't acquire some material goody. My plight has given me a strange kind of wealth, the most important kind. I value each moment that is not spent in pain, desperation, hunger, thirst, or loneliness. Even here, there is rich-ness all around me. As I look out of the raft, I see God's face in the smooth waves, His grace in the dorado's swim, feel His breath against my cheek as it sweeps down from the sky. I see that all of creation is made in His image. Yet despite His constant company, I need more. I need more than food and drink. I need to feel the company of other human spirits. I need to find more than a moment of tranquility, faith, and love. A ship. Yes, I still need a ship.

The sea has flattened. All is still. Inside of me I feel a symphony of excitement growing, like music that begins very low, almost inaudible, then grows stronger and stronger until the entire audience is swept up in it with a single synchronized, thumping heartbeat. I rise to scan the horizon. Blowing up from astern are gigantic clumps of cumulonimbus clouds. Rain bursts from their flat, black bottoms, above which thick, snowy fleece billows up to great heights, until it is blown off in anvil heads of feathery ice crystals. The clouds push bright blue sky ahead of their walls of gray rain streaking to earth. An invisible paintbrush suddenly splashes a full rainbow of sharply defined color from one horizon to the other. The top of its arc comes directly overhead, lost in turbulent white ten thousand feet up. The breeze caresses my face; the canopy of the raft snaps. The smooth, slate sea is broken with white tumbling cracks. The sun suddenly pops out between billowing sky sculptures far to the west and balances on the horizon. It sends warmth tracking to the east upon its path, heats my back, and sets the bright orange canopy aglow. Another invisible brush stroke paints another perfect rainbow inside and behind the first. Between their belts of color are walls of deep gray. The smaller rainbow is a cavernous mouth well lit on the rim, leading inward to a deeper, electric blue. I feel as if I am passing down the corridor of a heavenly vault of irreproducible grandeur and color. The dorados leap in very high arcs as if they are trying to reach the clouds, catching the setting sun on their sparkling skins. I stand comfortably, back to the sun, as cool rain splashes on my face, fills my cup, and washes me clean. Far away to the north and south the ends of the rainbows touch the sea. Four rainbow ends and no pots of gold, but the treasure is mine nonetheless. Perhaps until now I have always looked for the wrong kind of coin.

As the spectacle moves on, I empty the captured water into containers, pull the sleeping bag over me and close my eyes. My body is sore, but I am strangely at peace. For a short while I feel as if I've moved off of that seat in hell. The benign routine lasts three days. Sometimes for better, sometimes for worse, nothing lasts forever.

March 6, Day 30

By the night of March 6, it is blowing like hell again. All night I am thrown about; it's like trying to sleep in a bumper car. The next day the gale reachs forty knots. Combers crash down on *Rubber Ducky*, and I wonder if the strong wind will pick us up and fly us to Antigua. Keeping watch is out of the question. The entrance is lashed down tight. Even tending the still is impossible. If only I had windows, I could see what's going on outside before it leaps inside, and maybe I would see a ship that could get me out of this mess.

Patiently waiting for the gale to blow over, I chew on a fish stick. Dorado skin is much too tough to bite through, so I rake the meat off with my teeth. I feel a hard, sharp object in my mouth, like a shard of bone. I fish it out and find that it is plastic. Part of the cap that covers one of my front teeth has been chipped off. When I was young, the cap came off a few times, and I have vivid memories of the stabbing pain that ran down the exposed nerve of the uncapped tooth stub and shot into my brain. I can feel that some of the cap remains over the nerve, but it is loose and can't last much longer.

Water dribbles in constantly through the canopy. On March 8, *Ducky* is knocked down again. I bail out the gallons of water and begin to wring out the heavy lump that is supposed to be a sleeping bag. My cap is completely gone, but amazingly the tooth doesn't hurt at all. The nerve must have died. Thank heaven for small miracles. I haven't slept for two days. My skin is white, and even my wrinkles have wrinkles. My hair sits dripping and tangled on my head. Fish scales cling to me like ornamental slivers of nail polish. With a gap in the middle of my smile,

I must be quite a mess, a real hag. Well, we rafties can't be at our charming best all of the time.

Two hours later *Ducky* is knocked down again. I sit among the floating debris, exhausted, giving in, no longer able to keep cool. Beating my fists in a splashing tantrum, I yell, "You goddamned son-of-a-bitch ocean!" For five minutes I do nothing but curse the wind and sea. I break down sobbing: "Why me? Why does it have to be me? I just want to go home, that's all. Why can't I just go home?" Inside, a second voice scolds me to stop acting like a child. But I'm beyond control. I yell back at myself. "I don't give one damn about being reasonable! I'm hurt, hungry, tired, and scared. I want to cry." So I do.

What I do not know is that this same day, perhaps at this very moment, my father is calling the U.S. Coast Guard to notify them that *Napoleon Solo* is overdue. Sometime before, my mother had had a nightmare. She had seen me clawing through black waters, struggling to regain the surface. She awoke with a start, sweating, shaking, and had been tense ever since, awaiting word from me. None came.

After a few minutes, the fire inside me subsides. I set about the endless, heavy work of bailing and wringing things out. Perhaps when I get back I will have a picnic with friends and neighbors. Yes, I must return for that. There will be laughter and children and fresh-cut grass, pine trees and trout ponds. I'll have them at last. We will have a brontosaurus of a barbecue, trees of salads, and hills of ice cream. People will ask me what it was like. I will tell them I hated it, all of it. There was not one slimy corner that did not stink. You can never love it. You can only do what you must. I hated the sea's snapping off shots of heavy rifle fire next to my ear, rolling heavy stones over me, ripping wounds open, beating me, winning. Weeks on end, no bells, no rounds, continued onslaught. I even hated the equipment that saved my life—the primitive raft that was an aimless, drifting pig of a boat, the wretched tent that turned clean water foul. I hated having to catch drinking water in the same box I had to defecate in. I hated having to haul aboard lovely creatures and tear into their flesh like a beast. I hated counting minutes for thirty-two days. I hated . . . I hated . . .

I did not know a man could have so much hatred and so much long-ing within him. Yes, I will get home somehow. I must. Has the wind eased a little or is it my imagination?

March 10, Day 34

No. For the next two days the gale continues and life is hellish. I have managed to catch another triggerfish, my third, and another dorado, my fourth. The dorado bent the spear again. I must ration the use of my equipment. Who knows how many dorados it will take to break my spear beyond repair? And how long must the spear last?

The distillate collection bag of the solar still was nearly full an hour ago. Now it hangs flaccid. A tiny, burred hole has been bitten from one edge of the bag. Friggin' triggerfish. I've lost over six ounces of water. That's a half day of life gone, old boy. Won't you feel like a jerk if you die just one half day before being picked up?

By March 11 things have calmed again, and I resume my more placid routine. I'm about halfway to the West Indies. Once again I have time to count my blessings. *Solo* stayed afloat long enough for me to salvage what I needed. My equipment is all working, and doing a fair job of it, too. Mountain climbing, camping, Boy Scouts, boat building, sailing, and design, and my family's continued encourage-ment to confront life head on have all given me enough skill to "seastead" on this tiny, floating island. I am getting there. So far it is a tale of miracles.

March 13, Day 37

On March 13, however, I'm not feeling too chipper. Because of the bad weather, the last dorado that I caught never dried properly and turned pasty and rancid. I haven't eaten much, and I finally throw it out. I strain to do my yoga exercises, accomplishing in an hour and a half what usually takes only a half hour. Even in the calm of evening, I don't think I can last much longer.

Doing just enough to hang on will no longer do. I must keep myself in the best shape possible. I must eat more. I pull in the string farm trailing astern and rake off the barnacles with the blade of my knife. I scrape some rust from the peanut and coffee cans into my drinking water in the hope of absorbing some iron and alleviating anemia.

I talk to the lazy vagrant in control of my body. I coax him to kneel by the entrance to await another dorado. At first my body is slow. A dorado swims out. I clumsily splash down. Miss. Another. Miss. But the pumping of blood helps to revive my other self, the physical part. On the third shot I ram my weapon through the fish's back. It pulls me down over the tube as it twists and jerks to get away. I play the fish as if he's on a light line, because I don't want to break or bend my lance. However, I must also retrieve it as quickly as possible, before it can escape. So I let it twist and jerk while I reach down and grab the shaft close to the body; then I lift it up without the risk of bending the shaft. I flip the fish inside, onto the sailcloth blanket that protects the floor. When I get the dorado pinned down with my knees, I slip the cutting board under its head just behind the gills, push my knife into the lateral line, and break the spine with a quick twist of the blade. Usually I completely clean the fish before eating, but now I'm very hungry. I simply gut it and place the rest aside.

By midafternoon I am eating the organs, and I feel as if I have had a transfusion. The dorado's stomach seems full of something. I cut it open. Five partially digested flying fish spill out onto the floor. I hesitate, take a small taste of a flyer, and almost vomit. I gather them up and toss them out. As soon as they are in the air I think, Fool! You should have washed them off and then tried them. Next time. But such a waste of five fish. I mop up the spilled stomach juices and finish cleaning the dorado. Sweat pours off of my head as I squat over my catch and labor in the heat to slice up the body. I stop twice to stretch out my legs and to relieve my cramped knees and back. The work is hard, but I move fast so that I can rest sooner. I always work that way—pushing myself as hard as I can so I can finish quickly and then find complete rest.

As I poke holes through the fish sticks in order to string them up, SLAM! *Rubber Ducky* crushes me between her tubes. Water dribbles in and she springs back to her normal shape as though nothing has happened. It takes me a moment to get my wind back and recover from the shock. The average wave height is only about three feet, but a monster leisurely rolls off ahead. I set to work again with a shrug. I am getting used to various levels of disaster striking with no warning.

The still lies lifeless, draped flat over the bow. It must have gotten smacked pretty hard. Air jets out of it almost as quickly as I can blow it in. The cloth across the bottom, which allows excess seawater to drain through and which is airtight when wet, now sports a hole. The cloth has deteriorated from the constant cycles of wetting and drying and from chafing against *Ducky*'s tubes. Less than thirty days of use, and the still is gonzo. I've never been able to coerce my remaining still to work. As we have drifted west, the number of light showers has increased, but I am lucky when I can trap six or eight ounces of water within a week. Another critical safety margin has disappeared. I'm in big trouble—not that I've been out of big trouble for quite a while now.

I must get the other still to work and keep it working, perhaps for longer than thirty days. I blow it up until it's tight as a tick. Just below the skirt through which the lanyard passes, a tiny mouth whistles a single-note tune until the balloon's lungs are emptied. The hole is in a tight corner and on a lumpy seam, which makes it impossible to effectively wedge a piece of repair tape into it. Making something watertight is difficult enough, even for a boat builder in an equipped shop. To make something airtight is an even taller order.

For hours I try to think of a way to seal the leaking still. Perhaps I can burn some pieces of plastic from the old still or its packaging and drip the melted globs over the hole. But I find that my matches are sodden and my lighter has been drained of fluid. So I wedge the tape in as firmly as I can and grouchily reinflate the still every half hour. Each time, the still begins to slump as soon as I stop pumping. Water begins to collect in the distillate bag, but it is salty. At this pace, I already feel like I have a case of lockjaw, and my mouth is very dry. I must find an effective solution. If only I had some silicone seal or other kind of good goop.

March 16, Day 40

I have managed to last forty days, but my water stock is declining, and I have but a few hard pieces of fish dangling in the butcher shop. It is also a little disconcerting to realize that *Ducky* is guaranteed for forty days of use. If she fails me now, do you suppose I *can* get my money back?

Despite these problems, I have good reason to celebrate this milestone. I've lasted longer than I had dreamed possible in the beginning. I'm over halfway to the Caribbean. Each day, each hardship, each moment of suffering, has brought me another small step closer to salvation. The probability of rescue, as well as gear failure, continually increases. I imagine two stone-faced poker players throwing chips onto a pile. One player is named Rescue and the other is Death. The stakes keep getting bigger and bigger. The pile of chips now stands as tall as a man and as big around as a raft. Somebody is going to win soon.

The dorados begin their morning foray. They bang away at the bottom of the raft and sometimes run around the outside, cracking stiff shots against the raft with their tails. I grab my spear and wait. Sometimes I have a little trouble focusing. During the last gale I jabbed my eye with a piece of the polypropylene line I've rigged to keep the still in place. After a couple of days of oozing and swelling, my eye cleared up, but I was left with a spot in my vision, which I often take to be a glimpse of an airplane or the first hint of a fish shooting out before the tip of my spear. Dorados are so fast that my shot must be instantaneous, without thought, like a bolt of lightning. A head, a microsecond of hesitation, a splash, a strike, a hard pull on my arm, and an escape. On other days I've hit two or three morning and evening but most of the time come up with nothing. This morning I'm lucky and catch a nice fat female. Squatting over her for two hours on the rolling floor of the raft is hard work for my matchstick legs. Finally the job is done and the fish hung up to dry. I begin to mop up the blood and scales, but my sponges have turned to useless little globs. Evidently the stomach juices that I swabbed up from the last dorado have digested them. Since my sleeping bag has proven its ability to soak up water, I take out some of the batting and bind this up with pieces of codline to use as sponges.

Each day now I set my priorities, based on my continuing analysis of raft condition, body condition, food, and water. Each day at least one factor lags behind what I consider adequate. The dismal problem of collecting or distilling water is one I must find a solution to.

I take some of the black cloth wick from the first still, the one that I cut up early in the game. I affix it across the hole of the still with the rotted bottom, letting the still's weight keep it in place. I now have one still aft and one forward, in the only positions available for frequent tending. Every ten minutes throughout the day, I am a human bellows at the service of one or the other still. In between inflations, I empty the distillate just in case salt water sneaks in to pollute it while I'm not watching. By nightfall I have collected a full two pints of fresh water. I am continually paying higher prices for my small successes. The work is demanding and boils off a lot of body fluid. I can't decide if my steaming cells gain anything from the exercise. There is little time to dream these days, barely enough time to live, but fruit mountains still stand in the panorama of my mind's eye.

The next day my debate over the value of operating both stills becomes moot. The entire cloth bottom on the older still gives way. Throughout the day I keep the one still working and try to devise a patch for the old. I painstakingly poke holes around the rim of the opening, using my awl, then thread through sail twine and sew on a new cloth bottom. I try to seal it with the bits of tape that I have left, but the patch remains an utter failure. The still lies dead no matter how hard and fast I try to resuscitate it.

Luckily I'm learning about the personality of the new still. The inside black cloth wick is wetted by seawater dripping through a valve on the top of the still. The rate at which the inside wick is wetted is critical to production of fresh water. If it's too wet, it doesn't heat up efficiently. Instead, the excess, warm seawater just passes out through the bottom cloth. If the wick is too dry, there is less than the maximum amount of water available for evaporation. I must maximize the rates at which the water will evaporate, collect on the inside of the plastic balloon, condense, and finally drop into the distillate collection bag. It seems that the inside pressure of the still affects the rate of dripping through the valve. The still seems most efficient at a pressure that allows it to sag, but not so much that the wick hits the plastic balloon, because if that happens the salt water in the wick is drawn into the distillate. To keep her at just the right inflation requires constant attention.

To help prevent another failure of the bottom cloth, I make a diaper for the still out of a square of sailcloth and add padding, using the cloth wicking from the cut-up still. I blanket the bottom of the still by tying the diaper up by its corners to the lanyard skirt, hoping the diaper will take the chafe from *Ducky* and will keep the bottom cloth constantly wet to delay rotting.

My rain collection systems also need improvement. At the first *thrrrap* of water droplets from the sky, I usually wedge the Tupperware box against the aft side of the still. It's held in place by the still bridle. The arrangement is simple and is quick to rig or empty, which is important in order to minimize salt water pollution from breaking waves and spray. However, I think that I can catch more water if I can find a way to mount the Tupperware box on top of the raft. I need to put a bridle around the box so that I have something to secure it with. The awl on my jackknife has a cutting edge, so I wind it into the plastic lip that runs around the box, boring a hole in each corner. Through these I string a collar made of sail twine. I secure the two ends of one bridle to *Ducky*'s tail, lead the middle of it to the top of the arch tube, and equip it with a quick-release metal clip that I've stolen from one of the stills. Forward, I tie a short lanyard to the canopy entrance and affix a second clip to the other end, which I also lead to the peak of the canopy. When I have to use the Tupperware for some other purpose, I leave the two clips hooked together, so that they are always ready. As soon as it begins to rain, I can quickly flip the clips onto the collar of the box, which keeps it pretty secure on the apex of the arch tube, angled more directly into the wind and higher away from the waves. Its biggest benefit is that it is no longer blanketed from rainfall by the canopy, which is now below it. In fact, it will prove twice as effective this way.

Finally I must tend to my steel knives. My Cub Scout jackknife with the awl is one that I found when I was twelve. The spring on its main blade has always been broken, so the blade flops about a little. It's a ball of rust now. I scrape it clean. I sharpen both it and my sheath knife frequently. Rubbing the steel hard against fish skin that has a tissue of fat attached produces a tiny drool of fat, which greases the blades until they shine. I treasure raw materials and basic tools; so much can be done with them. Paper, rope, and knives have always been my favorite human inventions. And now, all three are essential to my own sanity and survival.

March 18, Day 42

Each day seems longer. On my forty-second in the raft, the sea is as flat and hot as an equatorial tin roof in August. The sun in the sky is joined by hundreds that flash from water ripples. It is all I can do to try to move about in *Ducky*. We sit like a period in a book of blank pages.

I find that my sleeping bag helps to keep me cool as well as warm. I spread it out over the floor to dry in the sun. When I stick my legs under it, they are shaded and sandwiched between the wet bag and the cool, damp floor. It is not very good for my sores, but they are not too bad now and the relief from the heat is quite noticeable. Without the bag covering, the black floor becomes very hot and the whole inside of *Ducky*, which is hot enough as is, becomes an unbearable oven.

Nothing to do but wait for the wind and try to score more food. Some good fresh guts should help lift my spirits. Triggers, a school of them, flap up toward the side of the raft, then disappear under it, come up again, pirouette, dive, loop, and roll about each other in an amazing underwater ballet. They are very wary of me now and are becoming more difficult to catch than the dorados. They don't have the same sustained speed, but in quick little jerks they can dodge my spear deftly. They flirt just outside of my reach. Jab. Miss. I must two-arm a hit on a dorado, but maybe I can get a quick and penetrating one-arm shot on a trigger. Jab. Jab. Their waving fins taunt me. My arm snaps out straight; a trigger takes the spear in his belly. Inside the fish, I find large white sacs—must be the male organs—that I will soon treasure as much as the female's golden eggs.

Ducky, can't you please stop flopping about? You're bound to be sending out a general invitation to every shark in the district. Maybe I should get more fish while things are so flat.

The sun sinks down to the horizon once again, and the dorados collect for evening recess. They seem mesmerized by the calm conditions and glide about like phantoms, gently nudging us. The emerald elders still skirt the vicinity, keeping an eye on their school. I am coming to know individuals not only by their size, markings, and scars but also by their personalities. I am getting very attached to them. Some like to strike one side of the raft, while others prefer another. Some strike aggressively and quickly fly away, as if they are angry or are testing my strength. Others softly slide along the bottom and wiggle out . . . right . . . in . . . front. Fire! I hit too far aft, near the tail. She churns the surface and shakes loose. I rest.

Clouds sit like dirty fingerprints across a silver sun that reaches down to touch the horizon. Bands of light, "Jesus rays," strike out across the heavens. On the eastern horizon, the sky has reached a deep blue, soon to be black and filled with twinkling stars. The soft, round waves remind me of long stretches of ripe wheat fields. Bending to a gentle breeze that marks where invisible heavens touch the earth, the heavy-headed stalks bow their heads and await the reaper's scythe. I haven't much time to fish. I take up my pose again.

A big form appears to my left. By now I'm used to awaiting the perfect shot, but I may not get another this evening. What the hell. Without thinking, without fear of battle with another male, I roll to the right and jab the spear to the left. Humph! Solid hit. All is still.

Where is the fury? I'm grasping the gun tightly, leaning over the tubes, frozen. In a second the battle will begin. But it doesn't. In his huge head the eye is glazed. His slightly opened mouth is paralyzed. His gills are glued shut. The tip of the spear rests in the stripe that runs down his side, which marks the position of his spine. The barb is still barely visible. The spear has not been driven straight through. I gently pull him toward me, grab the spear with my other hand, and ever so carefully, begin to lift. It's like juggling a ball on the end of a stick. What a relief not to endure another dangerous battle. He is food for a week. The glassy surface bubbles up as his body begins to rise. Taking the weight now . . . Splash. I lunge to grab him. Too late. His smooth skin slips from my fumbling fingers.

The big, stiff body whirls downward like a bright dead leaf falling from a limb. His blank stare goes round and round as he sinks deeper and deeper. All of the other dorados have been watching. Like fingers reaching down to him, they descend. Deeper, still deeper. Finally their shapes converge like living petals blooming from the stamen of the dead fish. The tiny flower whirls ever deeper, getting smaller and smaller, until it is no more. The sun is gone. The waters become black and empty. I stare into the depths.

from A World of My Own
by Robin Knox-Johnston

In 1968, Robin Knox-Johnston (born in 1939) set out to circle the globe single-handed and non-stop. He attempted the feat in his 44-foot (including bowsprit) double-ended Bermudan ketch the Suhaili (which he built). Knox-Johnston encountered serious difficulty in the Roaring Forties—the waters that circle the globe between the latitudes of 40°S and 50°S, where waves build to terrific heights.

We sailed into the Southern Ocean on September 3rd with three weeks of winter left. That night, perhaps a portent, the spinnaker split. There was, of course, no reason why I should suddenly feel that the weather would get more violent just because we had crossed the parallel of 40° South, but just the same it had a psychological effect on me, and I found myself half wanting the first storm to break so that I could see what I might expect during the next four months.

For two days we had very good weather, but there were obvious signs in the sky that a cold front was coming and the barometer's falling needle confirmed this. I had intended sailing along the 40° parallel right the way to Australia, but, naturally enough, the course zigzagged a good deal, depending upon the prevailing winds. To start with we went south and were about 42° South when the cold front arrived. This was my first experience of a Southern Ocean depression and it was quite an experience. As the cold front passed, the barome-

ter suddenly jumped up two millibars and the wind backed in minutes from north to west-south-west and rose to gale force. I reefed right
down on the mainsail and mizzen and replaced the jib with the storm
jib. These last jobs were done in a vicious hailstorm and I was glad to
get below to examine the level in the brandy bottle.

Suhaili was sailing along quite fast, and the Admiral seemed to like
the stronger winds and was reacting well. The wind soon built up the
sea, and as the old sea, left after the wind backed and coming from the
north, was still quite large, we soon had a confused cross sea which
was uncomfortable and potentially dangerous. I stayed in my wet
weather gear that evening, lying on a piece of canvas on my bunk so
that I could rush up immediately if anything went wrong. For an hour
or so I made a tape of my feelings and tried to describe the scene,
intending to send the tape home from Australia, but then as things
seemed safe I dropped off to sleep with the wind howling a lullaby in
the rigging, and the sound of the water rushing past the hull coming
through the planking quite clearly where I lay. The next thing I remember is being jerked awake by a combination of a mass of heavy objects
falling on me and the knowledge that my world had turned on its side.
I lay for a moment trying to gather my wits to see what was wrong, but
as it was pitch black outside and the lantern I kept hanging in the
cabin had gone out, I had to rely on my senses to tell me what had
happened. I started to try to climb out of my bunk, but the canvas
which I had pulled over me for warmth was so weighted down that
this was far from easy.

As I got clear *Suhaili* lurched upright and I was thrown off balance
and cannoned over to the other side of the cabin, accompanied by a
mass of boxes, tools, tins and clothing which seemed to think it was
their duty to stay close to me. I got up again and climbed through the
debris and out onto the deck half expecting that the masts would be
missing and that I should have to spend the rest of the night fighting to
keep the boat afloat. So convinced was I that this would be the case that
I had to look twice before I could believe that the masts were still in
place. It was then that I came across the first serious damage. The Admi-

ral's port vane had been forced right over, so far in fact that when I tried to move it I found that the stanchion was completely buckled and the ⅝-inch marine plywood of the vane had been split down about 10 inches on the mizzen cap shroud. The whole thing was completely jammed. Fortunately I was using the starboard vane at the time, because I could not hope to try and effect repairs until I could see, and the time was 2:50 a.m. It would not be light for another four hours. *Suhaili* was back on course and seemed to be comfortable and I could not make out anything else wrong; however, I worked my way carefully forward, feeling for each piece of rigging and checking it was still there and tight. I had almost gone completely round the boat when another wave came smashing in and I had to hang on for my life whilst the water boiled over me. This is what must have happened before. Although the whole surface of the sea was confused as a result of the cross-sea, now and again a larger than ordinary wave would break through and knock my poor little boat right over. I decided to alter course slightly so that the seas would be coming from each quarter and we would no longer have one coming in from the side, and went aft to adjust the Admiral accordingly.

Having checked round the deck and rigging, and set *Suhaili* steering more comfortably, I went below and lit the lantern again. The cabin was in an indescribable mess. Almost the entire contents of the two starboard bunks had been thrown across onto the port side and the deck was hidden by stores that had fallen back when the boat came upright. Water seemed to be everywhere. I was sloshing around in it between the galley and the radio as I surveyed the mess and I could hear it crashing around in the engine-room each time *Suhaili* rolled. That seemed to give me my first job and I rigged up the pump and pumped out the bilges. Over forty gallons had found its way into the engine-room and about fifteen more were in the main bilge, although how it had all got in I did not know at the time. Doing a familiar and necessary job helped to settle me again. Ever since I had got up I had been in that nervous state when you never know if in the next minute you are going to be hit hard for a second time. I could not really believe that the boat was still in one piece and, as far as I could see, undamaged. It's rather similar to when you uncover an ant nest. The exposed ants immediately wash their faces and this familiar task reassures them and prevents them panicking. Pumping the bilges was a familiar task to me and when it was completed I felt that I had the situation under control and set about tidying up quite calmly. The only real decision I had to make was where to start. I couldn't shift everything out of the cabin as there was nowhere else to put things, so I had to search for some large object amongst the mess, stow it away and then use the space vacated as a base. It was two hours before my bunk was cleared. I found books, films, stationery, clothes, fruit and tools all expertly mixed with my medical stores, and for days afterwards odd items kept appearing in the most out of the way places.

Working aft I started on the galley and put that straight, finding the pliers, which I had last seen on the radio shelf, tucked away behind a pile of saucers in their rack. It must have missed them by millimetres. The radio seemed all right, although it had got very wet. I mopped up what I could see, intending to do the job properly after daylight.

Whilst doing this I noticed a lot of water dripping down from the chart table immediately above the radio, and on following this up I discovered that water was pouring into the cabin round the edge each time a wave broke aboard. Tracing this back, I discovered that there were ominous cracks all round the edge of the cabin, and that the interior bulkheads had been shifted slightly by the force of the wave breaking over the boat. The sight of this, and the realization that if we took many more waves over the boat the weakened cabin top might be washed away, gave me a sick feeling in the pit of my stomach. If the cabin top went it would leave a gaping hole 6 feet by 12 in the deck; I was 700 miles south-west of Cape Town and the Southern Ocean is no place for what would virtually be an open boat. Just then another wave hit and I could feel the whole structure wince at the blow, but it did not appear to shift. Well, there would not be time to put extra fastenings in if it was going. I would just have to put lashings over it if things got worse and hope that the weather would ease and allow repairs to be made the next day.

The cabin was now clear so I found the torch and checked the engine-room for sources of leaks as water was already sloshing about in the bilges again. The first thing I noticed was that all the batteries were at a crazy angle and were fetched up against the port fuel tank. The side of the battery shelf had been knocked out by the weight of the batteries when the boat lurched and only the fact that the port fuel tank was in the way stopped the batteries from falling and being ruined. This would have meant no more radio and an end to getting the engine going. My two spare batteries were old, and could only be relied upon to work the Aldis signalling lamp and my tape recorder. I pushed the batteries back onto their shelf and lashed them in place, so that even if the other side of the shelf carried away they would not move again.

There was nothing else I could do until daylight, so I took a tot, folded the jib on the cabin deck, wrapped myself in a piece of canvas and fell asleep. Canvas may seem an odd covering, but it does keep the water out to a certain extent and once my own whisky induced heat had spread, the canvas kept me quite warm.

When I awoke three hours later and poked my head outside, the waves seemed less ferocious, but occasional squalls, usually accompanied by hail, were whipping across the surface and turning the dull grey sea into a milky white. After quickly checking that all was well on deck, I dived below again and started cooking up some porridge. By the time I had put this inside me and followed it with a mug of coffee and a cigarette, I was feeling quite happy. I obviously could not repair the Admiral in the present wind, as the vane would be blown away the moment I tried to unfasten it, so I decided to try and strengthen the cabin.

I got out my box of odd nuts and screws and selected the longest bolts and heaviest screws in order to try to reinforce the cabin top fastenings. The job kept me busy all day, but I slept a lot better knowing it was done.

That evening one of those infuriating little accidents occurred which, although it did not affect my ability to go on, nevertheless left me feeling rankled because it was so unnecessary. I had just opened a new bottle of brandy for my evening drink, and having poured out a good measure I put the bottle on the spare bunk, jammed by the sextant box. About an hour later a strong smell of brandy began to invade the cabin and I eventually traced it to the newly opened bottle. The bottle was sealed by one of these metal screw caps, and as the boat rolled in the sea, the movement had slowly loosened the top until the contents could escape. I was furious about this. As my allowance was half a bottle of spirits a week I had lost two weeks' supply, but I consoled myself with the thought that I had at least taken that day's ration from it!

On September 7th, two days after the knock down, the seas had eased sufficiently to allow me to tackle the Admiral. I had to do the job anyway as the wind direction had changed and I now needed to gybe round and use the port vane. The whole job was easier than I expected. I had two spare stanchions for the self-steering vanes so I decided to take the plywood fin out of the buckled stanchion and rebolt it into a new one. The job was complicated by the heavy rolls *Suhaili* was making and more than once I found myself completely immersed in the sea, which was most uncomfortable as no wet weather gear is completely waterproof and none is designed for swimming.

Until we reached the Southern Ocean we had met only one gale. The average had now changed dramatically, and five gales passed us in ten days. It was no good taking all sail in and letting *Suhaili* ride them out quietly, as we lost too much distance like that. The winds were from the west and I wanted to go east, and I was racing against time anyway. If I wanted to win I had to keep pushing the boat as much as I dared, but the frequency of the gales appalled me. . . .

Keeping the boat pressed left me on tenterhooks all day in case I was overdoing things, and it was even harder to stop myself from reducing sail at night when the wind always appeared stronger. I slept fully clothed, usually rolled up in the canvas on top of the polythene containers in the cabin. As I would quickly get cramped in that position, I would then try sleeping sitting up. This would be all right for a bit, but sooner or later the boat would give a lurch and I would be picked up and thrown across the cabin. If I tried wedging myself in the bunk I could not get out so quickly in an emergency, and if the boat received a really big bang I would get thrown out of the bunk and across the cabin anyway.

I became rather tired and irritable through lack of proper sleep; an idea of my feelings at this time can be seen in my diary for September 9th.

September 9th, 1968 (Day 87)

I finally awoke at 1100 having had three hours uninterrupted sleep in the bunk. The wind was down so I got up and set more sail. We were rolling very heavily and it was difficult to stand inside the cabin, but I managed to heat up some soup and in the afternoon, a superhuman effort, I made a prune duff, which was a great treat. I also made a new drink. Brandy, honey, hot water, sugar and a lemon, which tasted wonderful and bucked me up. I needed it. I felt very depressed on getting up. I cannot do anything in these conditions. (I am writing this late at night and the rolling has eased a bit.) The real trouble is I am so far from achieving anything at the moment. I used up a lot of nervous energy last night by leaving the jib up, for what— maybe an extra 20 miles if we're lucky—and what difference does 20 miles make when I have about 20,000 to go?

The future does not look particularly bright, and sitting here being thrown about for the next 150 days, at least with constant soakings as I have to take in or let out sail, is not an exciting prospect. After four gales my hands are worn and cut about badly and I am aware of my fingers on account of the pain from skin tears and broken fingernails. I have bruises all over from being thrown about. My skin itches from constant chafing with wet clothes, and I forget when I last had a proper wash so I feel dirty. I feel altogether mentally and physically exhausted and I've been in the Southern Ocean only a week. It seems years since I gybed to turn east and yet it was only last Tuesday night, not six days, and I have another 150 days of it yet. I shall be a Zombie in that time. I feel that I have had enough of sailing for the time being; it's about time I made a port, had a long hot bath, a steak with eggs, peas and new potatoes, followed by lemon meringue pie, coffee, Drambuie and a cigar and then a nice long uninterrupted sleep, although, come to think of it, to round it off properly. . . . Here, in a nutshell, is my problem; I have all this to look forward to, but it's so far ahead. I really want something in the more immediate future to look forward to. Australia possibly, and yet that is eight weeks ahead at least and will only be a brief contact with a boat, not something special I can look forward to, and even then I am only halfway; I still have a slightly greater distance to go. It's all a great prospect; why couldn't I be satisfied with big ships?

The life may be monotonous but at least one gets into port occasionally which provides some variety. A prisoner at Dartmoor doesn't get hard labour like this; the public wouldn't stand for it and he has company, however uncongenial. In addition he gets dry clothing and undisturbed sleep. I wonder how the crime rate would be affected if people were sentenced to sail round the world alone, instead of going to prison. It's ten months solitary confinement with hard labour.

Rather an interesting sight this evening. I was adjusting the Admiral at 2000 so that we would run better when I thought I saw a light ahead. I went forward and saw it again quite clearly low down on the surface. It rapidly drew close dividing into two as it did so and we passed between it. It, or rather they, were two wedge shaped lumps of luminescence, about 2 ft. 6 ins. long and about 8 ins. square at the thick end, narrowing down to about 4 ins. square at the other end. Possibly a leptocephalus but if so an unusual shape.

It's quiet just now, although I have one foot on the galley to hold myself steady, as we are rolling heavily. Note that the pressure has remained steady for over twenty-four hours. The wind seems to be veering which is good news.

The 10th was a bad day, and once again the diary carries the mood.

September 10th, 1968 (Day 88)

It is perhaps as well that I am more of an optimist, or perhaps fatalist would be a better word, than a realist, as if I were to be the latter I could give up after today. On thinking about it though, perhaps I am a realistic optimist—it's all speculative anyway. First, it was not too bad today; the weather on waking was reasonably fine and I managed to get sights. At noon we had covered a fantastic 314 miles in two days and were due south of Cape Town. Obviously leaving the sails up and hanging on gave us this terrific mileage—if only I could maintain it but, on account of the occurrence about to be related, I am going to limit the speed from now on.

I was just creating a bully beef and Ryvita sandwich, having plotted noon, when I noticed that we had yawed more off course than usual. I went up to investigate and discovered that the self-steering rudder had broken. It was blowing about Force 3 at the time and we were moving quite fast on a dead run so I took down the main and mizzen and just left the headsails to steady her.

After a difficult tussle I salvaged the bits and set about getting the spare ready to ship. This was not at all easy as although the bolts that held the rudder to the bar came undone, the female socket that takes the tiller securing bolt was rusted up and I had to scrape it out with a fork. This done I tried to ship the spare from aft, but only succeeded in bending the bar so, as this will weaken it, I hauled it out, stripped off, took a slug of brandy, and dived in and fitted the bar in its shoe. All well so far, except this description covers three hours' work. Having set the Admiral to work again, I hoisted the mizzen and went to hoist the main but the brake wouldn't work so I had to strip that. The main at last hoisted, I went back to check the course and knocked the lid off the binnacle. I fixed that; the hinge had broken. As I appeared to be accident prone I decided that the safest place for me was below and I made a mug of Barmene and had, I think, a well-earned cigarette.

The self-steering rudders gave me cause for concern. If one could break after about 8,000 miles, less than a thousand of which were in the Southern Ocean, how soon would the spare go? The cause of the trouble was obviously that the vertical bars on which the rudders were mounted were not strong enough, and the strain was too much for them. The last two days' fast going had been more than the first rudder could take and the spare was built the same way, so I would obviously have to reduce speed if I was going to keep any self-steering.

I lay in the next morning and spent the whole day reading Trollope's *Orley Farm*. There was a bit of psychology here, as I was feeling tired and not very enthusiastic and I knew that if I kept myself from doing anything but essential work, I would shortly get interested again. By the evening I was quite restless but I kept myself away from work, and sure enough the next day awoke raring to get on with repairing the rudder.

The repairs took me three days. The old rudder blade was hopelessly split, so I made a new one out of one of the teak bunkboards. The bar had broken by the middle of the blade, and to rejoin it I cut the handle of a pipe wrench and then filed it down until it fitted inside the bar, like an internal splint. I put the two broken ends of the bar together and then drilled through the bar and wrench handle, riveting them together with pieces of a 6-inch nail, heated on the primus stove. The final job looked pretty strong, but to make sure of it, I bound it with glass fibre.

Whilst I was working on the rudder the potentially most serious damage as a result of the knockdown came to light. I had left Falmouth with 15 gallons of fresh water stowed in polythene containers, and whilst passing through the Doldrums and Variables I had managed to catch quite a lot of rainwater and had not had to touch the fresh water tanks at all. Having watched *Suhaili*'s behaviour in the Southern Ocean, I decided that she would probably sail better if I could lift the bow a bit, so I decided to start using the forward fresh water tank. I connected the feed pipe to the pump and began to suck up water, but the pale brown and rather unpleasant smelling liquid that came out bore no resemblance to clean water. I kept pumping for a while, hoping that I might find that the bad water was just the contents of the pipe, but it stayed discoloured. Feeling thoroughly alarmed I uncovered the tank and took off the inspection cover. The putrid smell of bilgewater told me that I did not have to look farther to know that the water was contaminated and undrinkable. I tried the other tank but it was little better—I would poison myself if I tried drinking from either.

I lit a cigarette and sat down to consider the situation. Firstly, there was no immediate panic. I had well over ten gallons of water in the polythene containers, enough for forty days without discomfort. The Cape was 400 miles north of me so I was in no danger. Next, could I go on? I thought of the rain and hail that had accompanied the depressions of the last few days. There was obviously plenty of rain about in the Southern Ocean, so I should be able to collect enough to keep me going. Lastly, should I go on knowing that I would have to depend upon the rain to support my life? Well, there was a good forty days' supply in the containers to start with, and I had three hundred tins of fruit juices and beer to supplement this. If the worst came to the worst, I could distil drinking water by boiling sea water on the stove and condensing the steam, so long as my paraffin lasted out. Australia was about fifty days away and it looked as if I could manage that length of

time without catching any rain at all, so obviously the thing to do was
carry on and see how things went.

But now the radio began giving cause for concern. I failed to make a
scheduled contact with Cape Town, as although I could hear them they
couldn't hear me. This worried me as I had not failed to make a schedule so far. I waited until after dark when radio conditions are generally
better and then tried calling on the distress frequency. Much to my
relief, Port Elizabeth radio came through straight away and I was able to
send a message to Natie Ferreira letting him know that we had received
damage but were safe and that I was going to try to head north a few
degrees to find some better weather and give the boat a thorough check.
Port Elizabeth wanted me to report every eight hours just in case anything went wrong, but I managed to reduce this to twice a day in order
to conserve my batteries. To improve morale I listened to the South
African Radio for a while that evening, and picked up a magazine pro-
gramme dealing with the year 1947. At one point they mentioned that
in Britain that winter was the coldest on record, which I found amusing,
as I remembered it clearly as an excellent winter for tobogganing.

A day later I heard that Chay Blyth had been forced to pull into East
London. The last news I had had gave him as being off Tristan da
Cunha three weeks before and I had wondered how close we were to
each other in the Big Gale. I now knew he must have been about two
days ahead of me. We had been racing against each other for three
months and I had only closed the gap by four days. For my own sake I
was sorry to lose the competition.

Suhaili headed north-east for a few days and the weather got noticeably better. I was able to tidy her up properly and restow stores so that
they would not fall out so easily again. The boat itself was as good as I
could make her and I decided to start repairing the spinnaker as I should
need it if the weather continued fine. It had split completely down one
side and two corners were torn so I thought the best thing I could do
was sew rope along the edge all the way round. This was quite an enjoy-
able task and I got on with it quickly considering the difficulties of
holding myself steady whilst I sewed.

It was whilst I was in the middle of the job and halfway along the rope, which I had tied to opposite ends of the cabin to keep it taut and out of the way, that one of those silly incidents occurred which seem funny now but was far from being so at the time. I was standing braced in the middle of the cabin using one hand to steady myself and the other to sew. Coming to the end of a length of twine, I used my teeth to help tie a knot, and then tried to stand up. I had not moved more than three inches when I felt a painful wrench at my moustache. I tried to move again, very slowly, but as the spinnaker began to rise with me I decided not to continue the movement. With my free hand I groped around to discover the cause of the trouble and found that my moustache was firmly tied to the spinnaker. I thought for a moment and then tried to stretch to the nearest point where the rope was made fast, but I was a good foot short. I rolled my eyes round looking for the knife but it was tantalizingly out of reach. This was quite a problem. Here I was, hopelessly entangled. I could not undo or cut the knot that held me and it was getting on towards beer time. There was only one way out of it. I closed my eyes, gritted my teeth and jerked my head sharply back, tearing myself free. It hurt like hell and tears filled my eyes, but it soon passed off and at least, as I rushed to the mirror to reassure myself, the symmetry of the moustache was not badly upset. I gave it a trim with my surgical scissors, and while I was at it gave myself a haircut.

On the Admiralty weather charts that accompany *Ocean Passages of the World*, a book that not only gives the best routes to follow between ports, but also shows alternatives for the different seasons, we were heading out of the area round the Cape of Good Hope where for up to ten days in a month the winds will blow at gale force. The frequency of gales began to diminish; we even had some really fine weather which made my spirits rise and allowed me to air my sleeping-bag and a sailbag full of wet clothing which had accumulated whilst we rounded the Cape.

The radio batteries had been run very low and I got out the charger as soon as it was safe to do so. After removing the cylinder head to clear the valves, both of which were stuck, I left the motor going right through the night. The exhaust pipe and silencer had been broken when the boat was knocked down and the noise of the engine was frightful. The wind began to rise during the night but as I wanted to get the batteries up I left the charger at work, even though it made sleep impossible. During the night I went into the engine-room to check the batteries' strength with a hydrometer, and whilst I was doing this *Suhaili* broached before a wave, lurched, and I fell over. The hydrometer was in my hand and some acid from it was flicked over my face and into my left eye. I struggled out of the engine-room as fast as I could, and rushed on deck. The cockpit was awash and I scooped up a handful of water and threw it into the eye. I kept doing this for about five minutes, then went below again and washed it with fresh water.

The eye had begun to sting before I splashed water into it, and now it throbbed painfully. I found the medical box and took out the antiseptic eye drops. I could not see anything wrong with the eye in the mirror, but according to the *Ship Captain's Medical Guide* the eye should be rested after such an accident. One thing I had not thought of when checking my medical stores was an eye patch, so I had to put a bandage round my head at an awkward angle in order to leave my right eye free. The result was very piratical but not at all practical, and in fact I only left the bandage on for one night as it got in my way. It was not a pleasant night; I did not know the extent of the damage and having a fertile imagination I considered the possibility that I might lose the use of the eye. I debated turning back for Durban, but Commander King and Bernard Moitessier were in the race, I was in the lead and stood a slight chance of winning, and I felt that this would be worth giving an eye for, so I carried on. As it turned out, the eye was not damaged much and by the end of a week had ceased throbbing and has given no trouble since then.

When *Suhaili* broached, the charger was swamped and knocked over in the cockpit, so I decided to call it a day and took the unit below. I had to dry it out and clean the generators before it worked again. The other loss was my distilled water for replenishing the batteries. The top was off the container when we heeled over, and the container went flying. In my rush to wash my eye I had not noticed it, and by the time I found it all the contents had disappeared into the bilges. From this point on I had to use rain water in the batteries.

The next day, my one-hundredth out, found me some 1,400 miles east of Cape Town:

September 22nd, 1968 (Day 100)
Last Day of Southern Winter.

Awoke to find us heading north so got up and gybed. I banged my elbow badly during the night and what with that, numerous other bruises and an eye that throbbed, I felt as if I had just gone through ten rounds with Cassius Clay. As the wind was down I let out some sail and then went back to bed. It's warm and reasonably dry there and I feel very tired. I awoke at 1400 to another gale building up, this time from the S.W. so I had to start taking in sail again. Reefing is no longer an easy business. My hands are very sore and covered with blisters and whirling the handle is sheer hell. I noticed today over seven sail slides [the slides on the sail which run up a track on the mainmast] loose or missing on the mainsail so there's the first job when the wind goes down. I got up at 2000 and made a risotto which I followed with a tin of fruit to celebrate our 100th day, then I turned in again. This may seem very lazy, but I wanted to rest my eye as much as possible; also to give some idea of how tired I have become, each time I turned in I fell asleep at once and it was the alarm that woke me. We should get calmer weather shortly as the glass is rising steadily. Well, with this rest behind me I should feel energetic enough to get on with some of the jobs that need doing. I have set the alarm for just after midnight; it might be possible to set more sail then.

I was obviously trying to encourage myself with my headings. The one hundred and first day, September 23rd, begins '*The First Day of Spring Tra-La!*' and continues:

Up just after midnight to find it a lot calmer so I let out sail and turned in. Up again just after 0700 to find us virtually becalmed and the wind looking as if it was going to box the compass again. After a quick breakfast of coffee, Ryvita and damson jam, I took a sight and then I lowered the mainsail; for the first time since sailing the sail came off the mast. I spent all morning retying sail slides and replacing missing ones—seven were missing, two of which are at the top of the mast. I used one strand of the nylon Portuguese fishing line I bought in Lourenço Marques when on the *Congella*. It's better quality than British man-made fibre. I just hope they stay on. This was completed in time to take a Meridian Altitude. We have covered 243 miles in two days, not too bad considering we had light winds twice. I made a curry for lunch. I'm getting better at them, but onions are needed for best results. I wish I knew how to cook rice; Chris had it taped last voyage. After this I pottered—new halyard on staysail as the old one has chafed; tightened the port mizzen topmast shroud, went round with the oil can and grease tin and also whipped the thimble in the port storm jib sheet eye. The starboard one needs doing as well as the thimbles keep popping out, but it was wet so I left it for now. I set the charger to work; bless it, despite Saturday's knock over, it went. The batteries are coming up very slowly, there is something wrong somewhere but I cannot discover it. I have given up listening to the radio in the evenings to conserve power. I have just filled the charger again, the third fill today; none of the batteries has reached 1200 yet but they are getting close at last. I will run it as long as I dare but there will be no repeat of Saturday's performance. That was like a scene from the *Twilight of the Gods*, with the boat rushing through the sea, which was breaking over the bow, the wind howling in the sails and rigging almost drowning the sound of the unsilenced charger.

I decided to turn the engine today as it has not had any use for over two months. I tried to turn it by hand first, and even bent the handle of the pipe wrench which gives some idea of the force I was exerting on it, but it seems to have seized up. I checked all the cylinders, but the oil I put in is still there. I also checked the gearbox but that was clean. I'll take the starter motor off during the next calm spell and see if that is the cause of the trouble. Whatever the trouble it's my own fault for not turning it daily. Now I have a lot of work on my hands to get it free, even if I manage that—a stitch in time etc!

As expected, the wind has boxed the compass, and if everything goes according to pattern the wind will get up to another gale tonight—still I had today to get some work done for which I am very thankful. I would like to get working on some letters now, but writing when it is blowing is not easy and although my eye seems O.K.—it feels as if there is something in it at the moment—I don't want to take any risks for a while by reading or writing by oil lamp.

I seem to have got quite chatty about this time:

September 25th, 1968 (Day 103)

Awoke at 0800 to find us heading N.W. I don't know when the wind backed or veered to the S.S.E. as I slept or rather was unconscious most of the night. I did not sleep well and kept waking but was unaware of my whereabouts whilst awake. I gybed round and let out some sail; the motion is very uncomfortable. It poured with rain this morning but I was unable to catch any of it because the sail is rolled on the boom and the motion throws most of the water off the sail. In order to trap rainwater the booms must be rolled so that the sails are drawn down the lee side of the booms. The mizzen can only be reefed one way and so will only catch water when we are on the port tack. The main happens to be rolled the same way as the mizzen at present.

I held the sextant out in the rain for ten minutes to wash it off and then took out a cotton shirt to wipe it with. The shirt has miraculously remained dry and has a beautiful smell of soap about it. I conjure up memories of a life I have almost completely forgotten, where people daily immerse themselves in special containers filled with hot fresh water—a strange habit which cannot be healthy—sleep in sprung beds with clean white sheets and have special clothes to wear in their beds, and where, most peculiar of all, they transfer their food from the cooking pot to a plate before eating!

I remember reading an article once in an Insurance Company's House Magazine about people's 'off' days. This must be one of mine. *Suhaili* quietly gybed in the afternoon, so as we were hardly moving I held on to the port tack to gather water. As soon as the bucket was full I untied it and it dropped from my hand onto the deck. I caught it just before it went overside. As I have only two buckets left I gave this up and gybed back. The wind was about non-existent and one needed to be a Burmese Goddess to hang on [as *Suhaili* pitched and rolled in the swell], let alone do anything! I next decided to have a cup of coffee and of course everything played up. First I put methylated spirits into the primus to heat it up, but it failed to get hot enough and I had to add more meths. As I was pouring the boat lurched and I lost my balance. The meths spilt out of the can over the stove and my hand. Immediately the whole lot went up in flames which I managed to smother before any damage was done, but of course whilst I was doing that the meths in the stove went out and I was back to square one again. I started off again, got the stove alight this time and put the kettle on. Up to this moment the stove had not been rocking too badly; now for some reason it lurched and the kettle toppled over extinguishing the flame and wasting two pints of fresh water. I really lost my temper at this and gave the stove a good swipe with the pressure cooker which did not do either of them any good but made me feel a lot better, and I started again. I think I must have scared everything, because this time all went well and I got my coffee. I feel I have established the principle between the stove and myself that if I want it to work, it's bloody well going to work, and it will save itself a lot of bother by cooperating to start with!

Whilst on deck I noticed a seam going in the mainsail. In order to stop it going further until I can do a proper job on it, I got out needle and sailtwine. After half an hour I had made four stitches, and the rolling of the boat made this an achievement.

Suhaili will steer between north and west at present, and I'm damned if I'm hoisting more sail to try to improve things; the glass is still falling and you can bet your last shilling that the moment I have more sail up the wind will arrive with a rush and using a spanner it takes an age to reef the mainsail.

The remark about reefing with a spanner refers to the fact that I had lost my main reefing handle overside a few days before when I had slipped on the wet deck going forward. Reefing down using a spanner was a very slow business so I decided to see if I could make a new handle. All sorts of ideas occurred to me but I eventually decided to try and square a rigging screw whose internal circumference was the same as the circumference of the reefing gear lug. I cut the bottle part of the screw in half and then heated it on the primus until it was red hot.

Then I hammered it until it cooled and repeated the process until I had the right shape. I had to file out the corners a bit which took time but I ended up with a snug fit. The problem of a handle was solved by bending the screw and securing a bolt to the end, and presto! I had a reefing handle. I derived great satisfaction from the job and it put me in a thoroughly good mood.

By the end of September we had covered over 3,000 miles of the Southern Ocean and I had lost contact with Cape Town radio. As far as I could make out, my transmitter had packed up soon after the knock-down. I had been meant to contact Perth Radio Station in Western Australia, but had been unable to get through, and when I tried to meet my last schedule with Cape Town, I could hear them calling me for over half an hour but they obviously could not hear me. Cape Town had been most helpful and co-operative throughout my passage through their area, and I did not like leaving things in the present unsatisfactory state.

During the next spell of fine weather I stripped down the transmitter, cleaned out the encrusted salt and tried to find the fault, but I might as well have tried to sort out a railway timetable: in the first place the circuit diagram looked like a plan of Clapham Junction, and in the second, I am no electrician. I changed the valves and tried the transmitter again, but the fuses blew before the power started to come through. I spent two days trying to find out what was wrong and eventually had to admit defeat.

As I could not get the radio to work in the easier conditions clear of the Cape of Good Hope I decided to have another attempt at turning the engine. I stripped off the electric starter motor and exerted pressure directly on the flywheel. I calculated that I had to exert a turning moment of at least half a ton before the flywheel moved at all, and this was by means of a complicated system of levers that would have filled Emmett with awe. The main difficulty was finding bearing points and at one stage the lot slipped and my right forefinger was gashed down to the bone. I swabbed out the cut with Swarfega and then wiped it clean. Plaster would not stick to the skin and I had a terrible job covering the cut. Eventually I found a pair of heavy duty leather gloves and put these on before going back to try again. This time the flywheel moved, which gave me a terrific feeling of relief as I had been wondering what I should do if I could not shift it. Stripping the whole engine down in the middle of a heaving sea would have been next to impossible:

It took me forty minutes to turn it one revolution, but then it began to ease and I felt it was worth trying the self-starter. I ran the disconnected starter for a minute on the spare batteries just to make sure it was O.K. and give it a chance to clear any 'cobwebs', and then fitted it. It worked! It turned. Tra-La! Not fast, not easily, but it turned. I had removed the heater plugs so that the starter would not have to overcome the compression and the diesel oil I put in a few days ago came out as a thick mist. Rather rapidly I evacuated the engine-room and spliced the mainbrace. If it is still calm tomorrow I'll try to get it going and give it a run for an hour or so. There'll be a mammoth air lock to overcome and these always give me trouble.

I don't feel in the least tired this evening. I have the tape recorder running and feel very happy. I'm trying not to think about the lack of progress. I threw over an empty paper sack which had contained potatoes, the first of three empty, and an hour and a half later it was 20 yards away!

This was a trying period in some ways. The winds were generally light, but the gales round the Cape of Good Hope were fresh in my memory and I was still wary.

October 1st, 1968 (Day 109)

Calm all day. The diurnal variation in the barometric pressure gave me a few qualms, the wind builds up so quickly, but despite gusts in the morning which gybed her, there was very little wind and the day's run of 81 miles reflects this.

At midnight tonight it will be four weeks since we crossed the Greenwich Meridian and we should be 66° E [approximately 600 miles west of St Paul's Island], an average of $16^{1}/_{2}$° of longitude or in this latitude 740 miles a week. The last ten days have knocked the average down badly. At this rate we'll be off Melbourne on November 6th. I set the 'Big Fellow' this evening goosewinged out to port; it has made a little difference but I'll be glad when the spinnaker is ready. I worked on it, when allowed, all day.

I had a terrible job getting to sleep last night; I was feeling frustrated by our slow progress and this sort of thing causes me to tense up. I usually notice it in my legs; they feel as if they want exercise, rather like they do when you have been climbing all week; your legs get used to the work and want to go on doing it. I eventually dropped off at 0300 and awoke when we gybed just after 0900. There was so little wind that even with full sail set she drifted round. . . .

I have her with the sails, apart from the 'Big Fellow', boomed out to starboard at present, although I ought to be heading south a bit. The reason for this is that the port vane works better than the starboard one which sticks a bit, and I cannot afford to have the rudder stick with 890 sq. ft. of sail set.

The port halyard winch, the one I use for the storm jib and 'Big Fellow' caught it today. I put my foot on it so that I could reach the running boom slide and it spun round despite the fact that the brake was on. I was given a nasty jerk and found myself on the deck. Picking myself up, and commenting quietly upon the halyard winch's ancestors, I collected a screwdriver and attacked it. The brake now works!

We appear to be slightly down by the head again. I don't

know why, as I have added no weight forward. Tomorrow I'll decant some petrol from the tins in the foc's'le into my polythene containers. I am going to have to watch the petrol consumption, I have just over 20 gallons left and if I don't fix the main engine there is no reserve for charging. I have ceased to listen to commercial broadcasts to conserve power, but I think we'll have to miss a couple of weeks if the radio is to last all the way home.

It's a fine night, the wind has freshened slightly and we are making about 4 knots at the moment, increasing to 5 now and again. There is a bright gibbous moon. By this time next month we should be within a few days of Melbourne with any luck. At least there'll be plenty of moonlight so we should show up if there is any shipping around.

People talk about the empty sea and sky, but in my experience, more often than not, some form of life is in view. There are many varieties of seabirds which spend their whole lives, apart from the breeding season, living miles away from land. Most common during my voyage were petrels and albatross. The stormy petrels seem far too fluffy and delicate to live in such a merciless environment, yet even in the roughest weathers they are to be seen skitting low across the water, reacting instantly to the changing airflow caused by the waves inches below and extending one tiny, fragile leg beneath them to gauge their height above the waves. The old seamen watching them following in the wake of their ships for scraps of food used to call them Mother Carey's Chickens, a name which probably came from *madre cara* or *mater cara*, the Dear Mother or Virgin Mary.

The albatross is one of the most graceful of birds. I watched them in strong winds leisurely flapping their wings as they moved up wind, and then turning to glide down close to the waves across the wind. Until you see them close up, you just cannot appreciate their size. Wing spans of 6 to 8 feet were quite common. I had a trolling line out most of the voyage with a hook and lure on the end and this proved so irresistible to the albatross that I had to take the hook off to avoid injuring them, but I left the lure out because the birds gave me so much amusement. They did not seem to realize that the lure was moving, because they would land on the water, peck at the lure, usually missing, and then rise up on the water with their wings half extended, running along the surface uttering an irritated '*Squark! Squark!*' The whole picture was so reminiscent of Donald Duck in a temper that I often burst out laughing at their antics. What puzzled me, was why they ignored bully beef when I threw it to them!

When sitting on the water an albatross looks exactly like a dodo. They often sleep on the water, and more than once in the voyage there was a sudden commotion under the bow where some albatross had suddenly woken up as *Suhaili* came up to it. I think that on one occasion one of these birds must even have been dozing in the air because it flew straight into the mast. The impact shook the whole boat and brought me up on deck with a rush just in time to see the albatross recover itself a few feet above the water and fly on unconcernedly as if nothing had happened.

There are all sorts of superstitions concerning albatross, one of which is that seamen must never kill them. But this must be fairly new, because one of the names given to a species found in the Southern Ocean is Cape Sheep, a name that comes from the days when the seamen used to make jackets decorated with their feathers.

Albatross need a run along the surface before they can take off, and look like a heavily laden Lancaster bomber trundling along a runway as they struggle up into the air. In the days of the great steel-hulled barques running out to India, China, Australia and back, it used to be a favourite pastime amongst seamen to capture an albatross as a pet. It could be let loose on the deck as the bulwarks prevented it taking off, but as a pet its bad temper and snapping beak gave it marked disadvantages.

I never caught an albatross; I never tried to kill one either. I think being alone in a vast and hostile environment gave me a feeling of comradeship with any fellow animal—although I would certainly have killed them had I run short of food.

Regular visitors to us were dolphins and whales. I always welcomed the dolphins, as apart from the feeling of affinity with any warm-blooded creature of such a high intelligence, I have never grown tired of watching them race past a boat, manoeuvring with such agility that although the sea seems full of them, they never appear to touch each other. Whales I was frightened of. I saw many different species, most larger than *Suhaili*, and I had to trust that they would not decide to come too close to investigate. A large blue whale would not have to exert itself to turn over a boat of *Suhaili*'s size. But as with the birds and mammals, I always felt a little lonely when the whales left; even if we could not communicate, I felt that we shared the same difficulties.

I was still worried about the accuracy of my sextant. Despite the fact that I seldom had to make an adjustment, the feeling persisted that there was a slight error, which although it did not show at low altitudes, gradually increased as the observed altitude increased. Roughly halfway between the Cape of Good Hope and Australia lie two small, isolated islands, Amsterdam and St Paul's. I decided to make a check by heading in the direction of the islands and seeing if I made them when expected. No sooner had I made this decision than the wind, which had been light for a few days, freshened from the north, and in order to get the maximum speed I had to steer a course that took me well south of the islands. It did not really matter as I would find out if there was an error when I got near Melbourne anyway, and I think that the slight disappointment I felt was due to the fact that I rather wanted to see two completely uninhabited islands.

For four days we sailed fast. I left the large flying jib, the Big Fellow, set as long as I dared, in fact longer than I should, as it took me well over half an hour to get it in when I eventually decided the wind had risen high enough. It's not an easy sail to take in at the best of times as it is made fast at the end of the bowsprit, and that end has to be let go before one can start lowering the sail. In strong winds, once the sail is let go, it billows out, clear of the boat and out of reach. I took to putting a small length of rope on this end so that I could draw the sail in again, but if the boat yawed off course, and the sail filled, this rope would be torn from my hands. On one particular occasion I was further handicapped by the gash on my hand, which I was trying to protect; however, the rope ripped this wound open early on which gave me something less to worry about. The sail was ballooning right out of reach by this time and I did not have the strength to haul it in, so I just let go the halyard and tried to haul the sail in before it went into the water. I wasn't quite quick enough, and even the small part that remained in the water proved too heavy for me and dragged the whole sail from my hands.

My arms felt like lead by this time, and I was panting with the exertion, but the sail had to be brought in or be let go and lost. *Suhaili* could not be left dragging this huge sea anchor or something would be sure to break. I hauled in one corner of the sail and unshackled it and let it go again. This reduced the drag as that end now flowed out astern. Once again I threw my weight onto the main bulk of the sail and inch by inch I hauled it in. My fingers were no longer gripping by this time; all the strength had gone from them so I was having to use my hands like claws. The wind frequently caught the salvaged part of the sail on deck, blowing it up and enveloping me and I had to sit on it to hold it down. When the sail was inboard at last I bundled it up and sank down wearily on top of it. I must have stayed there for five minutes. I was completely exhausted and just did not have the strength, now the danger was over, to gather up the sail and take it below.

The wind stayed fresh, which made life difficult; however I was learning how to keep morale high:

October 5th, 1968 (Day 113)

We are moving about a lot; it took me over an hour to make some porridge this morning, during which the kettle fell over and I spilled sugar all over the radio. Fortunately this last accident made me lose my temper, so I got porridge.

I have had the tape recorder going most of the day; with it going the cabin seems more homely and less empty. It's a pity there was not time to make more tapes before I sailed—I know the words of all the songs now. One thing frustrates me. I cannot make out the first verse of 'I am a Pirate King'; I hope that Ken knows this one as we can add it to our selection on the way from Falmouth to London. Boy, am I looking forward to that trip. We'll load up with beer and set a course for Parker Bank south of Dungeness. That will keep us well clear of the shipping.

I wish the sea would ease just a bit. I would like to get shifting. Every time I look at the wake I think of the other boats and how much bigger their wakes will be. I'll be lucky to make Melbourne by November 7th at this rate, not good enough.

But the next night I was lying in my bunk when there was a terrific bang on the coach roof. I looked up at the skylight and saw the main boom much lower than usual. With a sinking feeling I climbed on deck and discovered what I had feared most—the main gooseneck had broken.

October 6th, 1968 (Day 114)

0130. Well this may be the end of it all. I don't know yet; I need time to think it out. The main gooseneck jaw has sheared as I rather feared it would. I've just come below from lashing the end of the boom to the mast end taking three reefs using the reefing points. We can still sail alright but under a further handicap in that the smallest I can make the mainsail is now three reefs; after that it has all to come in. I don't feel particularly depressed or angry even. I suppose I felt that this was inevitable; anyway I accept it as such. I shall fix something up I suppose, but what I don't know at the moment. I wish I had left some of the junk from last voyage on board; a bit comes to mind that would have been a perfect replacement. Well, I am having some brandy and then I'm going to bed, praying we don't gybe. The glass is falling to add to the fun. If the saying 'things happen in threes' is true, we're O.K. as this is the third thing to break.

Slept until 0830. It was too rough to think of unlashing the boom all morning so I spent the time rummaging for bolts and bits and pieces that might come in handy fixing the job. The simplest thing to do seems to be to drill out the old jaw and bolt it to the mast fitting. It could still swivel like that. Conditions eased for a while after lunch and I was able to remove the jaw. The stem of the jaw broke where pinned. I have been drilling out the remains of the stem all afternoon. I have given up now as I cannot see properly and I only have three drill bits left. The stem socket goes to within $^{1}/_{4}$ in. of the end of the metal which makes my job easier as the jaw appears to be hardened. My largest drill is $^{1}/_{4}$ in. so I am going to have to file out the last bit. It's going to take some time to do all this. I'm not helped by the weather. The wind is still strong and with the glass still falling is likely to increase if anything. The sea and swell are nasty and we are lurching heavily. *Suhaili* is yawing between east and south. It's a miracle I have not broken any bits so far. We are taking continuous bangs from the sea and all day at an average of five minute intervals a wave has broken right over the boat.

This is the second day I have been unable to see the sun so God knows where we are. Anyway we should be well south of the Islands.

I feel tired and a bit depressed this evening. This constant pounding worries me too; she's a good boat but there must be a limit. Things are beginning to go now; last night I fell against the mizzen and my elbow landed on a seam which broke the stitches. I don't seem able to keep up with the work at present, I wish I was fresh and had a few days of decent weather.

To add to my worries the wind kept up so I could not make repairs.

October 7th, 1968 (Day 115)

Awoke at 0600 and checked the course [which was SE] before rolling over again. I was dozing at 0635 when the wind increased and the boat's movement became bumpy. Feeling tired and a bit confused, it was a minute before I convinced myself that I had not just checked the course. I looked at the compass and got up in a hurry. We were heading north so obviously the cold front had just passed. I climbed on deck and looked around. The sea was already white with spray and appeared to be still getting up. I could feel the wind increasing. I quickly took in the staysail and most of the mizzen and then gybed, being as careful with the main boom as possible. It was freezing cold on deck; the temperature was actually 38°F but with a Force 10 wind it felt a lot colder. I nipped below and took a quarter of a bottle of brandy which made me feel better and then went back on deck. The mainsail was beginning to come apart along the leech so I took it down and she rode much more comfortably, but was still going a bit too fast for my liking especially as we had a rather vicious cross sea. I took in the rest of the mizzen, just leaving the storm jib set and then put out the orange warp as a bight, both ends fastened on board. The orange line floats anyway, but now it flew! I put a figure of eight knot in the main sheet and streamed that, and then did the same with the mizzen, jib and storm jib sheets. You could almost walk on the ropes astern! The glass had by this time started to rise. At 0640 it had been 1008, by 0900 it was 1010 which was comforting. She seemed quite comfortable so I went below and made a cup of coffee from the Thermos. The water was lukewarm so I heated it with the remains of the brandy. I ate half a packet of dates, three handfuls of peanuts and six digestive biscuits and was about to turn in where it was at least warm, when a cross wave caught us. We went over to about 90° and came up again immediately. Quite a lot of stuff shifted, but nothing like as much as on the previous occasion. I checked on deck but all was well, so I tidied up and climbed into my sleeping bag. There was nothing I could do but pray anyway. I got up at 1130 by which time the wind had eased quite a bit, down to about Force 7, so I reset the staysail and let out a bit of mizzen. She no longer needed the lines astern so they came in too. I could not work on the main-sail as it was much too wet on deck so I carried on with the gooseneck jaw. I was lucky enough to find another drill bit, a sharp one, and I soon discovered that the jaw was not hard-ened; the trouble had been blunt bits. By 1700 I had the job done, so I fitted it and put the main boom back in its proper position. Only one of its teeth had got damaged by banging against the mast and I soon had that filed down.

The only bolts I have that can do the job are not long enough to pass through both lugs on the mast, so I'll just have to hope that the one lug will take the strain. The bolts I am using, I have three left, were given me in Falmouth by Dad. Jim [Friend] had found them at home and sent them down. I would have been in trouble without them.

This done I started stitching up the sail. I managed to get both ends of the tear and the centre of it sewn up before the light failed, but as I did not want to waste twelve hours sailing I hoisted the sail anyway. This was quite a job, and a shackle I had put on the swivel piece jammed the boom guy. Whilst I was clearing this, the inevitable happened. A wave caught us and over we went. I was drenched and lucky not to be swept away. I went back to hoist having got the shackle off and the handle on the halyard winch flew back and cracked my wrist. The bloody brake had failed again. I was in agony, it hurt like hell. I moved my fingers to see if the wrist was broken; they moved O.K. but before going on I went below and put a bandage round the wrist, which was already swelling. The force of the blow, which was direct and not glancing, had cut the skin. I said a few polite things about halyard winches and their ancestors, and as soon as the pain was bearable went up and finished hoisting the sail, treating the winch with a great deal of respect.

It was 2030 by this time and I was cold, wet and hungry so I went below and got the heater going and changed my clothes. I then made one of the Vesta Risottos which tasted terrific. I wish I had brought more of that type of meal. It's so convenient. Having eaten, I thought about having a whisky, but decided that Horlicks was more what I needed, so after a strong cup of that I turned in.

A good night's sleep worked wonders, and by the next day I was quite light-hearted again:

October 8th, 1968 (Day 116)

I, today, discovered the magnetic properties of cheese! I do not expect the scientific world to gasp at this discovery which I will not put on quite the same plane as Newton's discovery of gravity. Nevertheless, it is a most important and interesting discovery. In order that posterity will not lose the record of how it came about, I give the details below. (*Alarums off! Commence soft guitar strumming!*) I was getting out some fresh tins for the ready use lockers round the galley, and as usual placed the butter and cheese in the locker above the galley (which Ken says is too hot for fats and which point I acknowledge but ignore, because I have always kept fats there!). My task completed I checked the course on the cabin compass. To my astonishment (*fast beat on guitars*) it was reading 60° off course. I checked the sun—it had not moved, noticeably anyway, so, being a quick thinker, I realized that the tins just placed in the locker, which is immediately behind the compass as I should have explained before, must have caused this elevation. I removed the butter—no change—so I removed the cheese (*guitars reach crescendo*) it swung back its full 60°. I next experimented with the jam, Ryvita, coffee, salt, Vit. Tabs., and others but they had no effect. Thus cheese is magnetic—Q.E.D.

I'm G & S'ing again this evening, at present walking my flowery way down Piccadilly with a Poppy or a Lily in my needy, evil hand!

On the 13th I thought we'd had it. The wind was blowing a good Force 10 and we were running under the storm jib when really big waves started to come up from the south and hit *Suhaili* with stunning force. This was by far the worst weather I had ever encountered and the terrifying shudders and cracks every time a wave hit the hull convinced me that the boat would not last long. I did not see how anything could stand up to this sort of continual punishment. Water was coming into the boat as if out of a tap from leaks all round the coachhouse I had never known before.

It is amazing how one's mind works in times like this. I can remember thinking that the boat might go any moment so I'd better get the liferaft out: Australia was a couple of thousand miles away, but the winds and currents would push a raft that way and I would stagger ashore eventually. I would put a couple of tins of dried fruit in the life-raft with anything else I could manage, and I would take the dinghy so that I could row myself north a bit to make sure of reaching land, and not miss Australia and carry on round the world in the Southern Ocean. For some irrational reason I also thought of poetry and the words of Robert Service's ballad 'The Quitter' came to mind.

> When you're lost in the Wild and you're scared as a child,
>   And Death looks you bang in the eye,
> And you're sore as a boil it's according to Hoyle
>   To cock your revolver . . . and die.
> But the Code of a Man says: 'Fight all you can,'
>   And self-dissolution is barred.
> In hunger and woe, oh, it's easy to blow . . .
>   It's the hell-served-for-breakfast that's hard.*

I think that saved me. It brought me up with a jolt. What was I doing getting the liferaft out? The boat hadn't gone yet; I had not really tried everything. I went back on deck and stood watching the sea for a while. Its character was slowly changing. The huge south-west seas were dominating now and the old northerly seas had been knocked flat by the wind. *Suhaili* was lying beam-on to this large sea, and if I could get her round to lie with the sea she might be all right.

> The decision facing me was this. Whether to put out more warps astern, or bring her round and put out the sea-anchor forward. She was lying nearly beam-on which was why the waves were hitting so heavily. I decided against the sea anchor because *Suhaili*'s bow is not really suitable, the bowsprit and attendant rigging gets in the way, so I got out the blue polypropylene line and put the whole coil out astern, both ends made fast to the kingpost forward and

*From Robert Service, *Collected Verse*, Ernest Benn Ltd., London, and Dodd, Mead, New York; Ryerson Press, Toronto.

led aft. The bight seemed to be on the horizon but it
dragged the stern up to the wind. Like this she yawed a bit
with the result that the storm jib was being thrown from
side to side with terrific bangs so I hardened up both
sheets and this, in fact, helped keep the bow down wind
nicely. I was a bit worried about the two rudders, but
although the seas were very heavy and moving past quite
fast, the rudders seemed O.K. The orange warp, the bight
of which was fairly close, seemed to break the crests up
slightly. It was quite amazing the difference the blue warp
made. From rolling beam on to the seas without it, and
being terribly battered, we were suddenly lying very quietly
stern to seas, which were occasionally breaking over the
decks. We were pooped twice but not heavily. I had been
having to pump the bilges frequently, about every two
hours, but ceased this as soon as we were round. In the
morning I tried to seal up the port cockpit locker as water
was pouring from there into the engine-room. Each time
she rolled about a gallon would get below which explains
why I was pumping so often. The four Diesel fuel drums
are still in the cockpit. One is empty and serves only to
jam the others in place. Another was filled up with water
which has forced the diesel oil out. The cap was no good.
I threw this drum overside to give myself room—it sank
immediately—and refixed the rag in the lower water hole.
But this was only half the problem, as most of the water
gets in via the locker lid, so I screwed that down and
caulked it. It helped a bit.

Quite why I got so depressed about the middle of the
day I don't know. It was after I had put out the orange warp
but before I put out the blue one, so I had not exhausted
all the possibilities. I think it may be due to the fact that I
am feeling very weary, and the low glass is not encouraging. Also the blows the boat was taking were very heavy.

After one of them I was convinced she had stove in the hull. It was cold on deck and I was wet, and I have not been eating properly the last few days.

Tonight I feel better; I've just eaten a curry, but terribly tired. She seems to be riding comfortably and the wind appears to be easing a bit. I've just been on deck, the fore-deck is dry!! I'm going to hope for the best and turn in. It tells on your nerves this sort of thing—you never know when she just might get hit by a big one, and it's so dark that you can only see the waves when they are on top of you. Can't hear 'em, too much noise from the wind.

Next morning I awoke with a stiff back and a bruise the size of a cricket ball at the base of my spine. I don't know how I came by the bruise, but I had been knocked about a good deal the day before, and when one is occupied one doesn't notice bangs. I had a strenuous task hauling the tangle of warps in again; 120 fathoms of 2-inch polypropylene being dragged at three knots weighs a good deal, and it took me twenty minutes to haul that in alone.

The self-steering began to give trouble again. It was stiff and operated slowly and then only in jerks. This meant I had to do a lot of steering myself. My diary entries became shorter because I was tired and when I did get below all I wanted to do was collapse into my bunk. Eating was another problem. I did not feel hungry, and the thought of the effort required to make a meal put me right off food. The succession of gales continued, and eventually I headed north to find better weather. The shearing of the main gooseneck worried me; I thought that if that could break then so could other things and this made me jittery. I wanted a rest and time to check everything. I also wanted to report to a passing ship if I could, and as the steamship routes are north of the sailing ship routes I hoped to kill two birds with one stone by heading northwards.

We were about 500 miles from Australia by this time; although the weather had been rough and uncomfortable, progress had been excellent, and I was beginning to pick up local radio stations in Western Australia.

This kept me abreast of the news and the Albany wool sales; every time I tuned in, it seemed, I picked up the latest market report, and after a few days I could have given anyone a full run down on every aspect of them.

Despite kinder conditions the self-steering rudder broke again on October 23rd after we were well into the Australian Bight. What was worse, I lost most of it and was left with no bits and pieces that could somehow be put together again. The weather was too rough to put in the now repaired original rudder, so I steered for a day myself. To add to my troubles, one of my primus burners developed a leak and I had to blank it off. This left one burner which had to last if I was going to have hot meals and coffee for the rest of the voyage. I could manage without hot food but not without coffee. I have a reputation for being ill-tempered before I get my coffee in the mornings!

The next day I managed to fit the last self-steering rudder. I did not try getting it into its slot from the deck but dived overside and connected it that way. It was much simpler and quicker, but the water was freezing cold, and took my breath away when I first entered. As usual I rushed to check the brandy bottle level on getting out. The rudder vibrated badly, and to ease it I put rope lashings around its bar to support it. This rather stiffened it, but it worked, though I wondered for how long. To reduce the strain I did not sail the boat as fast as I could have done, but even so, the rudder was not going to last. I wondered what I should do when it gave, but the thought was a bit depressing so I thought about other things.

The diary for the next day, October 25th, when I was 450 miles east-south-east of Cape Leeuwin begins with:

YIPPEE!!

Sighted a ship—the *Kooringa* of Melbourne at 1730 today. I had just finished writing a letter and glanced through the forward porthole and saw the superstructure. I rushed on deck and there she was about three miles away. I had reckoned on reaching the shipping lane at 1700 and was going to stay up all night if necessary, but to sight a ship within thirty minutes of getting there is phenomenal luck. I dashed below and grabbed the rifle, loaded a clip and fired three shots. I had hoisted *MIK* [the International Code for 'Please report me by radio to Lloyd's'] at lunchtime and I cleared these flags. For a while nothing happened, then as I fired off the remaining two rounds she turned towards me. As she came close she sounded one blast and then hoisted the answering pennant, so they saw my signal. At last people at home will know I'm safe. I got out the fog horn and sent 'All Well', which I hope they received. They came within a cable's length and then turned and came back for a look. The fact that they did this rather indicates that they realized who we are, so I hope the news gets out quickly. *Suhaili* was not looking very tidy I'm afraid. I should have spent the day on deck but I fiddled with the radio instead. I did screw a couple of bits of wood to the deck where the Highfield levers are wearing a bit. I also turned off the W.C. inlet valve as I don't use the W.C. and it has rather a lot of pipes on it.

In fact, I used a bucket instead of the W.C. It was much more convenient, although one had to be careful not to upset it.

from Two Years Before the Mast
by Richard Henry Dana, Jr.

Tyrannical captains are a staple of nautical literature, from Bligh of the Bounty *to Queeg of the* Caine. *Richard Henry Dana, Jr. (b. 1815; d. 1882) encoutered one when he shipped aboard the brig* Pilgrim *in 1834. Dana's account of the captain's brutality and the crew's response is keenly observed and surprisingly moving at a distance of more than 160 years.*

For several days the captain seemed very much out of humor. Nothing went right, or fast enough for him. He quarrelled with the cook, and threatened to flog him for throwing wood on deck; and had a dispute with the mate about reeving a Spanish burton; the mate saying that he was right, and had been taught how to do it by a man *who was a sailor!* This, the captain took in dudgeon, and they were at swords' points at once. But his displeasure was chiefly turned against a large, heavy-moulded fellow from the Middle States, who was called Sam. This man hesitated in his speech, and was rather slow in his motions, but was a pretty good sailor, and always seemed to do his best; but the captain took a dislike to him, thought he was surly, and lazy; and "if you once give a dog a bad name"—as the sailor-phrase is—"he may as well jump overboard." The captain found fault with everything this man did, and hazed him for dropping a marline-spike from the main-yard, where he was at work. This, of course, was an accident, but it was set down against him. The captain was on board all day Friday, and everything went on hard and disagreeably. "The more you drive a man, the less he will do," was as true with us as with any other people. We worked late Friday night, and were turned-to early Saturday morning. About ten o'clock the captain ordered our new officer, Russell, who by this time had become thoroughly disliked by all the crew, to get the gig ready to take him ashore. John, the Swede, was sitting in the boat alongside, and Russell and myself were standing by the main hatchway, waiting for the captain, who was down in the hold, where the crew were at work, when we heard his voice raised in violent dispute with somebody, whether it was with the mate, or one of the crew, I could not tell; and then came blows and scuffling. I ran to the side and beckoned to John, who came up, and we leaned down the hatchway; and though we could see no one, yet we knew that the captain had the advantage, for his voice was loud and clear—

"You see your condition! You see your condition! Will you ever give me any more of your *jaw*?" No answer; and then came wrestling and heaving, as though the man was trying to turn him. "You may as well keep still, for I have got you," said the captain. Then came the question "Will you ever give me any more of your jaw?"

"I never gave you any, sir," said Sam; for it was his voice that we heard, though low and half choked.

"That's not what I ask you. Will you ever be impudent to me again?"

"I never have been, sir," said Sam.

"Answer my question, or I'll make a spread eagle of you! I'll flog you, by G—d."

"I'm no negro slave," said Sam.

"Then I'll make you one," said the captain; and he came to the hatchway, and sprang on deck, threw off his coat, and rolling up his sleeves, called out to the mate—"Seize that man up, Mr. A——! I Seize him up! Make a spread eagle of him! I'll teach you all who is master aboard!"

The crew and officers followed the captain up the hatchway, and after repeated orders the mate laid hold of Sam, who made no resistance, and carried him to the gangway.

"What are you going to flog that man for, sir?" said John, the Swede, to the captain.

Upon hearing this, the captain turned upon him, but knowing him to be quick and resolute, he ordered the steward to bring the irons, and calling upon Russell to help him, went up to John.

"Let me alone," said John. "I'm willing to be put in irons. You need not use any force;" and putting out his hands, the captain slipped the irons on, and sent him aft to the quarter-deck. Sam by this time was *seized up*, as it is called, that is, placed against the shrouds, with his wrists made fast to the shrouds, his jacket off, and his back exposed. The captain stood on the break of the deck, a few feet from him, and a little raised, so as to have a good swing at him, and held in his hand the bight of a thick, strong rope. The officers stood round, and the crew grouped together in the waist. All these preparations made me feel sick and almost faint, angry and excited as I was. A man—a human being, made in God's likeness—fastened up and flogged like a beast! A man, too, whom I had dived with and eaten with for months, and knew almost as well as a brother. The first and almost uncontrollable impulse was resistance. But what was to be done? The time for it had gone by. The two best men were fast, and there were only two beside myself, and a small boy of ten or twelve years of age. And then there were (beside the captain) three officers, steward, agent and clerk. But beside the numbers, what is there for sailors to do? If they resist, it is mutiny; and if they succeed, and take the vessel, it is piracy. If they ever yield again, their punishment must come; and if they do not yield, they are pirates for life. If a sailor resist his commander, he resists the law, and piracy or submission are his only alternatives. Bad as it was, it must be borne. It is what a sailor ships for. Swinging the rope over his head, and bending his body so as to give it full force, the captain brought it down upon the poor fellow's back. Once, twice,—six times. "Will you ever give me any more of your jaw?" The man writhed with pain, but said not a word. Three times more. This was too much, and he muttered something which I could not hear; this brought as many more as the man could stand; when the captain ordered him to be cut down, and to go forward.

"Now for you," said the captain, making up to John and taking his irons off. As soon as he was loose, he ran forward to the forecastle. "Bring that man aft," shouted the captain. The second mate, who had been a shipmate of John's, stood still in the waist, and the mate walked slowly forward; but our third officer, anxious to show his zeal, sprang forward over the windlass, and laid hold of John; but he soon threw him from him. At this moment I would have given worlds for the power to help the poor fellow; but it was all in vain. The captain stood on the quarter-deck, bare-headed, his eyes flashing with rage, and his face as red as blood, swinging the rope, and calling out to his officers, "Drag him aft!—Lay hold of him! I'll *sweeten* him!" etc., etc. The mate now went forward and told John quietly to go aft; and he, seeing resistance in vain, threw the blackguard third mate from him; said he would go aft of himself; that they should not drag him; and went up to the gangway and held out his hands; but as soon as the captain began to make him fast, the indignity was too much, and he began to resist; but the mate and Russell holding him, he was soon seized up. When he was made fast, he turned to the captain, who stood turning up his sleeves and getting ready for the blow, and asked him what he was to be flogged for. "Have I ever refused my duty, sir? Have you ever known me to hang back, or to be insolent, or not to know my work?"

"No," said the captain, "it is not that that I flog you for; I flog you for your interference—for asking questions."

"Can't a man ask a question here without being flogged?"

"No," shouted the captain; "nobody shall open his mouth aboard this vessel, but myself;" and began laying the blows upon his back, swinging half round between each blow, to give it full effect. As he went on, his passion increased, and he danced about the deck, calling out as he swung the rope,—"If you want to know what I flog you for, I'll tell you. It's because I like to do it!—because I like to do it!—It suits me! That's what I do it for!"

The man writhed under the pain, until he could endure it no longer, when he called out, with an exclamation more common among foreigners than with us—"Oh, Jesus Christ! Oh, Jesus Christ!"

"Don't call on Jesus Christ," shouted the captain; *"he can't help you. Call on Captain T——, he's the man! He can help you!* Jesus Christ can't help you now!"

At these words, which I never shall forget, my blood ran cold. I could look on no longer. Disgusted, sick, and horror-struck, I turned away and leaned over the rail, and looked down into the water. A few rapid thoughts of my own situation, and of the prospect of future revenge, crossed my mind; but the falling of the blows and the cries of the man called me back at once. At length they ceased, and turning round, I found that the mate, at a signal from the captain had cut him down. Almost doubled up with pain, the man walked slowly forward, and went down into the forecastle. Every one else stood still at his post, while the captain, swelling with rage and with the importance of his achievement, walked the quarter-deck, and at each turn, as he came forward, calling out to us,—"You see your condition! You see where I've got you all, and you know what to expect!"—"You've been mistaken in me—you didn't know what I was! Now you know what I am!"—"I'll make you toe the mark, every soul of you, or I'll flog you all, fore and aft, from the boy, up!"—"You've got a driver over you! Yes, *a slavedriver—a negro-driver!* I'll see who'll tell me he isn't a negro slave!" With this and the like matter, equally calculated to quiet us, and to allay any apprehensions of future trouble, he entertained us for about ten minutes, when he went below. Soon after, John came aft, with his bare back covered with stripes and wales in every direction, and dreadfully swollen, and asked the steward to ask the captain to let him have some salve, or balsam, to put upon it. "No," said the captain, who heard him from below; "tell him to put his shirt on; that's the best thing for him; and pull me ashore in the boat. Nobody is going to lay-up on board this vessel." He then called to Mr. Russell to take those men and two others in the boat, and pull him ashore. I went for one. The two men could hardly bend their backs, and the captain called to them to "give way," "give way!" but finding they did their best, he let them alone. The agent was in the stern sheets, but during the whole pull—a league or more—not a word was spoken. We landed; the captain, agent, and officer went up to the house, and left us with the boat. I, and the man with me, staid near the boat, while John and Sam walked slowly away, and sat down on the rocks. They talked some time together, but at length separated, each sitting alone. I had some fears of John. He was a foreigner, and violently tempered, and under suffering; and he had his knife with him, and the captain was to come down alone to the boat. But nothing happened; and we went quietly on board. The captain was probably armed, and if either of them had lifted a hand against him, they would have had nothing before them but flight, and starvation in the woods of California, or capture by the soldiers and Indian blood-hounds, whom the offer of twenty dollars would have set upon them.

After the day's work was done, we went down into the forecastle, and ate our plain supper; but not a word was spoken. It was Saturday night; but there was no song—no "sweethearts and wives." A gloom was over everything. The two men lay in their berths, groaning with pain, and we all turned in, but for myself, not to sleep. A sound coming now and then from the berths of the two men showed that they were awake, as awake they must have been, for they could hardly lie in one posture a moment; the dim, swinging lamp of the forecastle shed its light over the dark hole in which we lived; and many and various reflections and purposes coursed through my mind. I thought of our situation, living under a tyranny; of the character of the country we were in; of the length of the voyage, and of the uncertainty attending our return to America; and then, if we should return, of the prospect of obtaining justice and satisfaction for these poor men; and vowed that if God should ever give me the means, I would do something to redress the grievances and relieve the sufferings of that poor class of beings, of whom I then was one.

The next day was Sunday. We worked as usual, washing decks, etc., until breakfast-time. After breakfast, we pulled the captain ashore, and finding some hides there which had been brought down the night before, he ordered me to stay ashore and watch them, saying that the boat would come again before night. They left me, and I spent a quiet day on the hill, eating dinner with the three men at the little house.

Unfortunately, they had no books, and after talking with them and walking about, I began to grow tired of doing nothing. The little brig, the home of so much hardship and suffering, lay in the offing, almost as far as one could see; and the only other thing which broke the surface of the great bay was a small, desolate-looking island, steep and conical, of a clayey soil, and without the sign of vegetable life upon it; yet which had a peculiar and melancholy interest to me, for on the top of it were buried the remains of an Englishman, the commander of a small merchant brig, who died while lying in this port. It was always a solemn and interesting spot to me. There it stood, desolate, and in the midst of desolation; and there were the remains of one who died and was buried alone and friendless. Had it been a common burying-place, it would have been nothing. The single body corresponded well with the solitary character of everything around. It was the only thing in California from which I could ever extract anything like poetry. Then, too, the man died far from home; without a friend near him; by poison, it was suspected, and no one to inquire into it; and without proper funeral rites; the mate, (as I was told,) glad to have him out of the way, hurrying him up the hill and into the ground, without a word or a prayer.

I looked anxiously for a boat, during the latter part of the afternoon, but none came; until toward sundown, when I saw a speck on the water, and as it drew near, I found it was the gig, with the captain. The hides, then, were not to go off. The captain came up the hill, with a man, bringing my monkey jacket and a blanket. He looked pretty black, but inquired whether I had enough to eat; told me to make a house out of the hides, and keep myself warm, as I should have to sleep there among them, and to keep good watch over them. I got a moment to speak to the man who brought my jacket.

"How do things go aboard?" said I.

"Bad enough," said he; "hard work and not a kind word spoken."

"What," said I, "have you been at work all day?"

"Yes! no more Sunday for us. Everything has been moved in the hold, from stem to stern, and from the waterways to the keelson."

I went up to the house to supper. We had frijoles, (the perpetual food of the Californians, but which, when well cooked, are the best bean in the world,) coffee made of burnt wheat, and hard bread. After our meal, the three men sat down by the light of a tallow candle, with a pack of greasy Spanish cards, to the favorite game of "treinta uno," a sort of Spanish "everlasting." I left them and went out to take up my bivouack among the hides. It was now dark; the vessel was hidden from sight, and except the three men in the house, there was not a living soul within a league. The coati (a wild animal of a nature and appearance between that of the fox and the wolf) set up their sharp, quick bark, and two owls, at the end of two distant points running out into the bay, on different sides of the hills where I lay, kept up their alternate, dismal notes. I had heard the sound before at night, but did not know what it was, until one of the men, who came down to look at my quarters, told me it was the owl. Mellowed by the distance, and heard alone, at night, I thought it was the most melancholy, boding sound I had ever heard. Through nearly all the night they kept it up, answering one another slowly, at regular intervals. This was relieved by the noisy coati, some of which came quite near to my quarters, and were not very pleasant neighbors. The next morning, before sunrise, the long-boat came ashore, and the hides were taken off.

We lay at San Pedro about a week, engaged in taking off hides and in other labors, which had now become our regular duties. I spent one more day on the hill, watching a quantity of hides and goods, and this time succeeded in finding a part of a volume of Scott's *Pirate*, in a corner of the house; but it failed me at a most interesting moment, and I betook myself to my acquaintances on shore, and from them learned a good deal about the customs of the country, the harbors, etc. This, they told me, was a worse harbor than Santa Barbara, for south-easters; the bearing of the headland being a point and a half more to windward, and it being so shallow that the sea broke often as far out as where we lay at anchor. The gale from which we slipped at Santa Barbara, had been so bad a one here, that the whole bay, for a league out, was filled with the foam of the breakers, and seas actually broke over the Dead Man's island. The *Lagoda* was lying there, and slipped at the first alarm, and in such haste that she was obliged to leave her launch behind her at anchor. The little boat rode it out for several hours, pitching at her anchor, and standing with her stern up almost perpendicularly. The men told me that they watched her till towards night, when she snapped her cable and drove up over the breakers, high and dry upon the beach.

On board the *Pilgrim*, everything went on regularly, each one trying to get along as smoothly as possible; but the comfort of the voyage was evidently at an end. "That is a long lane which has no turning"—"Every dog must have his day, and mine will come by-and-by"—and the like proverbs, were occasionally quoted; but no one spoke of any probable end to the voyage, or of Boston, or anything of the kind; or if he did, it was only to draw out the perpetual, surly reply from his shipmate— "Boston, is it? You may thank your stars if you ever see that place. You had better have your back sheathed, and your head coppered, and your feet shod, and make out your log for California for life!" or else something of this kind—"Before you get to Boston the hides will wear the hair off your head, and you'll take up all your wages in clothes, and won't have enough left to buy a wig with!"

The flogging was seldom if ever alluded to by us, in the forecastle. If any one was inclined to talk about it, the others, with a delicacy which I hardly expected to find among them, always stopped him, or turned the subject. But the behavior of the two men who were flogged toward one another showed a delicacy and a sense of honor, which would have been worthy of admiration in the highest walks of life. Sam knew that the other had suffered solely on his account, and in all his complaints, he said that if he alone had been flogged, it would have been nothing; but that he never could see that man without thinking what had been the means of bringing that disgrace upon him; and John never, by word or deed, let anything escape him to remind the other that it was by interfering to save his shipmate, that he had suffered.

Having got all our spare room filled with hides, we hove up our anchor and made sail for San Diego. In no operation can the disposition of a crew be discovered better than in getting under weigh. Where things are "done with a will," every one is like a cat aloft: sails are loosed in an instant; each one lays out his strength on his handspike, and the windlass goes briskly round with the loud cry of "Yo heave ho! Heave and paw! Heave hearty ho!" But with us, at this time, it was all dragging work. No one went aloft beyond his ordinary gait, and the chain came slowly in over the windlass. The mate, between the knightheads, exhausted all his official rhetoric, in calls of "Heave with a will!"—"Heave hearty, men!— heave hearty!"—"Heave and raise the dead!"—"Heave, and away!" etc., etc.; but it would not do. Nobody broke his back or his handspike by his efforts. And when the cattackle-fall was strung along, and all hands—cook, steward, and all— laid hold, to cat the anchor, instead of the lively song of "Cheerily, men!" in which all hands join in the chorus, we pulled a long, heavy, silent pull, and—as sailors say a song is as good as ten men—the anchor came to the cat-head pretty slowly. "Give us 'Cheerily!'" said the mate; but there was no "cheerily" for us, and we did without it. The captain walked the quarterdeck, and said not a word. He must have seen the change, but there was nothing which he could notice officially.

We sailed leisurely down the coast before a light fair wind, keeping the land well aboard, and saw two other missions, looking like blocks of white plaster, shining in the distance; one of which, situated on the top of a high hill, was San Juan Campestrano, under which vessels sometimes come to anchor, in the summer season, and take off hides. The most distant one was St. Louis Rey, which the third mate said was only fifteen miles from San Diego. At sunset on the second day, we had a large and well wooded headland directly before us, behind which lay the little harbor of San Diego. We were becalmed off this point all night, but the next morning, which was Saturday, the 14th of March, having a good breeze, we stood round the point, and hauling our wind, brought the little harbor, which is rather the outlet of a small river, right before us. Every one was anxious to get a view of the new place. A chain of high hills, beginning at the point, (which was on our larboard hand, coming in,) protected the harbor on the north and west, and ran off into the interior as far as the eye could reach. On the other sides, the land was low, and green, but without trees. The entrance is so narrow as to admit but one vessel at a time, the current swift, and the channel runs so near to a low stony point that the ship's sides appeared almost to touch it. There was no town in sight, but on the smooth sand beach, abreast, and within a cable's length of which three vessels lay moored, were four large houses, built of rough boards, and looking like the great barns in which ice is stored on the borders of the large ponds near Boston; with piles of hides standing round them, and men in red shirts and large straw hats, walking in and out of the doors. These were the hide-houses. Of the vessels: one, a short, clumsy, little hermaphrodite brig, we recognized as our old acquaintance, the *Loriotte*; another, with sharp bows and raking masts, newly painted and tarred, and glittering in the morning sun, with the blood-red banner and cross of St. George at her peak, was the handsome *Ayacucho*. The third was a large ship, with top-gallant-masts housed, and sails unbent, and looking as rusty and worn as two years' "hide-droghing" could make her. This was the *Lagoda*. As we drew near, carried rapidly along by the current, we overhauled our chain, and clewed up the topsails. "Let go the anchor!" said the captain but either there was not chain enough forward of the windlass, or the anchor went down foul, or we had too much headway on, for it did not bring us up. "Pay out chain!" shouted the captain; and we gave it to her; but it would not do. Before the other anchor could be let go, we drifted down, broadside on, and went smash into the *Lagoda*. Her crew were at breakfast in the forecastle, and the cook, seeing us coming, rushed out of his galley, and called up the officers and men.

Fortunately no great harm was done. Her jib-boom ran between our fore and main masts, carrying away some of our rigging, and breaking down the rail. She lost her martingale. This brought us up, and as they paid out chain, we swung clear of them, and let go the other anchor; but this had as bad luck as the first, for, before any one perceived it, we were drifting on to the *Loriotte*. The captain now gave out his orders rapidly and fiercely, sheeting home the topsails, and backing and filling the sails, in hope of starting or clearing the anchors; but it was all in vain, and he sat down on the rail, taking it very leisurely, and calling out to Captain Nye, that he was coming to pay him a visit. We drifted fairly into the *Loriotte*, her larboard bow into our starboard quarter, carrying away a part of our starboard quarter railing, and breaking off her larboard bumpkin, and one or two stanchions above the deck. We saw our handsome sailor, Jackson, on the forecastle, with the Sandwich Islanders, working away to get us clear. After paying out chain, we swung clear, but our anchors were no doubt afoul of hers. We manned the windlass, and hove, and hove away, but to no purpose. Sometimes we got a little upon the cable, but a good surge would take it all back again. We now began to drift down toward the *Ayacucho*, when her boat put off and brought her commander, Captain Wilson, on board. He was a short, active, well-built man, between fifty and sixty years of age; and being nearly twenty years older than our captain, and a thorough seaman, he did not hesitate to give his advice, and from giving advice, he gradually came to taking the command; ordering us when to heave and when to pawl, and backing and filling the topsails, setting and taking in jib and trysail, whenever he thought best. Our captain gave a few orders, but as Wilson generally countermanded them, saying, in an easy, fatherly kind of way, "Oh no! Captain T——, you don't want the jib on her," or "it isn't time yet to heave!" he soon gave it up. We had no objections to this state of things, for Wilson was a kind old man, and had an encouraging and pleasant way of speaking to us, which made everything go easily. After two or three hours of constant labor at the windlass, heaving and "Yo ho!"-ing with all our might, we brought up an anchor, with the *Loriotte*'s small bower fast to it. Having cleared this and let it go, and cleared our hawse, we soon got our other anchor, which had dragged half over the harbor. "Now," said Wilson, "I'll find you a good berth;" and setting both the topsails, he carried us down, and brought us to anchor, in handsome style, directly abreast of the hide-house which we were to use. Having done this, he took his leave, while we furled the sails, and got our breakfast, which was welcome to us, for we had worked hard, and it was nearly twelve o'clock.

After breakfast, and until night, we were employed in getting out the boats and mooring ship.

After supper, two of us took the captain on board the *Lagoda*. As he came alongside, he gave his name, and the mate, in the gangway, called out to the captain down the companion-way—"Captain T—— has come aboard, sir!" "Has he brought his brig with him?" said the rough old fellow, in a tone which made itself heard fore and aft. This mortified our captain a little, and it became a standing joke among us for the rest of the voyage. The captain went down into the cabin, and we walked forward and put our heads down the forecastle, where we found the men at supper. "Come down, shipmates! Come down!" said they, as soon as they saw us; and we went down, and found a large, high forecastle, well lighted; and a crew of twelve or fourteen men, eating out of their kids and pans, and drinking their tea, and talking and laughing, all as independent and easy as so many "wood-sawyer's clerks." This looked like comfort and enjoyment, compared with the dark little forecastle, and scanty, discontented crew of the brig. It was Saturday night; they had got through with their work for the week; and being snugly moored, had nothing to do until Monday, again. After two years' hard service, they had seen the worst, and all, of California;—had got their cargo nearly stowed, and expected to sail in a week or two, for Boston. We spent an hour or more with them, talking over California matters, until the word was passed—"Pilgrims, away!" and we went back with our captain. They were a hardy, but intelligent crew; a little roughened, and their clothes patched and old, from California wear; all able seamen, and between the ages of twenty and thirty-five. They inquired about our vessel, the usage, etc., and were not a little surprised at the story of the flogging. They said there were often difficulties in vessels on the coast, and sometimes knockdowns and fightings, but they had never heard before of a regular seizing-up and flogging. "Spread-eagles" were a new kind of bird in California.

Sunday, they said, was always given in San Diego, both at the hide-houses and on board the vessels, a large number usually going up to the town, on liberty. We learned a good deal from them about curing and stowing of hides, etc., and they were anxious to have the latest news (seven months old) from Boston. One of their first inquiries was for Father Taylor, the seamen's preacher in Boston. Then followed the usual strain of conversation, inquiries, stories, and jokes, which, one must always hear in a ship's forecastle, but which are perhaps, after all, no worse, nor, indeed, more gross, than that of many well-dressed gentlemen at their clubs.

from Desolation Island
by Patrick O'Brian

Patrick O'Brian (born in 1914) at last count had written 19 historical novels about two friends: English naval officer Jack Aubrey and naturalist, physician and spy Stephen Maturin. If O'Brian writes 19 more, I'll read them all: No writer has given me more pleasure and instruction. This passage from Desolation Island, *fifth in the series, finds Aubrey's outgunned ship fleeing a Dutch man-of-war into mountainous Antarctic seas.*

Dawn broke, and once again Jack was knocked up; once again he was torn from the arms of an ideal Mrs Wogan with the news of a ship fine on the larboard bow. This time the *Leopard*'s top-gallants had already vanished, but it was little more than a gesture to the conventions of war, because this time the *Waakzaamheid* was a good three miles nearer, perfectly recognizable in spite of the mist hanging over the cold milky sea—hanging and parting in the light air from the east, so that sometimes she almost entirely vanished and sometimes she looked spectral, unnaturally large, as she bore up, spread her wings, and headed for the *Leopard*.

They were already at the edge of the westerly current, and the breeze chopped up the pale surface; but there was nothing of a sea, nothing resembling the great rollers with the hills and dales that so favoured a heavier ship, and by noon the *Leopard*, setting all she could carry and steering south-west, had run the *Waakzaamheid* out of sight.

'May we cry *Io triumphe?*' asked Stephen at dinner. 'It is two hours since she vanished, wallowing in impotent rage.'

'I am not going to cry Io anything at all until we pick up our moorings in Simon's Bay,' cried Jack. 'With Turnbull and Holles here, I did not like to say anything at breakfast, but I do not know that I have ever seen anything so shocking in all my life as that Dutchman at dawn, sitting there to the windward, between us and the Cape. It was exactly as though he had been leaning over my shoulder last night, while I worked out our course. And I am by no means easy in my mind about this morning's performance, neither. It was too far off to be certain, with the haze, but I had an ugly feeling he was not chasing wholehearted. No skysails, as I dare say you remarked. Maybe his pole topgallantmasts will not bear 'em; but it seemed to me he was not so much eager to catch us as to drive us south, away to the leeward. In his place, and with his advantage in men, I should try to carry the ship by boarding, rather than batter her into matchwood and maybe have her sink on me: what a triumph to carry a sound fifty-gun ship with him to the Indies! And he may be waiting for his opportunity. However, I shall do all I can to cross his wake tonight, and if only l can get the weather-gage, with the wind anywhere east of south, I shall try a luffing match with him. We can lie closer to the wind, and those broadbottomed ships always sag to leeward more than we do. So in any sea where *Leopard* can stay, I believe we could leave him a great way astern by beating up, leave him for good and all; and I hope to be windward of him tomorrow.'

A vain hope. Jack's plan of crossing the Dutchman's wake in the night was frustrated by a dead calm; and in the afternoon of the next day, while all hands were bending a fresh suit of heavy-weather sails, the *Waakzaamheid* was seen in the north-east, bringing up the breeze. She was a noble sight, with studdingsails aloft and alow, gleaming under the clouded sky—towering canvas that gleamed with a more than ordinary and as it were inward glow, for she too had shifted her suit in preparation for the winds to be expected farther south—but the *Leopards* could not admire her. They had all seen the spent ball that damaged the figurehead, and they all knew that behind the lower deck ports of the approaching *Waakzaamheid* lay a long tier of Dutch thirty-two-pounders, throwing metal nearly half as heavy again as their own guns. The best part of the *Leopard*'s hull was heart of oak, so was the best part of her crew; but there was not a man aboard who concealed his delight when the breeze reached the *Leopard* too, filled her stout new canvas, and caused the water to gurgle under her counter as she gathered way. A little later the capricious air began to fail the *Waakzaamheid*: she put down her helm and opened a distant cannonade that effectually killed what little wind there was.

Slow, deliberate fire, gun by gun from her upper tier: single shot with a heavy charge of powder; almost always short, but remarkably good practice; and some of the ricochets came aboard. He could not hope to accomplish a great deal at this distance—his twelve-pound upperdeck shot could not do half as much harm after the first graze as the Dutchman's twenty-four-pounders—but there was always the chance of carrying away a spar or cutting up the rigging, which would be all to the good with the *Waakzaamheid* five or six thousand miles from her nearest source of supply. And then a stray shot might hit a cartridge-box or a lantern between decks, starting a fire and even blowing up the magazine: it was long, long odds, but he had known it happen. Yet there were other, far more important considerations. Since her captain delighted in gunnery, and since he was well-to-do, the *Leopard* was exceptionally rich in powder and shot; and if Jack, by provoking the *Waakzamheid*, could induce her to fire shot for shot, sending most of it into the sea, he would be relatively the gainer. Then he knew very well that even the most intrepid heroes did not much relish sitting mute, waiting to be fired at; and many of the *Leopard*'s landsmen were not heroic at all. Furthermore, experience had taught him that no target on earth could excite such a zeal, such careful, deliberate aiming, as one's fellow men: this was a perfect opportunity for getting the best into his gun-crews; the *Leopard* made the fullest use of it, and occasionally the fall of her shot would send water over the Dutchman's side, while twice, to rapturous cheers, the well-served number seven gun struck home, whereas the *Waakzaamheid* did nothing but send one spent ball into the *Leopard*'s hammock-netting. Yet Jack had a growing, disagreeable conviction that his colleague over the water had exactly the same thing in mind, that he too was profiting from the situation to work up his crew, his horribly numerous crew, to an even higher state of perfection. Jack could see him clearly through his telescope, a tall man in a light-blue coat with brass buttons, sometimes standing on his quarterdeck, smoking a short pipe at intervals of scrutinizing the *Leopard*, sometimes walking about among the upper-deck guns; and in spite of the cheering and pleasant spirit aboard, Jack was heartily pleased when another light air, neglecting the *Waakzaamheid*, enabled him to run out of range.

That night, the night of the new moon, they lay with very little movement until the morning watch, when cold rain came sweeping from the west, and a moderate swell made the *Leopard* pitch as she stood for the distant Cape, now considerably to the north as well as east.

No one had to wake the Captain this time. He was on the quarter-deck well before sunrise, muffled in a pilot jacket by the lee rail; as he had expected, the first light showed him the *Waakzaamheid*, far over between him and Africa, steering a course that would cut his own in a few hours' time. Jack brought the wind upon his starboard beam; the Dutchman did the same, but no more—he did not attempt to close. And so they ran all day through the rain, running parallel courses, south and south. Now and then a squall would hide one from the other, but every time it cleared, there was the *Waakzaamheid*, keeping station as faithfully as if she were the *Leopard*'s consort, attending to her signals. Sometimes one would gain a mile or two, sometimes the other, but by nightfall they were at much the same distance apart, having run off a hundred and thirty miles by dead reckoning—no sight of the sun at noon, with all that driving cloud. After dark Jack began beating up, tack upon tack, both watches on deck, hoping to shake off the *Waakzaamheid*, which was not such a windward ship, and then to fetch a wide cast northwards, to cross her wake far out of sight. And so he might have done, had not the wind failed him, leaving the *Leopard* with little more than steerage-way, drifting westward on the current, so that once again the morning sun showed her that odiously familiar shape, exact to the rendezvous.

It was that night, after a day of manoeuvring in light airs that boxed the compass, that the *Waakzaamheid* made her attempt at boarding. The sun set clear in a sky that promised a true breeze in the morning; there was a fair amount of starlight before the young moon rose, and it showed the Dutchman ghosting nearer under skysails, although there was not a ripple on the long oily swell. The movement was scarcely perceptible at first, and only the successive disappearance of the lowest stars betrayed it to the lookout's watchful eye: the seventy-four must have picked up the first whisper of the air as it was born, and when it brought her within gunshot she heaved to and opened up with a most spectacular series of rippling broadsides. The *Leopard* was already at action-stations; the battle-lanterns gleamed behind her open larboard ports; both tiers of guns peered out; the smell of burning match drifted along the decks; but until the ships were closer Jack would not give the order to fire. He stood on the poop, staring across the water with his night-glass; he did not wholly believe in this attack, and he was searching for the boats he would himself have launched. No sign, no sign at all: but then, when he had almost given up, he caught the flash of oars, very much farther from the ship than he had reckoned on. The Dutch captain had launched them on his blind side in the dark, and had sent them off, crammed with men, at least half an hour ago. They were pulling fast in a wide arc to take the *Leopard* on the starboard side while the *Waakzaamheid* engaged her with distant gunfire on the other. 'The fox,' said Jack, and he gave orders for boarding-netting, for the guns to be drawn and reloaded with grape, and for all the Marines to leave the guns for their muskets.

The attempt failed because a slant of wind wafted the *Leopard* southward faster than the boats could pull, so that she caught the leaders, cutting them up most dreadfully with grape-shot at two hundred yards; and because the *Waakzaamheid* lost too much time picking up the surviving boats and men to take advantage of the breeze. But it might very well have succeeded: Jack's ship could not fight both sides at once, and the men in the boats outnumbered his crew.

'I shall not run that risk again,' he said. 'Whatever wind we have, I shall beat up, even if it means going directly away from the Cape for days on end. By every sign, and by all the rules, it should come from the south, and so much the better. With luck,' he said, touching the wooden handle of his sextant, 'a southerly breeze should let us work up well into the forties, where we can be sure of no calms. He has to have a calm night for that kind of frolic.'

True to the rules for once, the morning's wind backed right round into the south. It was neither a steady nor a convincing breeze, but several mollymawks and one great albatross were seen, sure signs of stronger winds not far away; and it did allow the *Leopard* to work well ahead, tacking like clockwork every other glass and staying perfectly each time. The seventy-four did her best, whipping her heavy yards round like wands, but she could not lie so close; on every leg she lost several hundred yards, and once she was obliged to wear, which cost her the best part of a mile. A long, anxious day, with the surest helmsmen at the wheel, the leeward guns run in, the windward out, to make her stiffer still, every possible device to wring a little extra thrust from the breeze, and the clumsier hands nearly murdered by their mates for the slightest blunder; but a day that left *Waakzaamheid* hull down in the north, so that after the drum had beat the retreat, Jack ordered hammocks to be piped down in order to allow the exhausted larboard watch some sleep.

'Luff and touch her,' was the order of the night, as the *Leopard* held steady on the starboard tack, with the westerly current, now much stronger, to ease her way. In the morning the *Waakzaamheid* was no more than a pale wink against the dark clouds on the horizon; she had reduced sail, and she seemed discouraged.

More albatrosses appeared during the forenoon watch, and a more normal life began again. The wardroom was no longer part of a naked gun-deck; its cabins were set up once more, and the usual quite civilized dining-room had reappeared, decorations and all. The meal itself, glutinous soup, sea-pie, and duff, was no Lord Mayor's banquet, but it was hot, and Stephen, chilled through and through from watching albatrosses in the maintop, ate it eagerly. Between courses he gnawed a biscuit, tapping the weevils out in what was by now an automatic gesture, and he contemplated his messmates. In the article of clothes, the sailors were not a very creditable lot, being dressed in a disagreeable mixture of uniform and old warm garments, sometimes wool and sometimes cloth. Babbington wore a knitted Guernsey frock, inherited from Macpherson, that hung in folds upon his little form; Byron had on two waistcoats, one black, the other brown; Turnbull had come out in a tweed shooting-coat; and although Grant and Larkin were somewhat more presentable, on the whole they made a sad contrast to the neat Marines. Stephen had contemplated them from time to time since the beginning of this tension, and sometimes their reactions had surprised him. Benton the purser, for instance, never showed the least anxiety about being taken, sunk, burnt or destroyed, but the *Leopard*'s vast consumption of candles in the battle-lanterns and elsewhere rendered him gloomy, silent, irresponsive. Grant too was rather silent, and had been ever since the first shots were fired with intent to kill: silent, that is to say, when Stephen or Babbington were present. When they were not, as Stephen gathered from the chaplain's remarks, he spoke at length about the measures he would have adopted, had he been in command: the *Leopard* should either have attacked at once, relying on the effect of surprise, or have sailed north directly. Fisher was altogether of his mind, though he admitted that his opinion was of no great value: there was a growing sympathy between the two men, some underlying similarity. In other respects the chaplain was quite changed; he no longer visited Mrs Wogan, and he even asked Dr Maturin to carry her the books she had been promised. 'Ever since my near escape from death in battle,' he said, 'I have been thinking very seriously.'

'To what battle do you refer?' asked Stephen.

'To the first. A cannon-ball struck within inches of my head. Ever since then I have reflected upon the old adage about never allowing fire near inflammable material, and about the dangers of concupiscence.'

He was obviously willing to be questioned and to open his secret mind—but Stephen did not wish to hear. Since the gaol-fever he had lost interest in Mr Fisher, who seemed to him a commonplace man, too much concerned with himself and his own salvation, one whose attraction faded on acquaintance. He only bowed, and accepted the books.

He had the impression that both Grant and Fisher were in a state of powerful fear. There were no evident, direct signs of it, but both complained very often: a stream of blame and disapproval of the modern state of mind, the present generation, their useless, idle servants, the ill conduct of the government, of the political parties, and of those about the King: a general denigration, a frequent imputation of motives, always discreditable. They reminded him of his maternal grandmother in her last years, when, from being a strong, sensible, courageous woman, she grew weak and querulous, her expression of general discontent increasing with her vulnerability. He did not know how either of them would behave in a really bloody fight: whether their manliness would reassert itself in an obvious crisis. As for the others, he had little doubt. Babbington he had known since the lieutenant was a boy: as brave as a terrier. And Byron was of the same familiar naval genus. Turnbull would probably do well enough, for all his loud-mouthed hectoring. Moore had seen a great deal of service; he would shoot and be shot at with great good humour, as a matter of course—it was his profession. And Howard, the other lobster, would surely follow, in his phlegmatic military way: as far as Stephen could make out, there was almost no connection between the flute-playing Howard and the stuffed Marine lieutenant. He did have reservations about Larkin, however: the master's courage and professional ability might be very well, but by now he was fairly pickled in alcohol and unless Stephen's judgement were much at fault, his body was very near the limit of its resistance.

They drank the King; Stephen pushed back his chair, not choosing to stay with the execrable wine, tripped over Babbington's Newfoundland for the hundredth time, and stepped on to the quarterdeck for another glance at his albatross, a noble bird that had been sailing along with the ship since breakfast. Herapath was there, talking to the midshipman of the watch, and they gave him news of the *Waakzaamheid*, out of sight these two hours past, even from the jacks. 'Long may she stay so,' said Stephen, and returned to work in his cabin.

This cabin, being on the orlop, did not disappear when the ship cleared for action, and at intervals, even during these trying days, he had carried on with a task begun shortly after Herapath had confided in him. It consisted of drawing up a statement, in French, describing the British intelligence network in France and some other parts of western Europe, together with passing references to the United States and allusions to a separate document dealing with the situation in the Dutch East Indies; with its details of double agents, bribes offered and accepted, and treason in the ministries themselves, it was designed to cause disruption in Paris if there were in fact a connection between Mrs Wogan's chiefs and the French; and it was intended to be conveyed to those chiefs by Mrs Wogan herself, by means of Herapath. This statement was to have been found among the papers of a dead officer bound for the East Indies. The officer was not named, though of course Martin, who had spent half his life in France and whose mother-tongue was French, was clearly indicated. Copies of the document were to be made for the authorities, and Dr Maturin, knowing that Mr Herapath was fluent in that language, was to ask him to be so good as to help with the work. Stephen was certain that the artless young man would tell his Louisa, and that Mrs Wogan would soon get transcripts out of him, whatever honourable resistance he might put up at first. That she would then laboriously encode them, poor dear, and oblige Herapath to send them from the Cape. Stephen had poisoned many sources of intelligence in his time; but if all went well, this promised to be the prettiest piece of intoxication ever that he had brought about. Such a wealth of material at his disposition! Such utterly convincing details known only to himself, to Sir Joseph, and to a few men in Paris!

'What now?' he said, angrily.

'Come quick, sir,' cried a ghastly Marine. 'Mr Larkin's murdered our lieutenant.'

Stephen caught up his bag, locked his door, and ran to the ward-room. Three officers had pinned Larkin down, and they were tying his arms and legs. A bloody half-pike on the table. Howard lay back in his chair, his mouth and eyes wide open in his white astonished face. Larkin was still jerking and writhing with convulsive force in delirium tremens, making a hoarse, animal roaring. They overcame his violence and carried him away. Stephen probed the wound, found the aorta severed at the crest of the arch, and observed that death had been almost instantaneous.

The master had got up from the table, they told him, just as Howard began to screw his flute together, had taken a half-pike from the bulkhead, had said, 'There's for you, you flute-playing bugger', lunging straight across between Moore and Benton, and had then fallen roaring on the deck.

'You are strangely quiet,' said Mrs Wogan, as they walked upon the gangway an hour or two later. 'I have made at least two witty observations, and you have not replied. Surely, Dr Maturin, you should wrap up a little more, in this damp and horrid cold?'

'I am sorry, child, to seem so low,' he said, 'but a little while ago one of the officers killed another in a drunken fit, the sweetest flute I ever heard. Sometimes I feel that this is indeed an unlucky ship. Many of the men say there is a Jonah aboard.'

Some days later (for the Marines insisted upon a proper coffin and a plate for their lieutenant) they buried Howard in 41°15′S., 15°17′E., the *Leopard* heaving to the strong west wind for the purpose. Once again the log-book recorded 'committed the body of John Condom Howard to the deep' and once again Jack wrote Discharged Dead against his name.

After a melancholy, sober dinner at which Stephen was the only guest, Jack said, 'Tomorrow I think we may head north. With common luck we should raise the Table Mountain in three or four days, and then we can get rid of that poor raving maniac.'

They had been south of forty degrees since Thursday, and although at this season, the beginning of the austral summer, even the westerlies were not quite to be relied on north of forty-five or even forty-six, they had proved true enough for the *Leopard*, and together with the current they had carried her over two hundred nautical miles between one noon observation and the next day after day, with never a glimpse of the *Waakzaamheid*.

'Do you know, I wonder, whether the Americans have a consul at the Cape?' asked Stephen. His document was done; Herapath was copying it; the train was laid.

'I would not swear to it, but most probably they have: any number of their far eastern ships touch there, to say nothing of sealers and the like. Why do you—' He choked his question short, and said, 'What do you say to a turn on deck? The heat of that stove is killing me.'

On deck Stephen pointed out one particular albatross among the half dozen following the ship. 'That dark fowl is, I conceive, a nondescript species, and not exulans at all: see his cuneate tail. How I should love to visit his breeding-grounds! There, you may see his tail again.' Jack gazed politely and said, 'Upon my word,' but Stephen saw that the creature's tail was of no very great consequence to him, and said, 'So you think we have shaken off the Dutchman? What a persistent fellow he was, to be sure.'

'And devilish sly, too. I believe he was in league with the Devil, unless—' He had been about to say 'Unless we have a witch aboard that communicates with him by a familiar spirit, as many of the hands believe: they say it is your Gipsy' but he disliked being called superstitious and in any case he did not really give much credit to the tale, so he continued, 'That is to say, unless he could read my thoughts, and have private notice of the winds into the bargain. Still, this time I like to think we have lurched him good and hearty. By my reckoning he should only go north somewhere about seventy-five or eighty east, for the south-west monsoon. Indeed, I should be quite confident of it, but for one thing.'

'What thing is that, tell?'

'Why, the fact that he knows where we are bound; and that we did claw his boats most cruelly.'

'I beg your pardon, sir,' said Grant, walking across the deck, 'but they send to tell the Doctor that Larkin is at it again.'

They need scarcely have sent. The howling welled up from the master's cabin, where he lay bound, filling the quarterdeck in spite of the strong voice of the wind. 'I shall be with him directly,' said Stephen.

Jack paced on with a melancholy shake of his head. Ten minutes later the lookout hailed. 'Sail ho. On deck there; sail ho.'

'Where away?' called Jack, all thoughts of Larkin gone.

'Broad on the larboard beam, sir. Topsails on the rise.'

Jack nodded to Babbington, who raced up to the masthead with a glass: some moments later his voice came down, spreading relief throughout the attentive, silent ship. 'On deck, sir. A whaler. Steering south and east.'

The wardroom steward, pinned to the half-deck by the first awful hail, continued his course; and passing the Marine-sentry outside the master's cabin he said, 'It's not the Dutchman, mate: only a whaler, God be praised.'

On the other side of the door, Stephen said to Herapath, 'There. That should calm him. Pray put up the tundish and come along. We will have a dish of tea in my cabin: we have certainly deserved a dish of tea.'

Herapath came along, but he would not linger, nor would he drink his tea. He had a great deal of work to do, he said, avoiding Stephen's eye, and must beg to be excused.

'Poor Michael Herapath,' wrote Stephen in his book, 'he suffers much. I know the harrow's mark too well ever to mistake it, the harrow directed by a determined woman. Perhaps I shall give him a little of my laudanum, to tide him over till the Cape.'

Since her hands were protected from impressment, the whaler was not unwilling to be spoken by a British man-of-war: she was the *Three Brothers* from London river for the Great South Sea, she said, in answer to the *Leopard*'s 'What ship? What ship is that?' Last from the Cape: no, she had not seen a single sail since she cleared False Bay.

'Come aboard and crack a bottle,' called Jack over the wind and the grey heaving water. The whaler's words were balm to him; they did away with the lingering, almost superstitious doubt that had kept his eye perpetually turning to the windward for that white fleck on the horizon that, in spite of all his calculations, would prove to be the devilish *Waakzaamheid*. It was notorious that whalers had the sharpest eyes of any men afloat: their livelihood depended on seeing the distant spout, often in a torn, tormented, cloud-covered waste of sea, and they always had men up there in their crow's nests, watching with the most constant eagerness: the remotest gleam of topsails could not escape them by day, nor yet by these late moonlit nights.

The master of the *Three Brothers* came and cracked his bottle and talked about the pursuit of the whale in these largely unknown waters: he knew them as well as most men, having made three voyages, and he gave Jack some particularly valuable information about South Georgia, correcting his chart of the anchorages in that remote, inhospitable island, in case the *Leopard* should ever find herself in 54°S, 37°W, and about the few other specks of land in that vast far southern ocean. But presently, as the full bottles came in and the empty were carried away, his accounts became wilder; he spoke of the great continent that must lie round the pole, of the gold that was certainly there, and of how he should ballast his ship with the ore. Sailors rarely feel that they have done their duty if their guests leave them sober: but Jack was perfectly satisfied as he saw the whaler plunge into his boat. He bade the *Three Brothers* farewell and a happy return and worked out his course for the Cape: the *Leopard* brought the wind a little abaft the larboard beam in a fine fierce curve—white water sweeping over her waist—and began to run northwards under courses and reefed topsails, her deck sloping like a moderately pitched roof and her lee chains buried in the foam that came racing from her bows. She was heading for dirty weather, for a low bank of cloud with rain-squalls drifting across its face and hidden lightning within the mass; it was precious cold, and spray, whipping across the deck in the eddy of the mainsail, kept wetting the Captain's face. But he was warm within: not only had he a comfortable coat of blubber as well as his pilot-jacket, but he also had a glow of satisfaction. He continued his pacing, counting the number of turns on the fingers clasped behind his back. One thousand he would take before he went below. At each turn he glanced up at the sky and out over the sea: a mottled sky, blue and white to the south with a steely gleam on the farthest rim, grey, high-piled storm-breeders in the west, darkness north and east; and of course a mottled sea, though in quite different tones, running from middle blue through every shade of glaucous grey to black, and the whole streaked with a white that owed nothing to the sky but all to the broken water and the spindrift of former storms. The long, even fairly heavy swell lifted him and set him down at a measured pace, so that sometimes his horizon was no more than three miles away, and sometimes he saw an enormous disk of ocean, a cold, uneasy sea, endless miles of desolation, the comfortless element in which he was at home.

The surface of his mind was concerned with that unhappy man the master: his books had proved to be hopelessly confused, neglected these many weeks. One of Larkin's duties was to keep tally of the *Leopard's* water, but from the scrawled, haphazard notes Jack could not make out the present state: he and the mate of the hold would have to creep about in the depths, thumping casks and starting bungs. He would not ask Grant to do it, now that the first lieutenant had to keep a watch: a cantankerous, unwilling dog, with no desire to please, no goodwill—careful never to commit himself by a hasty word, but always ready with some objection, with general blame and discontent. A miserable sod. A good seaman, though: that must always be admitted. He thought of Breadfruit Bligh, and his nasty reputation: 'Before you judge a commander,' he said, on his seven hundredth turn, 'you must know just what he had to command.' Jack himself had had to speak to Grant in terms that might have earned him the name of a rough-tongued Turk; he had not lost his temper, but in the matter of Grant's interference with his orders about the storm-trysail he had spoken very plain.

He turned aft, seven hundred and fifty-one: he heard exclamations, saw faces staring, pointing hands. 'Sir, sir!' cried Turnbull, Holles and the quartermaster all at once; and from the masthead 'Sail ho,' with extreme urgency. 'On deck, on deck there . . .'

He whipped round, and there in the west-north-west, directly to windward, emerging from a black squall with lurid light behind, he saw the *Waakzaamheid*, no hanging threat on the far horizon but hull up, not three miles away.

'Port your helm,' he said. 'In driver. Out reefs. Fore topgallantsail.' The *Leopard* turned round on her heel so fast that Babbington's dog was flung outwards, colliding with a carronade. Hands raced for the brails, braces, sheets and tacks, and the ship steadied on her course, right before the wind.

The *Waakzaamheid* and the *Leopard* had seen one another at much the same moment, and aboard both ships the sails came flashing out as quickly as the hands could move. The *Waakzaamheid* carried away a maintopgallant the minute it was sheeted home, and the cloths streamed forward, fouling her stays. 'He is in earnest this time,' thought Jack. 'We must crack on.' But the *Leopard*'s masts would not stand another stitch of canvas without going by the board. He felt the backstays and shook his head, gazed up at the tall topgallant-masts and shook it again—no question of striking them down on deck at this juncture. 'Pass the word for the bosun,' he said. The bosun came running aft. 'Mr Lane, get warps and light hawsers to the mastheads.'

The bosun, a dark fellow in a perpetual ill-temper, opened his mouth: but the look on the Captain's face turned his remark to an 'Aye aye, sir,' and he plunged below, piping for his mates as he went.

'Let us try the main topgallantsail, Mr Babbington,' said Jack, when the ship had taken the full thrust of the wind right aft and all her way was on her. The upperyardsmen lay aloft, ran out on the yard, let fall. The yard rose, the mast complained, the backstays grew tauter still; but the good canvas held and the *Leopard*'s speed increased perceptibly. Jack looked aft, over the tearing wake: the seventy-four was a little far-ther off. 'So far, so good,' he said to himself, and to Babbington, 'Clew up, however: we will try again when the bosun has done his work.'

So far so good: the *Leopard* was just gaining, just outrunning the *Waakzaamheid* with the canvas she could bear at present. She could certainly hold her own and better in this wind and in this sea. But he did not want to go any further south, where the westerlies blew harder still.

After an hour he altered course due east. Instantly the *Waakzaamheid* steered to head him off, running the chord of the *Leopard*'s arc, gaining more than Jack liked to see, and at the same time setting a curious little triangular sail like an inverted skyscraper from the yardarms of her main topgallant to the cap.

'This is no time to jig,' reflected Jack. The *Waakzaamheid* had the masterhand as far as course was concerned, and he put the *Leopard* before the wind once more, a west-north-west wind with a distinct tendency to haul norther still. Then raising his voice to the foremast head, where Lane was toiling with his crew, clinging to what frail support there was, their pigtails streaming forward, stiff and straight, he called, 'Mr Lane, should you like your hammock sent aloft?'

If the bosun made any reply it was drowned by the striking of eight bells in the afternoon watch, followed by all the ritual gestures. The log was heaved, as clear of the huge wake as it would go; the reel whirled; the quartermaster bawled out 'Nip!'; the midshipman reported 'Just on the twelve, sir, if you please.' The officer of the watch chalked it up on the log-board. The carpenter made his report: 'Three inches in the well, sir,' and Jack said, 'Ah, Mr Gray, I was just about to pass the word for you. Deadlights in the cabin, if you please. I do not want to get my stockings wet, if a following sea should get up tonight.'

'Deadlights it is, sir; for nothing are so unwholesome as wet stockings.' Gray was an old old man, a master of his trade, and he might be a little chatty. 'Will it cut up tough, sir, do you reckon?' By most standards it had cut up rough long ago: the *Leopard* was pitching like a froward horse, white water over her bows, and although the wind was right aft, where in moderate weather it would be almost mute, they now conversed in a strong shout, while spray whipped off the rollers shot past them, to vanish forward. But they were in the forties, and in the forties this was not worth speaking of, not what would be called real weather at all.

'I doubt it may: look at the gleam to leeward, Mr Gray.'

The carpenter looked, and pursed his lips; glanced aft to catch the Dutchman on the rise, and pursed them again, muttering, 'What can you expect, when we got a witch aboard? Deadlights this minute, sir.'

'And hawse-bags, of course.'

So they ran another glass, and at the striking of the bell Jack moved to the poop: there, crouching with his telescope behind the taffrail, he inspected the *Waakzaamheid* The moment he had it focused on her forecastle he had a curious shock, for there, full in his glass, was the Dutch captain, looking straight at him. There was no doubt about his tall, burly form, the distinctive carriage of his head: Jack was familiar with the enemy. But now, instead of his usual light blue, he had a black coat on. 'I wonder,' thought Jack, 'whether it is just an odd chance, or whether we killed some relative of his? His boy, perhaps, dear God forbid.'

The seventy-four was gaining slightly now, and in the strong remaining light—for the evening was much longer down here, and the two ships had run well clear of the gloom of the north—Jack could make out the nature of those odd triangles. There was another at the foretopgallant now, and it was a storm-staysail, suspended by its tack.

'If you please, sir,' said a midshipman, young Hillier, 'the bosun says all is stretched along, and might he have a party.'

A tidy party it would have to be, for Jack's plan was to supplement the backstays with hawsers, no less, so that the immensely strengthened masts might bear a great press of sail with a following wind, the strain being transferred to the hull; but to bowse the massive cordage so taut that it would serve its office called for a most uncommon force. Once, when he was third of the *Theseus*, they had set the mainsail in a hurry to claw off the Penmarks, and a south-wester blew so hard that two hundred men were needed to haul the sheet right aft: he did not have two hundred valid men, but he did have a little more time than the captain of the *Theseus*, with the breakers under his lee.

None to waste, however, with the seventy-four only three miles away, and running off the mile in just five minutes: and above all, no time to make a mistake—a mast lost in this sea was sure destruction.

'A burton-tackle to the chess-tree,' he called, loud and clear. 'Lead aft to a snatch-block fast to the aftermost ring-bolts and forward free. Look alive, there, look alive. Light along that snatch-block, Craig.' Order came from apparent confusion in five minutes: the half-drowned bosun's party scrambled in from the chess-trees; and the whole ship's company crowded into the waist and along the gangways, standing by the cablets that were to act as horizontal falls, working with a threefold power.

'Silence fore and aft,' cried Jack. 'Starboard, tally on. At the word, now, and all together cheerly: like a bowline. Ho, one. Ho, two. Ho, belay. Larboard, clap on. Ho, one. Ho, two. Ho, belay.'

So it went, on either side: short sharp pulls aft from the chess-trees, forward from the snatch-blocks, and the hawsers tightened evenly, tighter and tighter yet, a most careful balancing of forces, until the wind sung the same note in each, and each pair was iron-taut, supporting its mast with extraordinary strength.

'Belay,' cried Jack for the last time. 'Well fare ye, lads. Are you ready, Mr Lane?'

'Ready, aye ready, sir.'

'Cast off all. Maintopgallantsail, there.'

The yard rose up; the mast took the strain without a groan; the *Leopard*'s bow-wave grew higher still with her increasing speed. Now the spritsail topsail followed, while to ease her plunging they hauled up the mainsail, giving all the wind to her forecourse: she sailed easier yet, with no slackening in her pace, clearly outrunning the Dutchman, although he had shaken out his foretopsail reef.

They raced furiously over the empty, heaving sea under a clear late evening sky, both ships driven very hard; and the first to lose an important spar or sail would lose the race that night. The sun was setting; in an hour and forty minutes the moon would rise, a little past her full. With the afterglow and then the strong moonlight, there would be small chance of jigging unperceived; yet half an hour before the moon he would bring the wind a point or so on the quarter, just so that the jibs and forward staysails would stand and give him another half knot or even more. And all things being considered, hammocks might be piped down: the larboard watch would turn in with all their clothes on in case of emergency, and there was no point in keeping them at quarters, shivering behind their tight-closed ports: the crisis, if it came to that, was some way off. Perhaps a great way to the east. He had chased forty-eight hours before this.

In the darkened cabin he found Stephen with his 'cello between his knees and a soup-tureen at his side. 'Judas,' he said, lifting the lid and beholding emptiness.

'Not at all, my dear. More is on the brew; but I cannot recommend it. You would be better with a glass of water, tempered with a few drops of wine, a very few drops of wine, and a piece of biscuit.'

'What did you eat it for, then? Why did you not leave a scrap, not a single scrap?'

'It was only that I felt my need was greater than thine, my business of greater importance than your business. For whereas yours is concerned with death, mine is the bringing forth of life. Mrs Boswell is in labour, and some time tonight or tomorrow I think I may promise you an addition to your crew.'

'Ten to one another—woman,' said Jack. 'Killick! Killick, there!'

More soup appeared, chops hot and hot, a jug of coffee, and a wedge of solid duff.

'Will this last long, do you suppose?' asked Stephen, over the booming of his 'cello.

'A stern chase is a long chase,' said Jack.

'And would you consider this a really stern one?'

'It could not well be more so. The Dutchman is in our wake. He is dead astern.'

'So that is the significance of the term. I had always supposed it to mean an eager, a grim, a most determined pursuit, inspired by inveterate animosity. Well: and so this is a stern chase. Listen till I tell you something for my part: a breech-presentation is a long, long labour too. It looks to me that the both of us have an active night ahead: you will allow me to call for another pot.'

Stephen's was active enough, with no proper forceps and no great experience of midwifery; but after Jack had gone on deck to alter course—southwards, since the Dutchman expected him to go north—and had stared at his pursuer for a while by the light of the risen moon, he stretched out on his cot and went straight to sleep. The outer jib and the foretopmast staysail were standing well, the *Leopard* was steering easy, and the seventy-four was between four and five miles astern; she had not perceived Jack's smooth change of direction for some time and she had not set her own headsails until the *Leopard* was close on another mile ahead.

He woke refreshed: yet his sleeping mind had recorded the crash of water against the deadlights, and coming on deck he was not surprised to find that both wind and sea had increased. The cold, brilliant moon showed an even ray of tall waves sweeping eastward, wide apart, with a deep trough between; and now their heads were curling over, streaming down the leeward side in a white cascade; and the general note of the wind in the rigging had risen half an octave.

If this grew worse, and from the look of the western sky, the feel of the air, it must grow worse, he would have to put the *Leopard* before the wind again; the ship could not stand a heavier sea upon her quarter without being thrown off her course. The *Waakzaamheid* was still at much the same distance, but that was not likely to last.

The graveyard watch wore on, bell by bell; and still they ran, starting neither sheet nor tack, an eager, grim, and most determined pursuit. At eight bells, with both watches on deck, he took in the spritsail, got the yard fore and aft, set the inner jib, and bore up another point. It might be his last chance of doing so, for the air was now filled with flying water and the ship was tearing through the sea at a rate he never would have believed possible, a rate that in fact would have been impossible without those hawsers to the mastheads. But this was no longer the exhilarating pace of a few hours ago; now there was a nightmare, break-neck quality about it; and now the wind was blowing very hard indeed.

Hour after hour towards the morning watch, and hour after hour the wind increased. Twice, just after seven bells, the *Leopard* was very nearly pooped by a freakish bursting sea: the steady progression of the rollers was losing its regularity, becoming disordered. Eight bells again, and he put the ship before the wind, taking in the staysails. It was impossible to get an accurate reading of the log, for the blast tossed the log-boat forward of her bows; and now the carpenter's mate reported two foot of water in the well. The *Leopard* had been working and straining so much that a good deal had come in through her sides, let alone that which made its way down from the decks in spite of the laid hatches and through the hawse holes in spite of the bags.

The sun rose on a sea in labour, the crests riding ahead of the swell and breaking: creaming water from horizon to horizon except in the bottom of the troughs, much deeper now; while from every height the wind tore foam, drops and solid water, driving it forward in a grey veil that darkened and filled the air. The *Waakzaamheid* lay within two miles. And now the extreme danger of sailing in a very heavy swell became more and more apparent: in the troughs, the valleys between the waves, the *Leopard* was almost becalmed, while on the crest the full force of the wind struck her, threatening to tear her sails from their boltropes or to carry away her masts: even worse, she lost some of her way at the bottom, whereas she needed all her speed to outrun the following seas, for if they were to overtake her she would be pooped, smothered in a mass of breaking water. Then ten to one she would slew round and broach to, presenting her broadside to the wind, so that the next sea would overwhelm her.

This was by no means the worst sea Jack had known; it was still far from the total chaos of a ten-days' blow—enormous waves with a fetch of a thousand miles running into one another, rising mountain-high, breaking, tumbling and bursting with enormous force—but it looked as though it might build up into something of the same kind; and already the *Waakzaamheid* was showing how much the larger ship was favoured. Her higher masts, her greater mass, meant that she lost less way when partially becalmed, and she was now not much more than a mile away: yet on the other hand she had either taken in or lost her odd triangles.

An albatross glided down the starboard side, turned on the wind and shot across the wake, picking something from the surface as it flew; and it was only when he saw the brilliant flash of its wings that he realized how yellow the foam was in fact. Even at this time of great concentration on his ship and the countless forces acting upon her he was astonished at the bird's perfect control, at the way its gleaming twelve-foot wings lifted it without the least effort and sent it flanking across the oncoming sea in an easy, unhurried curve. 'I wish Stephen could . . .' he was thinking as the *Leopard* climbed the crest ahead, but a crack forward and the sound of threshing canvas cut him short. The foretopsail had split. 'Clew up, clew up,' he cried—there was a chance of saving it. 'Halliards, there. Maintopsail.' He ran forward, calling for the bosun. No bosun, but Cullen, the captain of the foretop, was at the mast, and the bosun's mates: they secured the topsail, the yard lowered on the cap, while the ship plunged down the long slope among the smother of the breaking crest. The close-reefed maintopsail kept the *Leopard* ahead of the following seas after no more than a few minutes' hesitation, but it was too far aft for the ideal thrust—her speed was not so great, and she might steer wild.

It was still possible to bend another foretopsail. 'Pass the word for the bosun,' he shouted, and at last the man came stumbling aft: drunk, not dead drunk, but incapable. 'Get along forward,' said Jack to him: and to his older mate, 'Arklow, carry on. Number two foretopsail, and the best robins in the store.'

A cruel struggle out there on the yard, cruel and long, fighting with canvas animated by such a force, but they bent the sail at last and came down, hands bleeding, the men looking as though they had been flogged.

'Go below,' said Jack. 'Get your hands bound up: tell purser's steward I say you are to have a tot apiece, and something warm.'

Leaning over the rail, his eyes half-shut against the driving spray, he saw that the *Waakzaamheid* was now within a thousand yards. He shrugged: no ship, no first-rate, not even a Spanish four-decker, could show her broadside in such a sea. 'Mr Grant,' he said, 'let the pumps be rigged: we are steering rather heavy.' Then, with a look at the new foretopsail, tight as a drum, he went below for a bite himself.

Like the Dutch captain, Killick seemed able to read his thoughts: coffee and a pile of ham sandwiches were carrying in as Jack hung his streaming sou'-wester on its peg and walked into the gloomy cabin, where he sat on a locker by the starboard gun. Not a gleam came in from the stern windows, their glass replaced by solid wood; and even the skylight had a tarpaulin over it.

'Thankee, Killick,' he said, after a first ravenous gulp. 'Any news of the Doctor?'

'No, your honour. Only howls, and Mr Herapath took poorly. It must be worse before it can get better; that is what I always say.'

'No doubt, no doubt,' said Jack uneasily, and he applied himself to the sandwiches: thick cold pancake instead of bread, but welcome. Slowly champing, he mused on women, their hard lot; on the curse of Eve; on Sophie; on his daughters, growing fast. An immense crash of splintering wood, a surge of flying spray, a flood of light, and spent cannon-ball broke in upon his thought. He peered out through the broken deadlights and saw another flash in the *Waakzaamheid*'s bows. No sound in this universal roar, and the smoke was swept instantly away, but it was clear that the seventy-four had opened up with her chasers, trained sharp forward from the bridle-ports in her bluff bows and that a lucky shot had struck right home, smashing his coffee-cup— a chance in a million.

'Killick, another cup,' he called, carrying the rest of his breakfast into the dining-cabin. 'And let Chips come aft.'

'I had never expected that today,' he said to himself. Certainly the aim of warfare was the destruction of the enemy, and he had seen French ships totally destroyed in fleet-engagements; but in single-ship actions the idea of capture usually predominated. He had expected the seventy-four to hunt him down and take him, or try to take him, when the weather moderated: in this sea there was no possibility of capture and the Dutch captain's intent could only be to kill. Any engagement must mean the total loss of the first ship to lose a mast or a vital sail and thus the control of her run: the death of every soul aboard her. 'A bloody-minded man, I see.'

He did not spend long below, but how things had changed when he next came on deck! It was not that the wind was greater—indeed, there was a slight but certain lessening—but that the sea had grown steeper still. And the ship was labouring now, heavy on the rise, although the chain-pumps were shooting a great gush of water over her side. The storm-jib would have to come in: it was pressing her down, and in any case the boom was whipping like a bow. 'Mr Grant, we will get in the storm-jib and goose-wing the maincourse.'

'Surely, sir . . .' began the older man—he looked much older now—but went no further.

With the thrust lower, the *Leopard* fairly wallowed in the deeper troughs; yet her speed was still so great that she could certainly avoid the following seas with skilful handling: Jack named a team of men to take the wheel, prime seamen, four at a time, two glasses to a trick. The danger was more the shock when the wind took her full on the crests, and ordinarily Jack would have had her under a close-reefed foretopsail alone or even less—just enough to keep her ahead. But with the *Waakzaamheid* creeping up he dared not take more in; nor could he haul up the jib again. If this went on he would have to compensate the lack of thrust by lightening the load: he would have to pump out the tons and tons of fresh water down there in the hold. The *Waakzaamheid* was half a mile away. He saw two flashes, but never the pitch of the shot, quite lost in this white turmoil.

He made a tour of the ship—long, wind-hurried strides forward, a battle against it aft—which showed him that all was as snug as it could be in such a case, and that there was no likelihood of any change of sail for some while—no voluntary change—and he called for Moore, Burton and the best gun captains in the ship.

"Sir,' said Grant, as he was leaving the quarterdeck, 'the *Waak-zaamheid* has opened fire.'

'So I gather, Mr Grant,' said Jack, laughing. 'But two can play at that game, you know.'

He was surprised to see no answering smile at all, but this was not the moment for brooding over his lieutenant's moods, and he led his party into the cabin.

They cast loose the guns, removed the wing deadlights, and looked out on to a soaring green cliff of water fifty yards away with the *Leopard*'s wake trace down its side. It shut out the sky, and it was racing towards them. The *Leopard*'s stern rose, rose: the enormous wave passed smoothly under her counter, and there through the flying spume lay the *Waakzaamheid* below, running down the far slope. 'When you please, Mr Burton,' said Jack to the gunner. 'A hole in her foretopsail might make it split.' The larboard gun roared out and instantly the cabin was filled with smoke. No hole: no fall of shot either. Jack, to starboard, had the Dutchman in his dispart sight. A trifle of elevation and he pulled the lanyard. Nothing happened: flying spray had soaked the lock. 'Match,' he cried, but by the time he had the glowing end in his hand the *Waakzaamheid* was below his line of sight, below the depression of his gun. From down there in the trough she fired up, a distant wink of flame, and she got in another couple of shots before the grey-green hill of water parted them again.

'May I suggest a cigar, sir?' said Moore. 'One can hold it in one's mouth.' He was acting as sponger and second captain, and his face was six inches from Jack's: he was encased in oilskins and there was nothing of the Marine about him but his fine red face and the neat stock showing under his chin.

'A capital idea,' said Jack, and in the calm of the trough, before the *Waakzaamheid* appeared again, Moore lit him a cigar from the glowing match in its tub.

The *Leopard* began to rise, the Dutchman appeared, black in the white water of the breaking crests high up there, and both nine-pounders went off together. The guns leapt back, the crews worked furiously, grunting, no words, sponged, loaded, and ran them out again. Another shot, and this time Jack saw his ball, dark in the haze of lit water, flying at its mark: he could not follow it home, but the line was true, a little low. Now they were on the crest, and the cabin was filled with wind and water mingled, unbreathable: the gun-crews worked without the slightest pause, soaked through and through.

Down, down the slope amidst the white wreckage of the wave, the guns run out and waiting. Across the hollow and up the other side. 'I believe I caught his splash,' said Moore. 'Twenty yards short of our starboard quarter.'

'So did I,' said Burton. 'He wants to knock our rudder, range along, and give us a broadside, the bloody-minded dog.'

The *Waakzaamheid* over the crest again: Jack poured the priming into the touch-hole with his horn, guarding it with the flat of his hand, the cigar clenched between his teeth and the glow kept bright; and this bout each gun fired three times before the *Leopard* mounted too high, racing up and up, pursued by the Dutchman's shot. On and on: an enormous switchback, itself in slow, majestic motion, but traversed at a racing speed in which the least stumble meant a fall. Alternate bursts of fire, aimed and discharged with such an intensity of purpose that the men did not even see the storm of flying water that burst in upon them at each crest. On and on, the *Waakzaamheid* gaining visibly.

Here was Babbington at his side, waiting for a pause. 'Take over, Moore,' said Jack, as the gun ran in. He stepped over the train-tackle, and Babbington said, 'She's hit our mizen-top, sir, fair and square.'

Jack nodded. She was coming far too close: point-blank range now, and the wind to help her balls. 'Start the water, all but a ton; and try the jib, one-third in.'

Back to the gun as it ran out. Now it was the *Waakzaamheid*'s turn to fire, and fire she did, striking the *Leopard*'s stern-post high up: a shrewd knock that jarred the ship as she was on the height of the wave, and a moment later a green sea swept through the deadlights.

'Good practice in this sea, Mr Burton,' said Jack.

The gunner turned his streaming face, and its fixed fierce glare broke into a smile. 'Pretty fair, sir, pretty fair. But if I did not get home two shots ago, my name is Zebedee.'

The flying *Leopard* drew a little way ahead with the thrust of her jib, a hundred yards or so; and the switchback continued, the distances the same. It was the strangest gunnery, with its furious activity and then the pause, waiting to be fired at; the soaking at the crest, the deck awash; the intervening wall of water; the repetition of the whole sequence. No orders; none of the rigid fire-discipline of the gun-deck; loud, gun-deafened conversation between the bouts. The dread of being pooped by the great seas right there in front of their noses, rising to blot out the sun with unfailing regularity, and of broaching to, hardly affected the cabin.

A savage roar from Burton's crew. 'We hit her port-lid,' cried Bonden, the second captain. 'They can't get it closed.'

'Then we are all in the same boat,' said Moore. 'Now the Dutchmen will have a wet jacket every time she digs in her bows, and I wish they may like it, ha, ha!'

A short-lived triumph. A midshipman came to report the jib carried clean away—Babbington had all in hand—was trying to set a storm-staysail—half the water was pumped out.

But although the *Leopard* was lighter she felt the loss of the jib; the *Waakzaamheid* was coming up, and now the vast hill of sea separated them only for seconds. If the *Leopard* did not gain when all her water was gone, the upper-deck guns would have to follow it: anything to draw ahead and preserve the ship. The firing was more and more continuous; the guns grew hot, kicking clear on the recoil, and first Burton and then Jack reduced the charge.

Nearer and nearer, so that they were both on the same slope, no trough between them: a hole in the Dutchman's foretopsail, but it would not split, and three shots in quick succession struck the *Leopard*'s hull, close to her rudder. Jack had smoked five cigars to the butt, and his mouth was scorched and dry. He was staring along the barrel of his gun, watching for the second when the *Waakzaamheid*'s bowsprit should rise above his sight, when he saw her starboard chaser fire. A split second later he stabbed his cigar down on the priming and there was an enormous crash, far louder than the roar of the gun.

How much later he looked up he could not tell. Nor, when he did look up, could he quite tell what was afoot. He was lying by the cabin bulkhead with Killick holding his head and Stephen sewing busily; he could feel the passage of the needle and of the thread, but no pain. He stared right and left. 'Hold still,' said Stephen. He felt the red-hot stabbing now, and everything fell into place. The gun had not burst: there was Moore fighting it. He had been dragged clear—hit—a splinter, no doubt. Stephen and Killick crouched over him as a green sea gushed in: then Stephen cut the thread, whipped a wet cloth round his ears, one eye and forehead, and said, 'Do you hear me, now?' He nodded; Stephen moved on to another man lying on the deck; Jack stood up, fell, and crawled over to the guns. Killick tried to hold him, but Jack thrust him back, clapped on to the tackle and helped run out the loaded starboard gun. Moore bent over it, cigar in hand, and from behind him Jack could see the *Waakzaamheid* twenty yards away, huge, black-hulled, throwing the water wide. As Moore's hand came down, Jack automatically stepped aside; but he was still stupid, he moved slow, and the recoiling gun flung him to the deck again. On hands and knees he felt for the train-tackle in the smoke, found it as the darkness cleared, and tallied on. But for a moment he could not understand the cheering that filled the cabin, deafening his ears: then through the shattered deadlights he saw the Dutchman's foremast lurch, lurch again, the stays part, the mast and sail carry away right over the bows.

The *Leopard* reached the crest. Green water blinded him. It cleared, and through the bloody haze running from his cloth he saw the vast breaking wave with the *Waakzaamheid* broadside on its curl, on her beam-ends, broached to. An enormous, momentary turmoil of black hull and white water, flying spars, rigging that streamed wild for a second, and then nothing at all but the great hill of green-grey with foam racing upon it.

'My God, oh my God,' he said. 'Six hundred men.'

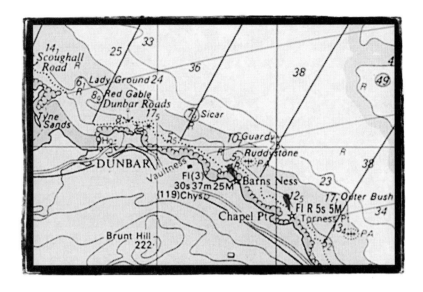

from The Breath of Angels
by John Beattie

John Beattie (born in 1951) worried that his plans to sail around the world were extremely ambitious, given his limited nautical experience and skills. He set out in July, 1992 with some trepidation—and quickly found that his concerns were justified.

Once we cleared the harbour entrance, all I wanted was a cup of tea and a cigarette. This always soothes the nerves. It would also give me a chance to get acquainted with John, who had joined at the last minute. The first thing I realised was that in the rush to depart I had forgotten to buy tobacco, but I knew that John also smoked roll-your-owns. 'How much tobacco do you have?' I asked. He told me that he had given up a few days ago and didn't have any! This was my first big problem. However, with an expected landfall in just over a day, I had enough to keep me going if I rationed it carefully.

With the wind blowing gently, we hoisted full sail. John had a new girlfriend in Edinburgh, with whom he was madly in love. He was planning to visit her after sailing with me as far as Inverness. As we sat in the cockpit, sipping the tea, John was happy to tell me about the 'good karma' that existed between them, and I was happy to listen. Shortly before dark, I advised him to turn in for a few hours' sleep. He went forward to the forepeak, closed the door, fell asleep, and no doubt dreamed about good karma.

Sitting alone in the cockpit at dusk, everything seemed so simple now that I was at last underway. The wind became a bit fitful, eventually dying away completely. I started the engine. The electronic autopilot was engaged. The motor for this was fitted below decks and couldn't be seen working—the boat gave the impression of being steered by an invisible helmsman, because the wheel in the cockpit would turn as if by magic with fine adjustments this way and that. I stretched out on the saloon berth to read the first book of my voyage. Plunging straight into the rich heritage of seafaring literature, I duly opened *Moby Dick*.

All was calm but I was too restless to make much progress with Melville's classic. I put it to one side and walked about the main cabin and cockpit, checking the engine instruments, compass, charts and navigation lights. Everything seemed to be in order. There was nothing much for me to do. The black silhouettes of a few fishing boats ghosted by, their navigation lights winking at me. None of them came too close to cause concern.

The British Admiralty chart for the North Sea was rolled out on the chart table. I studied its fine detail as if it were a painting in the Louvre. Charts of the sea are wonderful things. They show fishing grounds, shoals, banks, isolated dangers and rock outcrops. Every stretch of water has a name, as does each headland and bay. Every aid to navigation, be it a buoy, a beacon or a lighthouse, is clearly marked, as are the contours of the seabed. Even the seabed material is indicated—mud, clay, sand, shingle, rock. Currents, tides, magnetic variation, all are given, along with traffic-separation zones for inshore shipping. But there are few details of the land, apart from those visible from seaward —church spires, radio masts and old ruins perched on cliff-tops. The chartmakers of the sea tend to disregard the land. Theirs is another world, and its priorities and imperatives impose themselves upon the chart.

Each sea is different and because the North Sea is prone to bad weather, it is one of the biggest graveyards in the world. Wrecks lie all over the bottom. They are shown on the chart by a short horizontal line with two shorter perpendicular lines cutting through. I suppose this is an icon for the deck of a boat and two masts, but it also looks like two crucifixes joined together; one for the soul of the lost ship and one for the lost souls onboard. Each one is an untold or forgotten story. I always felt a strange feeling, sailing over these little marks on the chart. Such a tiny mark, such a big tragedy.

By now people were going to bed in Whitby. A man I hardly knew was fast asleep in the forepeak. Land was out of sight. After checking all the instruments time and again, I lifted the hatch in the cockpit to inspect the newly painted engine. With the help of a flashlight, everything looked fine. All the belts and pulleys were turning smoothly. The beam of the flashlight followed the fuel line, shining through the glass-bowled filter. It dipped down to the rubber engine mountings, which looked in good order, and travelled on to the gearbox at the back of the engine—no problem there. The stainless-steel propeller shaft was whizzing round, catching and reflecting back the brilliance of the light. The end of the shaft then passes through a watertight gland in the hull and out to sea to the propeller. Any through-hull fitting below the waterline is a potential source of disaster because if a leak is going to occur these are the most likely places. I craned my head to avoid the whirling pulleys and allow my eye to catch sight of the watertight gland. It had come undone!

Panic, surprisingly enough, is a response rarely encountered at sea because there is usually time to come to terms with problems. To my great relief, and even greater disbelief, there didn't seem to be any water coming aboard, but it was surely only a matter of time before water seeped though the grease already packed in the gland and came flooding in. But there were plenty of fishing boats around, my VHF radio was working, it was a calm night, I had a brand new life raft. Land was only 15 miles away. No need to panic, I kept thinking, but the engine must be shut down immediately. I pulled the stop handle. All fell silent. I felt a great sense of relief now that the engine was closed down. John, asleep in the forepeak, may have good karma with women, but I have always had bad karma with engines.

I didn't know what was the worst prospect: sinking or turning back? If I turned back to Whitby now, I had doubts that I would ever get going again before the equinoctial gales set in. There were safe harbours further north where I could put in for repairs. The wind was now starting to pick up again, probably the nightly offshore breeze. By making headway under sail and with the propeller not turning, there wouldn't be much strain on the stern gland. I kept a northerly course and a close eye on the gland.

The nightly offshore breeze stiffened, filling the sails. There is a compelling simplicity about making headway under sail: no moving parts, no lubrication or fuel, no noise—just the wind in the sails and the boat in harmony with nature.

Almost imperceptibly, the wind began to increase. With the sea beginning to get a bit lumpy, I shortened canvas. I had given considerable thought to the sailplan: a large headsail was attached to the forestay, which had roller reefing—a mechanism for reducing sail by pulling on a line that winds the canvas around a foil, like wrapping a piece of paper round a pencil. The other sail was the mainsail, which was hoisted up the mast and attached at the bottom to a swinging boom. This sail was shortened by hauling on a series of lines that pulled the sail down the mast in three stages, known as reefs. All sail control lines, which, for some reason that I have never understood, are called sheets, were led back to the cockpit to allow sail to be reduced without leaving its comparative safety.

Still the wind continued to rise. It was now blowing spray off the top of the waves. I rolled up more of the headsail and put the first-stage reef in the main. None of the new gear for reducing sail had been sea-trialed properly but it was being tested now. It proved inadequate. All the sheets had been re-routed back to the cockpit via a series of blocks. There was a single winch for gaining extra purchase on the sheets, along with a few rope jammers. I had seen this arrangement on other boats, and it looked eminently sensible. What I didn't realise is that each owner had a carefully worked-out configuration of winches, jammers and control lines that had been evolved and refined over two or three sailing seasons to meet each boat's particular needs. The set-up I had, although it looked fine on paper, simply didn't work in practice. I was finding this out for the first time at sea at night with a steadily increasing wind, a suspect stern gland, and an engine that I couldn't use.

There was no doubt that the weather was taking a turn for the worse, and the warm summer evening and settled sea that had enticed me out of the safety of the harbour in Whitby now seemed like a distant dream. Most of the people in bed in Whitby didn't care a hoot about the wind—the worst that could happen to them is that they might lose a slate from their roof—but the wind held me and the boat in its thrall: it had the power to change my world. I fumbled with the sheets to put the second reef in the mainsail.

When the wind blows hard and the seas build, the most uncomfortable place on a boat is the forepeak. As the troughs between waves get deeper and steeper, the bow of the boat falls into each one, slamming down hard. The sound of the water crashing against the hull is fearsome, and you start to wonder how the thin fibreglass skin of the boat can stand up to it. Sleeping in the forepeak is almost impossible, so I wasn't surprised when the door to this cabin opened and John stumbled out already fully dressed.

There was a look of anxiety on his face. 'What's going on?' he asked, making his way with difficulty through the main cabin to the companionway. When he went to bed there was daylight, the sea was flat calm, and there was very little wind. When he woke up four hours later, the whole world had changed. It wasn't surprising that he asked what was going on.

Alarmism is everyone's worst enemy aboard a boat, so I replied very casually, 'The wind's just getting up a bit, stick the kettle on.' John brewed a strong cup of tea, and the time spent doing it gave him a chance to wake up and get his wits about him. With the boat on autopilot, I came below. I smoked a couple of cigarettes with my tea, while John ate a few apples with his.

When the tea was finished, the wind was even stronger. I remembered reading somewhere that if the wind increases by more than three points on the Beaufort Scale in less than an hour, then a full-blown gale is approaching. John asked whether I had heard the forecast before we left. All I could say was, 'No.' Although the BBC issues a regular, comprehensive shipping forecast, it had never occurred to me to tune in. The evening transmission is just before the news at six—at that time I was stuffing gear into lockers. What's more, it had been a very settled summer so far, with hardly any wind at all for the last three or four weeks. The prospect of bad weather never entered my head. What was entering my head right then was the prospect of the stern gland bursting apart. In these deteriorating conditions, it would be no easy matter to launch the life raft and board it should the need arise. It wouldn't have served any purpose to tell John about the stern gland—I was doing enough worrying for the two of us—and there was no need to open the engine hatch to inspect it. It would be easy to establish whether we were taking water by regular pumping with the manual bilge pump, so I mentioned to John that we should pump the bilges every half hour, just to keep the boat nice and dry.

I had first go on the bilge pump, counting 42 strokes. As long as the number of strokes stayed at about this level, things were under control. With the full gale now nearly upon us, the boat was seriously overcanvased. Taking more canvas off the headsail was easy because the furling gear, which hadn't been changed in the refit, worked well. The long foil rotated, rolling the sail up neatly on the forestay until only a small amount remained—enough to help control the boat, but not too much to unbalance her. The seas were now too big for the electric autopilot to work. The invisible helmsman was being overwhelmed and couldn't turn the wheel fast or hard enough to counteract the effect of the waves which were breaking on the boat, knocking her off course.

Although the headsail had been brought under control, there was far too much mainsail up. The third and last reef had to go in without delay. When the new sails had been made, I had decided to opt for a very deep third reef in the main. The reasoning behind this was that it would allow me to carry a minimal amount of sail on the main, even in very bad conditions. It was needed now. When it was first hoisted up the mast a few days earlier in Whitby harbour, local yachtsmen, always eager to inspect any new gear on any boat, had commented that it was very deep and that I would probably never need it. They were wrong. So too was the boatyard owner who had fitted a new boom with all the sail control lines running inside. The arrangement of sliding blocks inside the boom restricted the number of lines available to four. I needed a single line for putting in the first reef, another for putting in the second, one for pulling the sail tight along the boom, and two for the third reef—that made five! That meant one short. I was advised that the best thing to do was not to worry about connecting one of the lines for the third reef—if I ever needed it, I could untie a line that was already used and feed it through the cringle in the sail for reef number three. Sounds great in theory, but now, with the wind blowing at gale force, darkness all around, the boat being knocked off course, heavy seas crashing on the deck and a wildly flogging main about to shred, it didn't seem so easy. The situation was made worse by the inadequate system of jammers and winches that I had installed.

With John's help, I tried again and again to put the third reef in. Even though it was late summer, our fingers became numb from the wet and cold. After many attempts we gave up. We couldn't use the engine because of the broken stern gland, and the boat couldn't be sailed because she had too much canvas. Had I been more experienced, I would have dropped the entire mainsail and lashed it to the boom, but I was so preoccupied with the third reef that this didn't occur to me. I thought, mistakenly, that some mainsail was necessary to balance the boat.

All the exertion of trying to tame the sail had taken its toll on both of us—John was starting to look very pale. He leaned over the side of the cockpit: I held on to his waist while he vomited up the apples and tea consumed an hour earlier. I had seen the debilitating effect that sea sickness can have on people and was worried that he would succumb completely. Seasickness is a curse, which, like all curses, afflicts some more than others. It can drain all the life out of the strongest man, making him feel miserable beyond belief. Hypothermia, weakness, lethargy and depression always accompany the wretching. The stomach heaves and contracts violently, almost turning itself inside-out to empty its contents, and the foul bile lingers in the mouth like the aftertaste of death. It can get so bad that sometimes a man with severe seasickness can fold like a house of cards, crawling into his bunk, almost wishing for death as a means of release. But there is no escape from it, which only makes it worse. As John wiped the last bits of green apple peel and white vomit from his mouth, he put a very brave face on it, saying almost apologetically, 'I don't normally get seasick.'

It takes real courage to keep going when you're sick. Not wanting to make him feel any worse than he already did, I replied, 'Don't worry, it'll do you good.'

Somehow or other, the boat had to be brought under control quickly. I decided to heave to. A long-keeled sailboat can be made to come virtually to rest in the water by backing the headsail, so that it tries to force the bow round one way, and putting the wheel hard over, to force the bow round the other way. The yacht lies at about 50 degrees to the wind, making slow forward progress, riding the oncoming seas. When the boat is hove to, no one needs to do anything and the gale can be waited out, provided you don't drift towards land. I hove so that whatever progress we made was to seaward. When I went down below to see John, who was recovering from his seasickness, and told him what I had done, I could see that he was a little concerned about drifting further out to sea in the teeth of a gale. He told me that if this was a fairground ride he wouldn't get on, but he was on and there was no getting off. He was somewhat reassured by the relative calm that settled upon us now that we were hove to. When I told him the old adage about land being the most dangerous thing you can see when at sea, we both managed to smile at one another.

The smile disappeared from my face when I suddenly remembered the bilge pump. We had completely forgotten about pumping her out while trying to tie and untie the sail lines. I went out to the cockpit, pump handle in hand, and started to empty her out once more. Sitting there huddled inside my foul-weather gear, forcing the handle up and down, I remembered all the fishing boats we had seen earlier that night. It occurred to me that I hadn't seen one in the last four or five hours. No doubt they knew more about the weather than I did, having picked up the gale warning issued in the shipping forecast. They had headed straight for port. Like a fool, I kept heading out to sea.

Once the weather had started to deteriorate, my consumption of cigarettes had escalated in line with the Beaufort Scale. I was now on my last one. As I finished the wet butt off, we were about level with Newcastle upon Tyne: there was a 24-hour shop in Newcastle—it sold cigarettes! Laura also lived there. She had just returned from her mother's funeral. I had asked her not to bother to take time off work to come down to see me off but to join me for a full week in Inverness to sail through the Caledonian Canal. It always made me sad to think of leaving her, and I couldn't bear the thought of being parted from her for a week, let alone two years. Most of my friends thought she was too good for me, and I agreed with them. She would have tuned in to the midnight shipping forecast and would know that I was out in a gale. She would probably be asleep now—all would be quiet and still. I could be lying in bed beside her, warm and safe—smoking a cigarette.

The wind was howling, the boat was pitching up and down, and the sea was raging about us. Land was out of sight, I was out of tobacco, and I must have been out of my mind. I strained my eyes to try to pick up a light on the shoreline to the west but could see none, and in time with the strokes of the pump, muttered to myself, 'What the hell . . . am I . . . doing here . . . ?'

We lay hove to, waiting for dawn. Neither of us got any sleep. The light came slowly at first, as it does in high latitudes, cheering us up a little. But the dawn was a bleak sight by any standards. It was a monochrome world. Everything was different shades of grey: the sky was overcast and grey, the sea was dark and grey, and the breakers on the tops of the waves were more grey than white.

Now that this dismal light was upon us, the best thing to do was to try to get going again. That meant putting the third reef in the main, which we had struggled unsuccessfully with the night before. The key to success lay in threading a line through a heavy cringle in the corner of the sail. Once this line was through, the sail could be reduced and the surplus canvas at the bottom could then be secured to the boom by pulling hard on the line. We zipped ourselves into our foul-weather gear and clipped on our life-harnesses and life-lines, before going out to the cockpit to try again. Life-lines are, in theory, a good idea. They secure you to the ship like an umbilical cord, stopping you from falling overboard, but they also severely restrict your movement and continually get in the way. When undertaking a difficult job, a moment sometimes occurs when you need an extra bit of reach quickly, and you have to unclip the life-line or the moment is lost.

When we dropped the sail it started to flog once more. John was trying to pull the canvas tight while I was trying to thread the line through. He was standing on the cockpit seat in order to reach the boom. His life-line was unclipped. As he struggled with the canvas, it slipped out of his wet, cold hands. He started to fall backwards. There was a hole in his face the size of an Italian tomato where his mouth should have been, but no sound came out. His eyes were open wide, staring straight at me. There was real terror in them—he didn't know where he was going to fall. I reached out and grabbed the front of his jacket. He stopped falling. Another failed attempt! John was visibly shaken by the fall—he had a haunted expression on his face even after the danger had passed. In that moment he was falling, he thought he was going to die. When someone has just had such thoughts they need time to come to terms with them, but there was no time to waste.

We tried again. This time John stayed on the wheel, trying to steer the boat so that the sail flogged as little as possible, while I tried on my own to get the line through. I just couldn't reach high enough for long enough to get it through the damn hole. If I climbed on to the end of the boom, I had a better chance of getting it through.

Above the noise of the wind and the breaking seas, I called out to John, 'Do you think you can hold her in this position?' There was a nod of desperation. I unclipped the harness and clambered on to the end of the boom. 'Make sure you hold her steady,' I yelled, trying, with one hand for the ship and one for myself, to get the line through. The sail, which seemed to be possessed, was thrashing about like a lunatic in a strait-jacket. It was impossible to manage with one hand. There was a big bag of billowing canvas hanging at the bottom of the boom. This was catching the wind, whipping the edge of the sail into a frenzy. I checked once more that John could hold her steady and jumped into the bag of canvas at the bottom of the leeward side of the boom. The thrashing lunatic was pinned to the ground and I now had two hands free to finish him off. The line went through the cringle and was secured. It was the most dangerous and stupid thing I had ever done, but it worked.

Once all the lines were made as tight as we could get them with the hopeless arrangement of winches and jammers I had installed, but never tested, the boat was brought under some sort of control. We swung her on to a north-westerly course and got underway. John remained on the wheel while I went below for a much-needed cup of tea. The tea just wasn't the same without a cigarette, and I craved one. As I sat sipping the tea, all I could think of was tobacco and how stupid I had just been. If the boat had been knocked round by a wave, the bag of sailcloth in which I had been standing would have flipped over to the other side of the boom, catapulting me into the raging sea and eternity. I vowed to myself that never again would I do anything with any risk attached to it without a life-line.

Visibility was poor, and we had made some miles to seaward while hove to. Even though we were now making good progress, land didn't appear for a long time. Shortly before noon, we caught our first glimpse of it off the coast of Northumberland. Bamburgh Castle, majestic and medieval, slowly appeared perched on a cragged cliff. The Northumberland coastline is steeped in history, and it wasn't long before Lindisfarne Priory on Holy Island, built in the eleventh century, came into view. St Cuthbert had once lived, prayed and scribbled away within its walls. He had, no doubt, on many occasions looked out to sea from his cell and seen ships struggling to make a landfall, and had probably said prayers for them.

We decided to try to put into Berwick upon Tweed. This, the most northerly town in England, has changed hands between that country and its old rival, Scotland, many times. The harbour, like most harbours on the east coast of England and Scotland, has a shallow entrance. It can only be approached by deep-draught vessels at certain states of the tide. The nautical almanac showed that high water occurred shortly after 2:00 p.m. There would be enough water for the *Warrior Queen* to go in up to about 3:30 p.m. We were making good progress and would probably get there in time.

When at sea, things don't go according to plan. By the time we were approaching the entrance to Berwick Harbour it was nearly 4:00 p.m. I hadn't had any sleep worth talking about for over 30 hours, had been through a gale, and the stern gland needed sorting out. I wanted to get into port badly. Berwick Harbour has a long wall that extends out to sea. You approach the harbour by heading for the end of this wall and then creep along the inside of it. The shallowest water is just before you reach the wall, and there is a vicious-looking outcrop of rocks close by. As long as we could reach the wall, we would be OK. We inched forward under power, keeping a close watch on the depth-sounder. With about 50 yards to go, as we were level with the rock outcrop, the depth fell off sharply. With 25 yards to go, we hit ground! There was a sickening, hard grating noise. The boat juddered on the bottom, losing its buoyancy in an instant. The rock outcrop, although still in the same place, now looked twice as big and twice as close.

The tide was on the ebb. If we didn't get off immediately, the ship would be lost. This wasn't a sandbank in a sheltered estuary on a calm day. There were rocks below us, and we were still in the open sea in bad weather. I slammed the engine into reverse. The engine was racing like mad and so was my mind. How could I ever cope with the humiliatlion of losing the boat at the start of the trip? People would say it was my fault, and they would be right. The local TV cameras would be here in no time, and I would never be able to look Laura in the face again. It would have been better to sink miles out to sea—at least that has a certain romance about it, but there is nothing romantic about piling your boat up at the entrance to a harbour. I could already see people shaking their heads when I tried to explain to them that I thought we *might* have had enough water to get in.

I willed her to come off. With the wind blowing from the bow and the propeller spinning like crazy, she started to move. We were backing off slowly, very slowly. I was worried that we might back into another clump of rocks on the seabed but she kept moving and we came clear. John and I were getting to the stage where we couldn't take much more of this. We couldn't carry on because of the stern gland, and we couldn't get into port because of the tide, but I did have a big insurance policy lashed to the bow of the boat—an anchor! There is a large bay south of the harbour entrance at Berwick. The chart showed that there was plenty of water and indicated that the bottom was sand and mud—perfect holding ground. We motored out to the middle of the bay and let go the anchor. It dug into the bottom, holding her fast with the bow to the wind. I remembered that someone had once told me that the most important gear aboard was good ground tackle. I now knew why.

We shut down the engine and, to allow access to the stern gland, cleared all the gear out of the cockpit lockers that had been stuffed in the day before. Although we were both dead tired, I couldn't go to sleep knowing that she might sink at anchor during the night. I clambered into the locker and lay prone in a space literally the size of a coffin. By removing an inspection plate at the aft end of this locker, I could stick my head through into the back of the engine bay. The stern gland was sorted out in less than half an hour. After a few sandwiches, John and I turned in and fell instantly into a deep sleep while the boat bobbed up and down on the sea, swinging on the anchor chain.

When we woke next morning, the wind had dropped off and was blowing gently from the north. This was bad news. It was now coming from where we wanted to go, but with the stern gland fixed we could motor. I felt an urgent need to make as much progress as possible. It looked as though summer was coming to an early close—the autumn would bring more gales. The evenings were already starting to draw in, so the sooner I got to more southerly latitudes, the better. We started the engine, checked the stern gland, hauled up the anchor chain and got underway. Before clearing the bay at Berwick, I called up the harbour master on the VHF radio to tell him we had hit ground when approaching the harbour entrance the day before. I asked him what was on the bottom. 'Rock covered with sand and mud,' came the disheartening reply, and I wondered how much damage had been done.

North of Berwick lies St Abb's Head, with its bird sanctuary. As we passed, the sky was filled with gannets, fulmers and puffins. The puffins flapped their wings furiously to make very little progress, while the fulmers, with their short tails and stocky bodies, seemed to be able to catch every shift in the wind, skipping over the waves with an effortlessness that belied their appearance. The gannets soared majestically above the rest, folding their wings flat every once in a while, before plunging like arrows into the sea below to catch a fish.

I made sure to tune in to the lunchtime shipping forecast—northerly winds of force four to six were predicted. The force of the wind is measured on the Beaufort Scale, with force 0 representing flat calm and force 12 being a hurricane with winds over 100 miles an hour. Force four to six represents a good stiff breeze, which is ideal for sailing, provided it blows from the right direction. We needed the wind to blow anywhere from east through south to west, but today it was coming from where we wanted to go. The open sea at the mouth of the Firth of Forth lay in front of us, and we had no alternative but to motor across. It was only about 20 miles wide. Provided we made four or five knots, we should make it before nightfall. As the wind picked up to the predicted force six, it whipped up the sea before us. The waves were not particularly big but we were heading straight into them, and the ride was a bit uncomfortable. Engines on sailboats don't have much power. They perform well in harbour or in calm conditions, but when going to windward they have to fight against each oncoming wave and the drag of the wind. St Abb's Head behind us seemed to stay where it was forever—we were not making much progress. By regularly checking our position on the chart, it was clear that instead of doing the expected four or five knots, we were barely making one knot. By nightfall we were only a third of the way across.

As we got further out into the open sea and the wind had more time to stir up the waves, our speed across the ground fell off to about half a knot. Spray broke over the bow, soaking the helmsman. When you spend an hour being soaked with freezing water to cover half a mile and have the prospect of another 20 or 30 hours in store, you start to get a bit demoralised. With the boat pitching up and down, the propeller rises out of the water every now and again and the engine screeches. All the time you struggle with the futility of asking yourself pointless questions such as, 'Why doesn't the wind go round to the west or the east?', because you know that if it did, you could hoist the sails, close down the drone of the engine, and take flight.

John was beginning to miss his girlfriend and I was starting to miss mine. We got the charts out to explore the options. It was now slowly dawning on me that it was pointless to simply look at a destination, in this case Inverness in the north of Scotland, and try to head straight for it regardless of where the wind blew from. There was a small harbour in Dunbar, round the corner from St Abb's Head. We could turn round and sail straight to it. There wouldn't be much progress to show from Berwick but there would be some. At about three in the morning we brought the bow round and started heading back.

At daybreak, we were sailing close along the coast, looking for the entrance to Dunbar. A friend, who had once sailed in there, had told me that it was the most dramatic harbour entrance he had ever seen. The harbour is not visible from seaward but there are two large beacons situated on a hillside near the town which guide you in. The beacons are some distance apart and at different heights. The closest of the two has a triangle pointing upwards and the furthest has a triangle pointing downwards. Having spotted the beacons, we sailed along until both triangles were lined up. I made sure that the two apexes of each triangle kept pointing together as I sailed in. This line took us between pinnacles of isolated rock on either side, along the edge of a tall cliff and seemingly straight to the shore. No harbour could be seen. As we approached the shore, and I was just beginning to say to myself, 'This can't be right', a small gap appeared in the cliff. Sheer rock towered above the mast as we edged in through this gap, whereupon a small, tranquil fishing harbour appeared in front of us. Fishing boats were getting ready to leave as we tied up alongside the harbour wall.

It had been a miserable trip. The newly installed reefing gear hadn't worked, the stern gland fell apart, and John had been sick. We had been caught in a gale, then ran aground, and, finally, had turned back. I had probably come as close to going overboard as I ever wanted to, and we were nowhere near Inverness. It had taken us nearly three hard days to cover a distance that you could do in a car in comfort in less than three hours. Sydney Opera House seemed a very long way away.

Although the harbour is sheltered, it is subject to heavy swell in northerly winds. This swell was running up the side of the harbour wall. The only way to secure the boat was with two very long lines tied bow and stern. The boat was swept up and down the harbour wall with the incoming swell and kept banging up against the side. The harbour master gave us some help in adjusting the lines but there was nothing that we could do to get her to lie steady.

We both climbed up the steel ladder on the harbour wall. The first thing that John did, before we went off to find a telephone, was to kneel down to kiss the ground. He was so serious that he didn't even bother trying to make a joke about it. Laura had, as I expected, been listening to the shipping forecasts. She was full of sympathy and concern but her first words were what they would always be for the time I was at sea. 'Where are you?' she asked. I was hoping that she would join me that day and as often as possible in the future, so I played down the drama of the last three days and lied, saying we had just had one or two minor problems. She said she would get a train up in the afternoon. John, who had also been in touch with his girl, was going to leave at

Dunbar. He was good with his hands, and there were a couple of broken hinges and fastenings that he said he would fix before leaving. We both went back to the boat and started work.

It would have been easy for John to pack up his gear and leave there and then, but he spent all morning helping me sort out a few problems. He was as shattered as I was and would probably never sail on the *Warrior Queen* again. But he got stuck in. Nothing pleases the owner of a boat more than having someone aboard who is able and willing to help fix broken gear. I was very touched that he took the time to help. Before leaving round about lunchtime, he told me that the last three days had been the worst and the longest of his life but he was still glad he had made the trip. I think he now had a keener appreciation of everything in life after nearly having lost his own. Just as he was going, he put his hand in his pocket, pulled out a half-ounce of rolling tobacco that was still wrapped in the cellophane, and said as he handed it to me, 'I had this with me all the time.'

'I thought you'd given up?'

'I have, but I just needed it in my pocket for reassurance.'

'But why didn't you give it to me when I ran out?'

'Because I thought that if you didn't have any, you would be more likely to put in sooner, and all I wanted was to get off the boat.'

'Well, why are you telling me this now?'

'Because . . . because I feel guilty about it.' A craving for cigarettes is, like fear, intensely experienced when it occurs but it leaves no memory. We both laughed about it, before shaking hands warmly and saying goodbye. I climbed back down the ladder, stretched out on my bunk and was so exhausted that I couldn't be bothered to take my shoes off before falling fast asleep.

from The Loss of the S. S. Titanic
by Lawrence Beesley

Lawrence Beesley was a young science teacher aboard the Titanic *when it struck an iceberg on April 14, 1912. He published his account of the disaster in part to correct the misimpressions left by contemporary accounts—"where they err," he wrote, "they err on the highly dramatic side." His story in its simplicity and compassion is more affecting than better-known versions of the sinking that have appeared in print and on screen.*

had been fortunate enough to secure a two-berth cabin to myself—D 56—quite close to the saloon and most convenient in every way for getting about the ship; and on a big ship like the *Titanic* it was quite a consideration to be on D deck, only three decks below the top or boat-deck. Below D again were cabins on E and F decks, and to walk from a cabin on F up to the top deck, climbing five flights of stairs on the way, was certainly a considerable task for those not able to take much exercise. The *Titanic* management has been criticized, among other things, for supplying the boat with lifts: it has been said they were an expensive luxury and the room they took up might have been utilized in some way for more life-saving appliances. Whatever else may have been superfluous, lifts certainly were not: old ladies, for example, in cabins on F deck, would hardly have got to the top deck during the whole voyage had they not been able to ring for the lift-boy. Perhaps nothing gave one a greater impression of the size of the ship than to take the lift from the top and drop slowly down past the different floors, discharging and taking in passengers just as in a large hotel. I wonder where the lift-boy was that night. I would have been glad to find him in our boat, or on the *Carpathia* when we took count of the saved. He was quite young— not more than sixteen, I think—a bright-eyed, handsome boy, with a love for the sea and the games on deck and the view over the ocean—and he did not get any of them. One day, as he put me out of his lift and saw through the vestibule windows a game of deck quoits in progress, he said, in a wistful tone, "My! I wish I could go out there sometimes!" I wished he could, too, and made a jesting offer to take charge of his lift for an hour while he went out to watch the game; but he smilingly shook his head and dropped down in answer to an imperative ring from below. I think he was not on duty with his lift after the collision, but if he were, he would smile at his passengers all the time as he took them up to the boats waiting to leave the sinking ship.

After undressing and climbing into the top berth, I read from about quarter-past eleven to the time we struck, about quarter to twelve. During this time I noticed particularly the increased vibration of the ship, and I assumed that we were going at a higher speed than at any other time since we sailed from Queenstown. Now I am aware that this is an important point, and bears strongly on the question of responsibility for the effects of the collision; but the impression of increased vibration is fixed in my memory so strongly that it seems important to record it. Two things led me to this conclusion—first, that as I sat on the sofa undressing, with bare feet on the floor, the jar of the vibration came up from the engines below very noticeably; and second, that as I sat up in the berth reading, the spring mattress supporting me was vibrating more rapidly than usual: this cradle-like motion was always noticeable as one lay in bed, but that night there was certainly a marked increase in the motion. Referring to the plan, it will be seen that the vibration must have come almost directly up from below, when it is mentioned that the saloon was immediately above the engines as shown in the plan, and my cabin next to the saloon.

From these two data, on the assumption that greater vibration is an indication of higher speed—and I suppose it must be—then I am sure we were going faster that night at the time we struck the iceberg than we had done before, i.e., during the hours I was awake and able to take note of anything.

And then, as I read in the quietness of the night, broken only by the muffled sound that came to me through the ventilators of stewards talking and moving along the corridors, when nearly all the passengers were in their cabins, some asleep in bed, others undressing, and others only just down from the smoking-room and still discussing many things, there came what seemed to me nothing more than an extra heave of the engines and a more than usually obvious dancing motion of the mattress on which I sat. Nothing more than that—no sound of a crash or of anything else: no sense of shock, no jar that felt like one heavy body meeting another. And presently the same thing repeated with about the same intensity. The thought came to me that they must have still further increased the speed. And all this time the *Titanic* was being cut open by the iceberg and water was pouring in her side, and yet no evidence that would indicate such a disaster had been presented to us. It fills me with astonishment now to think of it. Consider the question of list alone. Here was this enormous vessel running starboard side onto an iceberg, and a passenger sitting quietly in bed, reading, felt no motion or list to the opposite or port side, and this must have been felt had it been more than the usual roll of the ship—never very much in the calm weather we had all the way. Again, my bunk was fixed to the wall on the starboard side, and any list to port would have tended to fling me out on the floor: I am sure I should have noted it had there been any. And yet the explanation is simple enough: the *Titanic* struck the berg with a force of impact of over a million foot-tons; her plates were less than an inch thick, and they must have been cut through as a knife cuts paper: there would be no need to list; it would have been better if she had listed and thrown us out on the floor, for it would have been an indication that our plates were strong enough to offer, at any rate, some resistance to the blow, and we might all have been safe to-day.

And so, with no thought of anything serious having happened to the ship, I continued my reading; and still the murmur from the stewards and from adjoining cabins, and no other sound: no cry in the night; no alarm given; no one afraid—there was then nothing which could cause fear to the most timid person. But in a few moments I felt the engines slow and stop; the dancing motion and the vibration ceased suddenly after being part of our very existence for four days, and that was the first hint that anything out of the ordinary had happened. We have all "heard" a loud-ticking clock stop suddenly in a quiet room, and then have noticed the clock and the ticking noise, of which we seemed until then quite unconscious. So in the same way the fact was suddenly brought home to all in the ship that the engines—that part of the ship that drove us through the sea—had stopped dead. But the stopping of the engines gave us no information: we had to make our own calculations as to why we had stopped. Like a flash it came to me: "We have dropped a propeller blade: when this happens the engines always race away until they are controlled, and this accounts for the extra heave they gave"; not a very logical conclusion when considered now, for the engines should have continued to heave all the time until we stopped, but it was at the time a sufficiently tenable hypothesis to hold. Acting on it, I jumped out of bed, slipped on a dressing-gown over pajamas, put on shoes, and went out of my cabin into the hall near the saloon. Here was a steward leaning against the staircase, probably waiting until those in the smoke-room above had gone to bed and he could put out the lights. I said, "Why have we stopped?" "I don't know, sir," he replied, "but I don't suppose it is anything much." "Well," I said, "I am going on deck to see what it is," and started towards the stairs. He smiled indulgently at me as I passed him, and said, "All right, sir, but it is mighty cold up there." I am sure at that time he thought I was rather foolish to go up with so little reason, and I must confess I felt rather absurd for not remaining in the cabin: it seemed like making a needless fuss to walk about the ship in a dressing-gown. But it was my first trip across the sea;

I had enjoyed every minute of it and was keenly alive to note every new experience; and certainly to stop in the middle of the sea with a propeller dropped seemed sufficient reason for going on deck. And yet the steward, with his fatherly smile, and the fact that no one else was about the passages or going upstairs to reconnoiter, made me feel guilty in an undefined way or breaking some code of a ship's régime—an Englishman's fear of being thought "unusual," perhaps!

I climbed the three flights of stairs, opened the vestibule door leading to the top deck, and stepped out into an atmosphere that cut me, clad as I was, like a knife. Walking to the starboard side, I peered over and saw the sea many feet below, calm and black; forward, the deserted deck stretching away to the first-class quarters and the captain's bridge; and behind, the steerage quarters and the stern bridge; nothing more: no iceberg on either side or astern as far as we could see in the darkness. There were two or three men on deck, and with one—the Scotch engineer who played hymns in the saloon—I compared notes of our experiences. He had just begun to undress when the engines stopped and had come up at once, so that he was fairly well-clad; none of us could see anything, and all being quiet and still, the Scotchman and I went down to the next deck. Through the windows of the smoking-room we saw a game of cards going on, with several onlookers, and went in to enquire if they knew more than we did. They had apparently felt rather more of the heaving motion, but so far as I remember, none of them had gone out on deck to make any enquiries, even when one of them had seen through the windows an iceberg go by towering above the decks. He had called their attention to it, and they all watched it disappear, but had then at once resumed the game. We asked them the height of the berg and some said one hundred feet, others, sixty feet; one of the onlookers—a motor engineer traveling to America with a model carburetor (he had filled in his declaration form near me in the afternoon and had questioned the library steward how he should declare his patent—said, "Well, I am accustomed to estimating distances and I put it at between eighty and ninety feet." We accepted his estimate and made guesses as to what had happened to the *Titanic*: the general impression was that we had just scraped the iceberg with a glancing blow on the starboard side, and they had stopped as a wise precaution, to examine her thoroughly all over. "I expect the iceberg has scratched off some of her new paint," said one, "and the captain doesn't like to go on until she is painted up again." We laughed at his estimate of the captain's care for the ship. Poor Captain Smith!— he knew by this time only too well what had happened.

One of the players, pointing to his glass of whiskey standing at his elbow, and turning to an onlooker, said, "Just run along the deck and see if any ice has come aboard: I would like some for this." Amid the general laughter at what we thought was his imagination—only too realistic, alas! for when he spoke the forward deck was covered with ice that had tumbled over—and seeing that no more information was forthcoming, I left the smoking-room and went down to my cabin, where I sat for some time reading again. I am filled with sorrow to think I never saw any of the occupants of that smoking-room again: nearly all young men full of hope for their prospects in a new world; mostly unmarried; keen, alert, with the makings of good citizens. Presently, hearing people walking about the corridors, I looked out and saw several standing in the hall talking to a steward—most of them ladies in dressing-gowns; other people were going upstairs, and I decided to go on deck again, but as it was too cold to do so in a dressing-gown, I dressed in a Norfolk jacket and trousers and walked up. There were now more people looking over the side and walking about, questioning each other as to why we had stopped, but without obtaining any definite information. I stayed on deck some minutes, walking about vigorously to keep warm and occasionally looking downwards to the sea as if something there would indicate the reason for delay. The ship had now resumed her course, moving very slowly through the water with a little white line of foam on each side. I think we were all glad to see this: it seemed better than standing still. I soon decided to go down again, and as I crossed from the starboard to the port side to go down by the vestibule door, I saw an officer climb on the last lifeboat on the port side—number 16— and begin to throw off the cover, but I do not remember that any one paid any particular attention to him. Certainly no one thought they were preparing to man the lifeboats and embark from the ship. All this time there was no apprehension of any danger in the minds of passengers, and no one was in any condition of panic or hysteria; after all, it would have been strange if they had been, without any definite evidence of danger.

As I passed to the door to go down, I looked forward again and saw to my surprise an undoubted tilt downwards from the stern to the bows: only a slight slope, which I don't think anyone had noticed—at any rate, they had not remarked on it. As I went downstairs a confirmation of this tilting forward came in something unusual about the stairs, a curious sense of something out of balance and of not being able to put one's feet down in the right place: naturally, being tilted forward, the stairs would slope downwards at an angle and tend to throw one forward. I could not see any visible slope of the stairway: it was perceptible only by the sense of balance at this time.

On D deck were three ladies—I think they were all saved, and it is a good thing at least to be able to chronicle meeting some one who was saved after so much record of those who were not—standing in the passage near the cabin. "Oh! why have we stopped?" they said. "We did stop," I replied, "but we are now going on again." "Oh, no," one replied; "I cannot feel the engines as I usually do, or hear them. Listen!" We listened, and there was no throb audible. Having noticed that the vibration of the engines is most noticeable lying in a bath, where the throb comes straight from the floor through its metal sides—too much so ordinarily for one to put one's head back with comfort on the bath—I took them along the corridor to a bathroom and made them put their hands on the side of the bath: they were much reassured to feel the engines throbbing down below and to know we were making some headway. I left them and on the way to my cabin passed some stewards standing unconcernedly against the walls of the saloon: one of them, the library steward again, was leaning over a table, writing. It is no exaggeration to say that they had neither any knowledge of the accident nor any feeling of alarm that we had stopped and had not yet gone on again full speed: their whole attitude expressed perfect confidence in the ship and officers.

Turning into my gangway (my cabin being the first in the gangway), I saw a man standing at the other end of it fastening his tie. "Anything fresh?" he said. "Not much," I replied; "we are going ahead slowly and she is down a little at the bows, but I don't think it is anything serious." "Come in and look at this man," he laughed; "he won't get up." I looked in, and in the top bunk lay a man with his back to me, closely wrapped in his bedclothes and only the back of his head visible. "Why won't he get up? Is he asleep?" I said. "No," laughed the man dressing, "he says——" But before he could finish the sentence the man above grunted: "You don't catch me leaving a warm bed to go up on that cold deck at midnight. I know better than that." We both told him laughingly why he had better get up, but he was certain he was just as safe there and all this dressing was quite unnecessary; so I left them and went again to my cabin. I put on some underclothing, sat on the sofa, and read for some ten minutes, when I heard through the open door, above, the noise of people passing up and down, and a loud shout from above: "All passengers on deck with lifebelts on."

I placed the two books I was reading in the side pockets of my Norfolk jacket, picked up my lifebelt (curiously enough, I had taken it down for the first time that night from the wardrobe when I first retired to my cabin) and my dressing-gown, and walked upstairs tying on the lifebelt. As I came out of my cabin, I remember seeing the purser's assistant, with his foot on the stairs about to climb them, whisper to a steward and jerk his head significantly behind him; not that I thought anything of it at the time, but I have no doubt he was telling him what had happened up in the bows, and was giving him orders to call all passengers.

Going upstairs with other passengers—no one ran a step or seemed alarmed—we met two ladies coming down: one seized me by the arm and said, "Oh! I have no lifebelt; will you come down to my cabin and help me to find it?" I returned with them to A deck—the lady who had addressed me holding my arm all the time in a vise-like grip, much to my amusement—and we found a steward in her gangway who took them in and found their lifebelts. Coming upstairs again, I passed the purser's window on F deck, and noticed a light inside; when halfway up to E deck, I heard the heavy metallic clang of the safe door, followed by a hasty step retreating along the corridor towards the first-class quarters. I have little doubt it was the purser, who had taken all valuables from his safe and was transferring them to the charge of the first-class purser, in the hope they might all be saved in one package. That is why I said above that perhaps the envelope containing my money was not in the safe at the bottom of the sea: it is probably in a bundle, with many others like it, waterlogged at the bottom.

Reaching the top deck, we found many people assembled there—some fully dressed, with coats and wraps, well-prepared for anything that might happen; others who had thrown wraps hastily round them when they were called or heard the summons to equip themselves with lifebelts—not in much condition to face the cold of that night. Fortunately there was no wind to beat the cold air through our clothing: even the breeze caused by the ship's motion had died entirely away, for the engines had stopped again and the *Titanic* lay peacefully on the surface of the sea—motionless, quiet, not even rocking to the roll of the sea; indeed, as we were to discover presently, the sea was as calm as an inland lake save for the gentle swell which could impart no motion to a ship the size of the *Titanic*. To stand on the deck many feet above the water lapping idly against her sides, and looking much farther off than it really was because of the darkness, gave one a sense of wonderful security: to feel her so steady and still was like standing on a large rock in the middle of the ocean. But there were now more evidences of the coming catastrophe to the observer than had been apparent when on deck last: one was the roar and hiss of escaping steam from the boilers, issuing out of a large steam pipe reaching high up one of the funnels: a harsh, deafening boom that made conversation difficult and no doubt increased the apprehension of some people merely because of the volume of noise: if one imagines twenty locomotives blowing off steam in a low key it would give some idea of the unpleasant sound that met us as we climbed out on the top deck.

But after all it was the kind of phenomenon we ought to expect: engines blow off steam when standing in a station, and why should not a ship's boilers do the same when the ship is not moving? I never heard any one connect this noise with the danger of boiler explosion, in the event of the ship sinking with her boilers under a high pressure of steam, which was no doubt the true explanation of this precaution. But this is perhaps speculation; some people may have known it quite well, for from the time we came on deck until boat 13 got away, I heard very little conversation of any kind among the passengers. It is not the slightest exaggeration to say that no signs of alarm were exhibited by any one: there was no indication of panic or hysteria; no cries of fear, and no running to and fro to discover what was the matter, why we had been summoned on deck with lifebelts, and what was to be done with us now we were there. We stood there quietly looking on at the work of the crew as they manned the lifeboats, and no one ventured to interfere with them or offered to help them. It was plain we should be of no use; and the crowd of men and women stood quietly on the deck or paced slowly up and down waiting for orders from the officers.

Now, before we consider any further the events that followed, the state of mind of passengers at this juncture, and the motives which led each one to act as he or she did in the circumstances, it is important to keep in thought the amount of information at our disposal. Men and women act according to judgment based on knowledge of the conditions around them, and the best way to understand some apparently inconceivable things that happened is for any one to imagine himself or herself standing on deck that night. It seems a mystery to some people that women refused to leave the ship, that some persons retired to their cabins, and so on; but it is a matter of judgment, after all.

So that if the reader will come and stand with the crowd on deck, he must first rid himself entirely of the knowledge that the *Titanic* has sunk—an important necessity, for he cannot see conditions as they existed there through the mental haze arising from knowledge of the greatest maritime tragedy the world has known: he must get rid of any foreknowledge of disaster to appreciate why people acted as they did.

Secondly, he had better get rid of any picture in thought painted either by his own imagination or by some artist, whether pictorial or verbal, "from information supplied." Some are most inaccurate (these, mostly word-pictures), and where they err, they err on the highly dramatic side. They need not have done so: the whole conditions were dramatic enough in all their bare simplicity, without the addition of any high coloring.

Having made these mental erasures, he will find himself as one of the crowd faced with the following conditions: a perfectly still atmosphere; a brilliantly beautiful starlight night, but no moon, and so with little light that was of any use; a ship that had come quietly to rest without any indication of disaster—no iceberg visible, no hole in the ship's side through which water was pouring in, nothing broken or out of place, no sound of alarm, no panic, no movement of any one except at a walking pace; the absence of any knowledge of the nature of the accident, of the extent of damage, of the danger of the ship sinking in a few hours, of the numbers of boats, rafts, and other life-saving appliances available, their capacity, what other ships were near or coming to help—in fact, an almost complete absence of any positive knowledge on any point. I think this was the result of deliberate judgment on the part of the officers, and perhaps, it was the best thing that could be done. In particular, he must remember that the ship was a sixth of a mile long, with passengers on three decks open to the sea, and port and starboard sides to each deck: he will then get some idea of the difficulty presented to the officers of keeping control over such a large area, and the impossibility of any one knowing what was happening except in his own immediate vicinity. Perhaps the whole thing can be summed up best by saying that, after we had embarked in the lifeboats and rowed away from the *Titanic*, it would not have surprised us to hear that all passengers would be saved: the cries of drowning people after the *Titanic* gave the final plunge were a thunderbolt to us. I am aware that the experiences of many of those saved differed in some respects from the above: some had knowledge of certain things, some were experienced travelers and sailors, and therefore deduced more rapidly what was likely to happen; but I think the above gives a fairly accurate representation of the state of mind of most of those on deck that night.

All this time people were pouring up from the stairs and adding to the crowd: I remember at that moment thinking it would be well to return to my cabin and rescue some money and warmer clothing if we were to embark in boats, but looking through the vestibule windows and seeing people still coming upstairs, I decided it would only cause confusion passing them on the stairs, and so remained on deck.

I was now on the starboard side of the top boat deck; the time about 12.20. We watched the crew at work on the lifeboats, numbers 9, 11, 13, 15, some inside arranging the oars, some coiling ropes on the deck— the ropes which ran through the pulleys to lower to the sea—others with cranks fitted to the rocking arms of the davits. As we watched, the cranks were turned, the davits swung outwards until the boats hung clear of the edge of the deck. Just then an officer came along from the first-class deck and shouted above the noise of escaping steam, "All women and children get down to deck below and all men stand back from the boats." He had apparently been off duty when the ship struck, and was lightly dressed, with a white muffler twisted hastily round his neck. The men fell back and the women retired below to get into the boats from the next deck. Two women refused at first to leave their husbands, but partly by persuasion and partly by force they were separated from them and sent down to the next deck. I think that by this time the work on the lifeboats and the separation of men and women impressed on us slowly the presence of imminent danger, but it made no difference in the attitude of the crowd: they were just as prepared to obey orders and to do what came next as when they first came on deck. I do not mean that they actually reasoned it out: they were the average Teutonic crowd, with an inborn respect for law and order and for traditions bequeathed to them by generations of ancestors: the reasons that made them act as they did were impersonal, instinctive, hereditary.

But if there were any one who had not by now realized that the ship was in danger, all doubt on this point was to be set at rest in a dramatic manner. Suddenly a rush of light from the forward deck, a hissing roar that made us all turn from watching the boats, and a rocket leapt upwards to where the stars blinked and twinkled above us. Up it went, higher and higher, with a sea of faces upturned to watch it, and then an explosion that seemed to split the silent night in two, and a shower of stars sank slowly down and went out one by one. And with a gasping sigh one word escaped the lips of the crowd: "Rockets!" Anybody knows what rockets at sea mean. And presently another, and then a third. It is no use denying the dramatic intensity of the scene: separate it if you can from all the terrible events that followed, and picture the calmness of the night, the sudden light on the decks crowded with people in different stages of dress and undress, the background of huge funnels and tapering masts revealed by the soaring rocket, whose flash illumined at the same time the faces and minds of the obedient crowd, the one with mere physical light, the other with a sudden revelation of what its message was. Every one knew without being told that we were calling for help from any one who was near enough to see.

The crew were now in the boats, the sailors standing by the pulley ropes let them slip through the cleats in jerks, and down the boats went till level with B deck; women and children climbed over the rail into the boats and filled them; when full, they were lowered one by one, beginning with number 9, the first on the second-class deck, and working backwards towards 15. All this we could see by peering over the edge of the boat-deck, which was now quite open to the sea, the four boats which formed a natural barrier being lowered from the deck and leaving it exposed.

About this time, while walking the deck, I saw two ladies come over from the port side and walk towards the rail separating the second-class from the first-class deck. There stood an officer barring the way. "May we pass to the boats?" they said. "No madam," he replied politely, "your boats are down on your own deck," pointing to where they swung below. The ladies turned and went towards the stairway, and no doubt were able to enter one of the boats: they had ample time. I mention this to show that there was, at any rate, some arrangement—

whether official or not—for separating the classes in embarking in boats; how far it was carried out, I do not know, but if the second-class ladies were not expected to enter a boat from the first-class deck, while steerage passengers were allowed access to the second-class deck, it would seem to press rather hardly on the second-class men, and this is rather supported by the low percentage saved.

Almost immediately after this incident, a report went round among men on the top deck—the starboard side—that men were to be taken off on the port side; how it originated, I am quite unable to say, but can only suppose that as the port boats, numbers 10 to 16, were not lowered from the top deck quite so soon as the starboard boats (they could still be seen on deck), it might be assumed that women were being taken off on one side and men on the other; but in whatever way the report started, it was acted on at once by almost all the men, who crowded across to the port side and watched the preparation for lowering the boats, leaving the starboard side almost deserted. Two or three men remained, however: not for any reason that we were consciously aware of; I can personally think of no decision arising from reasoned thought that induced me to remain rather than to cross over. But while there was no process of conscious reason at work, I am convinced that what was my salvation was a recognition of the necessity of being quiet and waiting in patience for some opportunity of safety to present itself.

Soon after the men had left the starboard side, I saw a bandsman— the 'cellist—come round the vestibule corner from the staircase entrance and run down the now deserted starboard deck, his 'cello trailing behind him, the spike dragging along the floor. This must have been about 12:40 a.m. I suppose the band must have begun to play soon after this and gone on until after 2 a.m. Many brave things were done that night, but none more brave than by those few men playing minute after minute as the ship settled quietly lower and lower in the sea and the sea rose higher and higher to where they stood; the music they played serving alike as their own immortal requiem and their right to be recorded on the rolls of undying fame.

Looking forward and downward, we could see several of the boats now in the water, moving slowly one by one from the side, without confusion or noise, and stealing away in the darkness which swallowed them in turn as the crew bent to the oars. An officer—I think First Officer Murdock—came striding along the deck, clad in a long coat, from his manner and face evidently in great agitation, but determined and resolute; he looked over the side and shouted to the boats being lowered: "Lower away, and when afloat, row around to the gangway and wait for orders." "Aye, aye sir," was the reply; and the officer passed by and went across the ship to the port side.

Almost immediately after this, I heard a cry from below of, "Any more ladies?" and looking over the edge of the deck, saw boat 13 swinging level with the rail of B deck, with the crew, some stokers, a few men passengers and the rest ladies—the latter being about half the total number; the boat was almost full and just about to be lowered. The call for ladies was repeated twice again, but apparently there were none to be found. Just then one of the crew looked up and saw me looking over. "Any ladies on your deck?" he said. "No," I replied. "Then you had better jump." I sat on the edge of the deck with my feet over, threw the dressing-gown (which I had carried on my arm all of the time) into the boat, dropped, and fell in the boat near the stern.

As I picked myself up, I heard a shout: "Wait a moment, here are two more ladies," and they were pushed hurriedly over the side and tumbled into the boat, one into the middle and one next to me in the stern. They told me afterwards that they had been assembled on a lower deck with other ladies, and had come up to B deck not by the usual stairway inside, but by one of the vertically upright iron ladders that connect each deck with the one below it, meant for the use of sailors passing about the ship. Other ladies had been in front of them and got up quickly, but these two were delayed a long time by the fact that one of them—the one that was helped first over the side into boat 13 near the middle—was not at all active: it seemed almost impossible for her to climb up a vertical ladder. We saw her trying to climb the swinging rope ladder up the *Carpathia*'s side a few hours later, and she had the same difficulty.

As they tumbled in, the crew shouted, "Lower away"; but before the order was obeyed, a man with his wife and a baby came quickly to the side: the baby was handed to the lady in the stern, the mother got in near the middle and the father at the last moment dropped in as the boat began its journey down to the sea many feet below.

Looking back now on the descent of our boat down the ship's side, it is a matter of surprise, I think, to all the occupants to remember how little they thought of it at the time. It was a great adventure, certainly: it was exciting to feel the boat sink by jerks, foot by foot, as the ropes were paid out from above and shrieked as they passed through the pulley blocks, the new ropes and gear creaking under the strain of a boat laden with people, and the crew calling to the sailors above as the boat tilted slightly, now at one end, now at the other, "Lower aft!" "Lower stern!" and "Lower together!" as she came level again—but I do not think we felt much apprehension about reaching the water safely. It certainly was thrilling to see the black hull of the ship on one side and the sea, seventy feet below, on the other, or to pass down by cabins and saloons brilliantly lighted; but we knew nothing of the apprehension felt in the minds of some of the officers whether the boats and lowering-gear would stand the strain of the weight of our sixty people. The ropes, however, were new and strong, and the boat did not buckle in the middle as an older boat might have done. Whether it was right or not to lower boats full of people to the water—and it seems likely it was not—I think there can be nothing but the highest praise given to the officers and crew above for the way in which they lowered the boats one after the other safely to the water; it may seem a simple matter, to read about such a thing, but any sailor knows, apparently, that it is not so. An experienced officer has told me that he has seen a boat lowered in practise from a ship's deck, with a trained crew and no passengers in the boat, with practised sailors paying out the ropes, in daylight, in calm weather, with the ship lying in dock—and has seen the boat tilt over and pitch the crew headlong into the sea. Contrast these conditions with those obtaining that Monday morning at 12:45 a.m., and it is impossible not to feel that, whether the lowering crew were trained or not, whether they had or had not drilled since coming on board, they did their duty in a way that argues the greatest efficiency. I cannot help feeling the deepest gratitude to the two sailors who stood at the ropes above and lowered us to the sea: I do not suppose they were saved.

Perhaps one explanation of our feeling little sense of the unusual in leaving the *Titanic* in this way was that it seemed the climax to a series of extraordinary occurrences: the magnitude of the whole thing dwarfed events that in the ordinary way would seem to be full of imminent peril. It is easy to imagine it—a voyage of four days on a calm sea, without a single untoward incident; the presumption, perhaps already mentally half realized, that we should be ashore in forty-eight hours and so complete a splendid voyage—and then to feel the engine stop, to be summoned on deck with little time to dress, to tie on a lifebelt, to see rockets shooting aloft in call for help, to be told to get into a lifeboat—after all these things, it did not seem much to feel the boat sinking down to the sea: it was the natural sequence of previous events, and we had learned in the last hour to take things just as they came. At the same time, if any one should wonder what the sensation is like, it is quite easy to measure seventy-five feet from the windows of a tall house or a block of flats, look down to the ground and fancy himself with some sixty other people crowded into a boat so tightly that he could not sit down or move about, and then picture the boat sinking down in a continuous series of jerks, as the sailors pay out the ropes through cleats above. There are more pleasant sensations than this! How thankful we were that the sea was calm and the *Titanic* lay so steadily and quietly as we dropped down her side. We were spared the bumping and grinding against the side which so often accompanies the launching of boats: I do not remember that we even had to fend off our boat while we were trying to get free.

As we went down, one of the crew shouted, "We are just over the condenser exhaust: we don't want to stay in that long or we shall be swamped; feel down on the floor and be ready to pull up the pin which lets the ropes free as soon as we are afloat." I had often looked over the side and noticed this stream of water coming out of the side of the *Titanic* just above the water-line: in fact so large was the volume of water that as we ploughed along and met the waves coming towards us, this stream would cause a splash that sent spray flying. We felt, as well as we could in the crowd of people, on the floor, along the sides, with no idea where the pin could be found—and none of the crew knew where it was, only of its existence somewhere—but we never found it. And all the time we got closer to the sea and the exhaust roared nearer and nearer—until finally we floated with the ropes still holding us from above, the exhaust washing us away and the force of the tide driving us back against the side—the latter not of much account in influencing the direction, however. Thinking over what followed, I imagine we must have touched the water with the condenser stream at our bows, and not in the middle as I thought at one time: at any rate, the resultant of these three forces was that we were carried parallel to the ship, directly under the place where boat 15 would drop from her davits into the sea. Looking up we saw her already coming down rapidly from B deck: she must have filled almost immediately after ours. We shouted up, "Stop lowering 14,"* and the crew and passengers in the boat above, hearing us shout and seeing our position immediately below them, shouted the same to the sailors on the boat deck; but apparently they did not hear, for she dropped down foot by foot—twenty feet, fifteen, ten—and a stoker and I in the bows reached up and touched her bottom swinging above our heads, trying to push away our boat from under her. It seemed now as if nothing could prevent her dropping on us, but at this moment another stoker sprang with his knife to the ropes that still held us and I heard him shout, "One! Two!" as he cut them through. The next moment we had swung

---

*In an account which appeared in the newspapers of April 19 I have described this boat as 14, not knowing they were numbered alternately.

away from underneath 15, and were clear of her as she dropped into the water in the space we had just before occupied. I do not know how the bow ropes were freed, but imagine that they were cut in the same way, for we were washed clear of the *Titanic* at once by the force of the stream and floated away as the oars were got out.

I think we all felt that that was quite the most exciting thing we had yet been through, and a great sigh of relief and gratitude went up as we swung away from the boat above our heads; but I heard no one cry aloud during the experience—not a woman's voice was raised in fear or hysteria. I think we all learnt many things that night about the bogey called "fear", and how the facing of it is much less than the dread of it.

The crew was made up of cooks and stewards, mostly the former, I think; their white jackets showing up in the darkness as they pulled away, two to an oar: I do not think they can have had any practise in rowing, for all night long their oars crossed and clashed; if our safety had depended on speed or accuracy in keeping time it would have gone hard with us. Shouting began from one end of the boat to the other as to what we should do, where we should go, and no one seemed to have any knowledge how to act. At last we asked, "Who is in charge of this boat?" but there was no reply. We then agreed by general consent that the stoker who stood in the stern with the tiller should act as captain, and from that time he directed the course, shouting to other boats and keeping in touch with them. Not that there was anywhere to go or anything we could do. Our plan of action was simple: to keep all the boats together as far as possible and wait until we were picked up by other liners. The crew had apparently heard of the wireless communications before they left the *Titanic*, but I never heard them say that we were in touch with any boat but the *Olympic*: it was always the *Olympic* that was coming to our rescue. They thought they knew even her distance, and making a calculation, we came to the conclusion that we ought to be picked up by her about two o'clock in the afternoon. But this was not our only hope of rescue: we watched all the time the darkness lasted for steamers' lights, thinking there might be a chance of other steamers coming near enough to see the lights which some of our boats carried. I am sure there was no feeling in the minds of any one that we should not be picked up next day: we knew that wireless messages would go out from ship to ship, and as one of the stokers said: "The sea will be covered with ships to-morrow afternoon: they will race up from all over the sea to find us." Some even thought that fast torpedo boats might run up ahead of the *Olympic*. And yet the *Olympic* was, after all, the farthest away of them all; eight other ships lay within three hundred miles of us.

How thankful we should have been to know how near help was, and how many ships had heard our message and were rushing to the *Titanic*'s aid. I think nothing has surprised us more than to learn so many ships were near enough to rescue us in a few hours.

Almost immediately after leaving the *Titanic* we saw what we all said was a ship's lights down on the horizon on the *Titanic*'s port side: two lights, one above the other, and plainly not one of our boats; we even rowed in that direction for some time, but the lights drew away and disappeared below the horizon.

But this is rather anticipating: we did none of these things first. We had no eyes for anything but the ship we had just left. As the oarsmen pulled slowly away we all turned and took a long look at the mighty vessel towering high above our midget boat, and I know it must have been the most extraordinary sight I shall ever be called upon to witness; I realize now how totally inadequate language is to convey to some other person who was not there any real impression of what we saw.

But the task must be attempted: the whole picture is so intensely dramatic that, while it is not possible to place on paper for eyes to see the actual likeness of the ship as she lay there, some sketch of the scene will be possible. First of all, the climatic conditions were extraordinary. The night was one of the most beautiful I have ever seen: the sky without a single cloud to mar the perfect brilliance of the stars, clustered so thickly together that in places there seemed almost more dazzling points of light set in the black sky than background of sky itself; and each star seemed in the keen atmosphere, free from any haze, to have increased its brilliance tenfold and to twinkle and glitter with a staccato flash that made the sky seem nothing but a setting made for them in which to display their wonder. They seemed so near, and their light so much more intense than ever before, that fancy suggested they saw this beautiful ship in dire distress below and all their energies had awakened to flash messages across the black dome of the sky to each other; telling and warning of the calamity happening in the world beneath. Later, when the *Titanic* had gone down and we lay still on the sea waiting for the day to dawn or a ship to come, I remember looking up at the perfect sky and realizing why Shakespeare wrote the beautiful words he puts in the mouth of Lorenzo:

> Jessica, look how the floor of heaven
> Is thick inlaid with patines of bright gold.
> There's not the smallest orb which thou behold'st
> But in his motion like an angel sings,
> Still quiring to the young-eyed cherubims;
> Such harmony is in immortal souls;
> But whilst this muddy vesture of decay
> Doth grossly close it in, we cannot hear it.

But it seemed almost as if we could—that night: the stars seemed really to be alive and to talk. The complete absence of haze produced a phenomenon I had never seen before: where the sky met the sea the line was as clear and definite as the edge of a knife, so that the water and the air never merged gradually into each other and blended to a softened rounded horizon, but each element was so exclusively separate that where a star came low down in the sky near the clear-cut edge of the water-line, it still lost none of its brilliance. As the earth revolved and the water edge came up and covered partially the star, as it were, it simply cut the star in two, the upper half continuing to sparkle as long as it was not entirely hidden, and throwing a long beam of light along the sea to us.

In the evidence before the United States Senate Committee the captain of one of the ships near us that night said the stars were so extraordinarily bright near the horizon that he was deceived into thinking that they were ships' lights: he did not remember seeing such a night before. Those who were afloat will all agree with that statement: *we* were often deceived into thinking they were lights of a ship.

And next the cold air! Here again was something quite new to us: there was not a breath of wind to blow keenly round us as we stood in the boat, and because of its continued persistence to make us feel cold; it was just a keen, bitter, icy, motionless cold that came from nowhere and yet was there all the time; the stillness of it—if one can imagine "cold" being motionless and still—was what seemed new and strange.

And these—the sky and the air—were overhead; and below was the sea. Here again something uncommon: the surface was like a lake of oil, heaving gently up and down with a quiet motion that rocked our boat dreamily to and fro. We did not need to keep her head to the swell: often I watched her lying broadside on to the tide, and with a boat loaded as we were, this would have been impossible with anything like a swell. The sea slipped away smoothly under the boat, and I think we never heard it lapping on the sides, so oily in appearance was the water. So when one of the stokers said he had been to sea for twenty-six years and never yet seen such a calm night, we accepted it as true without comment. Just as expressive was the remark of another—"It reminds me of a bloomin' picnic!" It was quite true; it did: a picnic on a lake, or a quiet inland river like the Cam, or a backwater on the Thames.

And so in these conditions of sky and air and sea, we gazed broadside on the *Titanic* from a short distance. She was absolutely still—indeed from the first it seemed as if the blow from the iceberg had taken all the courage out of her and she had just come quietly to rest and was settling down without an effort to save herself, without a murmur of protest against such a foul blow. For the sea could not rock her: the wind was not there to howl noisily round the decks, and make the ropes hum; from the first what must have impressed all as they watched was the sense of stillness about her and the slow, insensible way she sank lower and lower in the sea, like a stricken animal.

The mere bulk alone of the ship viewed from the sea below was an awe-inspiring sight. Imagine a ship nearly a sixth of a mile long, 75 feet high to the top decks, with four enormous funnels above the decks, and masts again high above the funnels; with her hundreds of portholes, all her saloons and other rooms brilliant with light, and all round her, little boats filled with those who until a few hours before had trod her decks and read in her libraries and listened to the music of her band in happy content; and who were now looking up in amazement at the enormous mass above them and rowing away from her because she was sinking.

I had often wanted to see her from some distance away, and only a few hours before, in conversation at lunch with a fellow-passenger, had registered a vow to get a proper view of her lines and dimensions when we landed at New York: to stand some distance away to take in a full view of her beautiful proportions, which the narrow approach to the dock at Southampton made impossible. Little did I think that the opportunity was to be found so quickly and so dramatically. The background, too, was a different one from what I had planned for her: the black outline of her profile against the sky was bordered all round by stars studded in the sky, and all her funnels and masts were picked out in the same way: her bulk was seen where the stars were blotted out. And one other thing was different from expectation: the thing that ripped away from us instantly, as we saw it, all sense of the beauty of the night, the beauty of the ship's lines, and the beauty of her lights—and all these taken in themselves were intensely beautiful—that thing was the awful angle made by the level of the sea with the rows of porthole lights along her side in dotted lines, row above row. The sea level and the rows of lights should have been parallel—should never have met— and now they met at an angle inside the black hull of the ship. There was nothing else to indicate she was injured; nothing but this apparent violation of a simple geometrical law—that parallel lines should "never meet even if produced ever so far both ways"; but it meant the *Titanic* had sunk by the head until the lowest portholes in the bows were under the sea, and the portholes in the stern were lifted above the normal height. We rowed away from her in the quietness of the night, hoping

and praying with all our hearts that she would sink no more and the day
would find her still in the same position as she was then. The crew, however, did not think so. It has been said frequently that the officers and
crew felt assured that she would remain afloat even after they knew the
extent of the damage. Some of them may have done so—and perhaps,
from their scientific knowledge of her construction, with more reason at
the time than those who said she would sink—but at any rate the stokers in our boat had no such illusion. One of them—I think he was the
same man that cut us free from the pulley ropes—told us how he was
at work in the stoke-hole, and in anticipation of going off duty in quarter of an hour—thus confirming the time of the collision as 11:45—had
near him a pan of soup keeping hot on some part of the machinery;
suddenly the whole side of the compartment came in, and the water
rushed him off his feet. Picking himself up, he sprang for the compartment doorway and was just through the aperture when the watertight
door came down behind him, "like a knife," as he said; "they work them
from the bridge." He had gone up on deck but was ordered down again
at once and with others was told to draw the fires from under the boiler,
which they did, and were then at liberty to come on deck again. It seems
that this particular knot of stokers must have known almost as soon as
any one of the extent of injury. He added mournfully, "I could do with
that hot soup now"—and indeed he could: he was clad at the time of
the collision, he said, in trousers and singlet, both very thin on account
of the intense heat in the stoke-hole; and although he had added a short
jacket later, his teeth were chattering with the cold. He found a place to
lie down underneath the tiller on the little platform where our captain
stood, and there he lay all night with a coat belonging to another stoker
thrown over him and I think he must have been almost unconscious.
A lady next to him, who was warmly clad with several coats, tried to
insist on his having one of hers—a fur-lined one—thrown over him,
but he absolutely refused while some of the women were insufficiently
clad; and so the coat was given to an Irish girl with pretty auburn hair
standing near, leaning against the gunwale—with an "outside berth"
and so more exposed to the cold air. This same lady was able to dis-

tribute more of her wraps to the passengers, a rug to one, a fur boa to another; and she has related with amusement that at the moment of climbing up the *Carpathia*'s side, those to whom these articles had been lent offered them all back to her; but as, like the rest of us, she was encumbered with a lifebelt, she had to say she would receive them back at the end of the climb. I had not seen my dressing-gown since I dropped into the boat, but some time in the night a steerage passenger found it on the floor and put it on.

It is not easy at this time to call to mind who were in the boat, because in the night it was not possible to see more than a few feet away, and when dawn came we had eyes only for the rescue ship and the icebergs; but so far as my memory serves the list was as follows: no first-class passengers; three women, one baby, two men from the second cabin; and the other passengers steerage—mostly women; a total of about 35 passengers. The rest, about 25 (and possibly more), were crew and stokers. Near to me all night was a group of three Swedish girls, warmly clad, standing close together to keep warm, and very silent; indeed there was very little talking at any time.

One conversation took place that is, I think, worth repeating: one more proof that the world after all is a small place. The ten-months-old baby which was handed down at the last moment was received by a lady next to me—the same who shared her wraps and coats. The mother had found a place in the middle and was too tightly packed to come through to the child, and so it slept contentedly for about an hour in a stranger's arms; it then began to cry and the temporary nurse said: "Will you feel down and see if the baby's feet are out of the blanket! I don't know much about babies but I think their feet must be kept warm." Wriggling down as well as I could, I found its toes exposed to the air and wrapped them well up, when it ceased crying at once: it was evidently a successful diagnosis! Having recognized the lady by her voice—it was much too dark to see faces—as one of my *vis-à-vis* at the purser's table, I said—"Surely you are Miss——?" "Yes," she replied, "and you must be Mr. Beesley; how curious we should find ourselves in the same boat!" Remembering that she had joined the boat at

Queenstown, I said, "Do you know Clonmel? a letter from a great friend of mine who is staying there at——[giving the address] came aboard at Queenstown." "Yes, it is my home: and I was dining at—— just before I came away." It seemed that she knew my friend, too; and we agreed that of all places in the world to recognize mutual friends, a crowded lifeboat afloat in mid-ocean at 2 a.m. twelve hundred miles from our destination was one of the most unexpected.

And all the time, as we watched, the *Titanic* sank lower and lower by the head and the angle became wider and wider as the stern porthole lights lifted and the bow lights sank, and it was evident she was not to stay afloat much longer. The captain-stoker now told the oarsmen to row away as hard as they could. Two reasons seemed to make this a wise decision: one that as she sank she would create such a wave of suction that boats, if not sucked under by being too near, would be in danger of being swamped by the wave her sinking would create—and we all knew our boat was in no condition to ride big waves, crowded as it was and manned with untrained oarsmen. The second was that an explosion might result from the water getting to the boilers, and débris might fall within a wide radius. And yet, as it turned out, neither of these things happened.

At about 2:15 a.m. I think we were any distance from a mile to two miles away. It is difficult for a landsman to calculate distance at sea but we had been afloat an hour and a half, the boat was heavily loaded, the oarsmen unskilled, and our course erratic: following now one light and now another, sometimes a star and sometimes a light from a port lifeboat which had turned away from the *Titanic* in the opposite direction and lay almost on our horizon; and so we could not have gone very far away.

About this time, the water had crept up almost to her sidelight and the captain's bridge, and it seemed a question only of minutes before she sank. The oarsmen lay on their oars, and all in the lifeboat were motionless as we watched her in absolute silence—save some who would not look and buried their heads on each other's shoulders. The lights still shone with the same brilliance, but not so many of them:

many were now below the surface. I have often wondered since whether they continued to light up the cabins when the portholes were under water; they may have done so.

And then, as we gazed awe-struck, she tilted slowly up, revolving apparently about a center of gravity just astern of amidships, until she attained a vertically upright position; and there she remained— motionless! As she swung up, her lights, which had shone without a flicker all night, went out suddenly, came on again for a single flash, then went out altogether. And as they did so, there came a noise which many people, wrongly I think, have described as an explosion; it has always seemed to me that it was nothing but the engines and machinery coming loose from their bolts and bearings, and falling through the compartments, smashing everything in their way. It was partly a roar, partly a groan, partly a rattle, and partly a smash, and it was not a sudden roar as an explosion would be: it went on successively for some seconds, possibly fifteen to twenty, as the heavy machinery dropped down to the bottom (now the bows) of the ship: I suppose it fell through the end and sank first, before the ship. But it was a noise no one had heard before, and no one wishes to hear again: it was stupefying, stupendous, as it came to us along the water. It was as if all the heavy things one could think of had been thrown downstairs from the top of a house, smashing each other and the stairs and everything in the way.

Several apparently authentic accounts have been given, in which definite stories of explosions have been related—in some cases even with wreckage blown up and the ship broken in two; but I think such accounts will not stand close analysis. In the first place the fires had been withdrawn and the steam allowed to escape some time before she sank, and the possibility of explosion from this cause seems very remote. Then, as just related, the noise was not sudden and definite, but prolonged—more like the roll and crash of thunder. The probability of the noise being caused by engines falling down. . . . As the *Titanic* tilted up they would almost certainly fall loose from their bed and plunge down through the other compartments.

No phenomenon like that pictured in some American and English papers occurred—that of the ship breaking in two, and the two ends being raised above the surface. I saw these drawings in preparation on board the *Carpathia,* and said at the time that they bore no resemblance to what actually happened.

When the noise was over the *Titanic* was still upright like a column: we could see her now only as the stern and some 150 feet of her stood outlined against the star-specked sky, looming black in the darkness, and in this position she continued for some minutes—I think as much as five minutes, but it may have been less. Then, first sinking back a little at the stern, I thought, she slid slowly forwards through the water and dived slantingly down; the sea closed over her and we had seen the last of the beautiful ship on which we had embarked four days before at Southampton.

And in place of the ship on which all our interest had been concentrated for so long and towards which we looked most of the time because it was still the only object on the sea which was a fixed point to us—in place of the *Titanic,* we had the level sea now stretching in an unbroken expanse to the horizon: heaving gently just as before, with no indication on the surface that the waves had just closed over the most wonderful vessel ever built by man's hand; the stars looked down just the same and the air was just as bitterly cold.

There seemed a great sense of loneliness when we were left on the sea in a small boat without the *Titanic*: not that we were uncomfortable (except for the cold) nor in danger: we did not think we were either, but the *Titanic* was no longer there.

We waited head on for the wave which we thought might come— the wave we had heard so much of from the crew and which they said had been known to travel for miles—and it never came. But although the *Titanic* left us no such legacy of a wave as she went to the bottom, she left us something we would willingly forget forever, something which it is well not to let the imagination dwell on—the cries of many hundreds of our fellow-passengers struggling in the ice-cold water.

I would willingly omit any further mention of this part of the disaster from this book, but for two reasons it is not possible—first, that as a matter of history it should be put on record; and secondly, that these cries were not only an appeal for help in the awful conditions of danger in which the drowning found themselves—an appeal that could never be answered—but an appeal to the whole world to make such conditions of danger and hopelessness impossible ever again; a cry that called to the heavens for the very injustice of its own existence; a cry that clamored for its own destruction.

We were utterly surprised to hear this cry go up as the waves closed over the *Titanic*: we had heard no sound of any kind from her since we left her side; and, as mentioned before, we did not know how many boats she had or how many rafts. The crew may have known, but they probably did not, and if they did, they never told the passengers: we should not have been surprised to know all were safe on some life-saving device.

So that unprepared as we were for such a thing, the cries of the drowning floating across the quiet sea filled us with stupefaction: we longed to return and rescue at least some of the drowning, but we knew it was impossible. The boat was filled to standing-room, and to return would mean the swamping of us all, and so the captain-stoker told his crew to row away from the cries. We tried to sing to keep all from thinking of them; but there was no heart for singing in the boat at that time.

The cries, which were loud and numerous at first, died away gradually one by one, but the night was clear, frosty and still, the water smooth, and the sounds must have carried on its level surface free from any obstruction for miles, certainly much farther from the ship than we were situated. I think the last of them must have been heard nearly forty minutes after the *Titanic* sank. Lifebelts would keep the survivors afloat for hours; but the cold water was what stopped the cries.

from Albatross

by Deborah Scaling Kiley
and Meg Noonan

Adversity at sea doesn't always bring out the best in people. Deborah Scaling Kiley and a motley collection of four young crewmates on a casual cruise from Maine to Florida lost their 58-foot yacht in a sudden storm. Matters continued to deteriorate as the five—one badly injured—waited for rescue in their rubber dinghy. Kiley wrote about the experience with the help of writer Meg Noonan (not the Meg in the story).

need more fucking room!" Somebody was screaming at me and hitting me. I opened my eyes. Mark.

"You're taking up too much room." He kicked me again. "She's dying. I have to get away from her."

I felt the dinghy rocking. I tried to get oriented. It was dark and my teeth were chattering. I couldn't feel my feet at all. Seaweed was tangled around my body, and I had an awful taste in my mouth. Meg was moaning and Mark was yelling at me and I had been sleeping and I couldn't get ahold of where I was or what was happening.

"Brad?" I called, reaching out. He wasn't there. I shouted for him again and pulled myself out from under the bow cover. I tried to focus in the blackness. I could make out John and Meg, huddled together, and Brad, sitting on the starboard side of the dinghy.

"What are you doing?" I asked.

"I'm just giving Mark some more room so he'll be quiet," he said flatly, never taking his eyes off John and Meg. John had his arms around Meg, and the two of them were rocking back and forth. Meg moaned, John rocked. Meg moaned, John rocked. I wanted to look away, but I kept staring.

"I need water," John said. "I need water."

"My ankle's cut," Mark said, clutching his foot. "It's infected. I know it's infected. What if I get the same disease she has? I have to move, I need more bloody room. Look at her, she's gonna die. She's gonna die. I have to get away from her. She's gonna die."

I knew I should try to shut him up, but I said nothing. I didn't have the energy. Maybe Meg couldn't even hear him now. What was the point of trying to stop anyone from doing anything? Mark was screaming and John was rocking and Meg was moaning and Brad was just sitting there staring at nothing. The stench and the filth and the rot and the emptiness—it was the darkest, darkest nightmare.

If only it would rain, I thought. A warm rain, soft and steady. Everything would be better if I could feel the rain on my skin, let it run over me, wash it all away. I started reciting the Twenty-third Psalm— the Lord is my shepherd, I shall not want. I wanted to see if I could remember the words, the simple, soothing words—words that fell like raindrops, leaving soft circles of hope.

Sometime later, everyone was quiet again. Brad was up on the side. Meg, John, and Mark all seemed to be asleep. The dinghy moved from wave to wave, my teeth chattered, the wind blew. Silence is so loud, I thought.

"Brad," I whispered.

"What?" I had startled him.

"Why don't you come down here and get some sleep? Aren't you freezing up there?"

"I'm okay," he said and looked away.

"Please, Brad. I need you down here."

He didn't move. I was so afraid he would fall asleep and then drop off the Zodiac if we hit a wave.

"Please. I'd just feel a lot better if you were down here. It's not very safe sitting up there."

Without a word he lowered himself down next to me. We huddled together and I felt better. I allowed myself the great luxury of sleep.

Meg was moaning again. Mark was whining about not having any room. John was babbling about water. They were driving me insane, the three of them. If Meg would just shut up—my God, how could I be angry at Meg for moaning? How could I be so heartless? I started in on the whys again. Why this? Why now? Why me? I was imperfect. I had done some not-so-great things in my life. But this? This was my punishment? I felt I was supposed to learn something from this ordeal, some key, something magical and pure. And when I found it I would take it . . . Shit, where would I take it now? I dozed off again.

"Debbie," Brad was whispering. It was still dark.

"Yeah?"

"Listen. What do you think they're doing?"

I lifted my head and strained to see the others. I could see two forms—John and Mark—leaning over the stern.

"What are they doing?" Brad said again.

I couldn't hear what they were saying. I felt a rush of panic. Were they doing something to the boat? Or to Meg? No. Meg was all right. She was sitting with her head on her knees, asleep. I could hear the two guys splashing water. Then I understood. They were drinking sea-water. I was stunned. How could they be so stupid?

"They're drinking it," I said to Brad. "Should we stop them?"

"It's probably too late," Brad said.

I felt such sadness listening to them. They had given in, they had lost control. I knew that drinking seawater was a terrible mistake—I remembered hearing that you should drink your own urine first. I didn't know what would happen to them. Would they go mad, or had they already? Would they die? Would they try to do something to the rest of us?

"Brad. Promise me you won't drink it," I whispered.

He didn't answer. That scared me even more. I dropped my head back down, and the water in the dinghy sloshed up around my mouth. I imagined myself opening my mouth and drinking; hanging my head over the side and letting the ocean flow in. How would it taste? How would it feel?

Dawn broke, and for the first time since the sinking it looked as if we might see the sun. The clouds were breaking up. The thought of feeling the sun on my skin gave me a renewed sense of hope. Maybe the Coast Guard was coming after all. Of course they were. So they had some problems getting to us, okay. But now the sea was calmer and there was no reason they couldn't get to us today—hell, maybe they'd be here within the hour.

Don't be a fool, Debbie. If the Coast Guard was looking for us they would have found us by now. They aren't coming; that's all there is to it. "God helps those who helps themselves," my grandmother Queenie used to say. I will help myself, I thought. All I have is myself. I will not fall apart.

Brad ducked out from under the bow. Mark and John stirred, and Meg groaned. Her bad leg looked even worse; the gruesome red streaks had become wider, and now they ran all the way up, disappearing under her shirt.

"They'll come today," John said.

"They better. Look at my ankle," Mark said. The infection in his ankle had spread down to his foot. "What am I going to do?"

"The sun is over there," Brad said slowly, "so it seems like the wind is northerly and the seas are from the northeast. We should be drifting toward land. We might just wash ashore sometime in the next couple of days."

"South Carolina or Georgia, maybe," Mark said.

I was cheered by that image, washing up on a low barrier beach.

"What do we do when we get there?" Meg asked. "Go to the Coast Guard station?"

"Hell, no," John said. "I'm flying home. Those bastards left us out here. Fuck 'em."

"You know I hate to fly," Meg said. "Let's just go to the Coast Guard station and let them take care of us."

John shrugged. Then he sat up straight and pointed.

"I see land," he said.

We all turned and looked.

"Right there, man. See it? It's right in front of us!"

I strained to see it, but I could see nothing but water. "I think you're seeing things, bro," Brad said.

John slumped against the stern and sighed.

"So where would we fly, anyway?" Meg asked John.

"Probably to Portland. We'd go to my mom's."

"I don't want to fly there. I want to go to the Coast Guard station. I can't get on a plane like this. I might give someone this disease."

"What are you talking about?" I said to Meg.

"This thing I have. I don't want to give it to anyone."

"That's not a disease, Meg," I said. "It's blood poisoning. Nobody can catch it."

"I don't want to fly!" Meg said. Tears were spilling down her face. "John knows I can't fly. Please don't make me."

John put his arm around her.

"It's okay, Meg," I said. "You don't have to fly. When we get there we'll put you on a train or rent a car or something . . ."

"Yeah, we'll do whatever you want," Brad said.

She continued to sob.

"Christ, Meg, shut up," Mark said and kicked at her. She wailed harder.

John didn't seem to notice. "We won't have to fly. We'll just get the car," he said. "We're right off Falmouth, so we'll just drive to the hospital where my mom works. She'll take care of us."

I couldn't believe John would tell Meg such a cruel lie. Then I realized that he believed what he was saying.

"We're not off Falmouth," Brad said. "We're out in the middle of the Atlantic Ocean somewhere. We're nowhere near Falmouth."

"Bullshit. It's right over there," John said with conviction.

"What the hell is wrong with you?" Mark said.

"Nothing's wrong with me," John said angrily.

Brad suggested Meg move up to the bow for a while. He thought if she tucked her legs up under the bow no one would be able to bump them. "Deb and I can sit on the sides. And Mark can scoot to the back and you could stretch out a little more."

I nodded in agreement, though I wasn't happy about having to give up my spot.

"What about my foot?" Mark whined. "I need to stretch out, too. I want to get up there."

"Meg's in worse shape than you, Mark," I said.

"I'm going to sit up there next," Mark said.

John and Brad helped Meg slide up to the bow. John moved as if he were in a trance. His eyes were fixed and his movements slow and unnaturally deliberate. I sat up on the side for a few minutes, but I was too exposed to the wind, so I dropped down to the floor and leaned against the stern. Nobody said anything. I searched what I thought was the western horizon, looking for land, for anything.

"Quit it," I heard Meg say. "You're kicking me."

"I'm not kicking you," John replied.

"Cut it out."

"Quit bitching. All you do is bitch," John snapped.

"Where are my fucking cigarettes?" Mark suddenly shouted. His eyes were wide and wild-looking, and he was digging through the small mound of rotting seaweed in the bottom of the dinghy. "Who took them?"

"What are you talking about?" Brad said. "You don't have any cigarettes."

"What the fuck? You took them, didn't you?" Mark said to Brad.

"There aren't any cigarettes. Even if you did have some they would be sopping wet by now."

"I have cigarettes," Mark said slowly.

"Where'd you get them?" Brad asked.

"I just went to the Seven-Eleven and I bought beer and cigarettes. And I want to know who took them."

I stared at Mark in disbelief. He was out of his mind. Totally gone.

"Mark," I said, thinking I might be able to reason him back to reality. "If you did just go to the Seven-Eleven, then why the hell did you come back?"

Mark sat in the rotten seaweed and stared down at his palms. He looked at Brad, then at me, then at Brad again. He blinked fast, as if he was trying to focus, then pulled his shoulders up toward his ears and winced and closed his eyes. He tried to speak, but the words seemed to get jammed up in his mouth.

"Wh-where a-are m-m-mmy bl-bl-oody cig-a-re-rettes?" he stammered and resumed pawing through the stinking weed.

Then Meg was shouting at John again and John was shouting back and Mark was ranting and I felt myself drowning in the sound of their voices, the whining, the shouting, the crying, the complaining. Why couldn't everyone just be quiet? I saw John kick Meg. He was doing it on purpose. She wailed and he kicked her again.

"Stop it, John," I said. "Don't you think she's in enough pain without you making it worse? Leave her alone."

John continued to jostle Meg. Meg continued to scream and cry. Mark was still trying to find his cigarettes. Finally Meg said she didn't want to be next to John anymore, so Brad and I helped her back to the stern. Mark immediately said it was his turn in the bow. While Brad and I were easing Meg back into position, I heard a strange noise. I turned in time to see John at the bow ripping off the rubber patch that secured the painter to the dinghy.

Brad and I hollered at John, but he pulled it off cleanly and threw it into the water before falling back against the stern. My knees buckled. I knew that in the next second the air would come hissing out of the Zodiac. I crawled forward, and Mark shouted, "Where the hell do you think you're going! It's my turn!"

I fell onto the bow and ran my hand over the rubber where the patch had been. Maybe I could plug the hole somehow, maybe there was a chance. To my relief, it seemed to be intact. There was no hole, no escaping air, no damage at all.

"Are you trying to kill us all?" I said to John, but I could see that he had no idea what he had done. His eyes were flat and dull. He was a million miles away. I knew he was in big trouble—maybe it was hypothermia or maybe the effects of drinking salt water.

Mark pushed me aside so he could claim his spot in the bow. I moved back to the spot where Mark had been sitting. Meg sat crumpled in the corner whimpering. I followed John's every move, terrified of what he might do next. I spotted the air valves in the stern. Please don't notice them, I said to myself. I willed John to look the other way.

I had to stretch. My legs were cramped and stiff. Mark had become engrossed again in searching for his phantom cigarettes, so I didn't think he would notice if I stretched my legs out straight just for a minute. As I unfolded them I saw how swollen they had become. The saltwater sores had grown, too. My skin looked as if someone had stubbed out big cigars on it. Some of the sores were red and hot and oozing. I wondered whether I would be able to walk once we got back to land.

Suddenly I felt a searing bolt of pain shoot up my left leg, through my groin, and up to the top of my head. I screamed and flew forward and slammed my fist into Mark's back.

"Bastard!" He had twisted my wounded toe. Blood spurted from it.

"Why can't you leave everyone alone?" Brad shouted.

"She's in my place," he said. "I want it back."

He pushed me out of the way and crawled to the port side. Brad and I moved back to the bow. I kept my eyes on Mark and John.

"Hey," Mark said to John. "Want a smoke?"

"Sure," John said. "Got any?"

"Under the seaweed. Up there." Mark moved toward the bow again.

"Mark. Listen to me, man. There aren't any smokes or beer or anything up here," Brad said. "We're out in the middle of the ocean."

"I got some sandwiches," John said. "You want one?"

It was pure horror, watching Mark and John carry on about their cigarettes and their sandwiches. They seemed to genuinely believe they had just been to the store and picked up supplies—as if they were just out on a day sail. They had both moved, simultaneously, into some other reality.

"Okay, where are they?" John hollered, picking up seaweed and tossing it overboard. "I know they were here."

"Where are my bloody fags?" Mark asked me. "I know you took them." He started to come at me, but Brad put up his hand to protect me.

"She doesn't have them, Mark," Brad shouted. "Leave her alone." Mark stared at us, then collapsed back against the side of the Zodiac. John slid down next to him, looking confused.

I slept. It was a tortured, fitful sleep, full of voices and cries. I awoke with the feeling that a shadow had just crossed my face. I sat up. Everyone was sleeping. It was dusk again. The clouds that had blocked the sun for so long were finally gone. I knew that this night was going to be colder than the others—the clouds, at least, had held in some warmth. Now I knew for sure where the west was, and I tried to convince myself that we were drifting in that direction. I watched the sky as we rode the swells and slid westward, toward land, toward life.

Meg's moans startled me. Had I been asleep again? The eastern sky was indigo-black now and pricked with a few bright stars. The western horizon still held some light.

"Meg," I said quietly. I didn't want to wake John and Mark.

She moaned again.

"Meg. Do you want to try sitting up here? You could stretch your legs out again."

"I want to sit up on the side," she said, and John's eyes opened.

"What?" John said with alarm.

"It's okay, John," I said. "Meg just needs to stretch out. She wants to get up on the side."

John immediately started to help Meg lift herself up. I was relieved to see him respond to her. Maybe he was okay. Whatever it was that had made him so irrational had been temporary.

Once Meg was up on the side, she said, "I've been thinking about it, and I've decided that if the Coast Guard wants to fly us to your mom's, it's okay with me. I just want to go home."

"We'll go straight home," John said.

"I don't normally like to fly, but—"

"I know, but just this once—"

"Yeah. I mean, it's probably the best way to go."

Brad woke up and listened to the two of them talk. Then Mark stirred. I felt myself go rigid with apprehension.

"See, that's west," Brad said. "We're definitely heading toward land. We have to wash up on shore eventually."

"When do you think?" Meg asked.

"Tomorrow, maybe the day after."

"I can't wait to see the look on the faces of those Coast Guard guys when we show up on their bloody doorstep," Mark said.

"Do you think they'll fly us in a private plane or a commercial plane?" Meg said.

"I can't believe they just left us out here," I said. "They never do that."

"What do you think, John, private or commercial plane?"

"Quit talking about planes," John said sharply. "I'm sick of hearing you talk about planes."

"I was just wondering—"

"We're not going on a plane. That would be stupid. I'm just going to go get the car."

"There isn't any car, John," I said.

"We're just off Falmouth. I know right where the car is. I'll go get it," he said. "You guys bring the boat in and I'll get the car. Then we can unload."

He sounded so sure, I had to fight to keep from being sucked into the fantasy. Was he right? Were we just off Falmouth? Then why . . . no, that wasn't right. It couldn't be. I closed my eyes and shook my head, trying to clear it, trying to stay focused on what was real. When I looked up again I saw John lowering himself over the side of the Zodiac.

"What are you doing?" Brad and I both hollered.

"I'll be back in a few," John said matter-of-factly.

"What about the sharks?" Mark asked.

"John, if you leave this dinghy we may not be able to get you back in," I said. "It's almost dark. Why don't you just come on back in now."

I was trying to keep my voice even and calm. I had no idea what John was going to do, what might set him off. Was he just trying to get warm? Did he really think we were close to home?

"I can't take this anymore," he said. "I'm going to go get the car."

Brad and I looked at each other. John's hands slid away from the gunwale and he began to swim. He stopped for a minute, treading water and looking back at us. I thought he might be playing a sick joke. Meg was begging him to come back, pleading with one of us to go get him.

"Should I go after him?" Brad said to me.

I didn't know. I couldn't think. Was he really going to just swim away?

"Should I?" Brad sounded panicky. John turned and started stroking away from the Zodiac.

"John!" Meg cried.

"You can't go after him, Brad," I said. There was almost no light left in the sky. It would be impossible to force him back to the dinghy—and it could be suicidal to try. What if Brad went in and we lost him, too? We all watched John swim. Meg, her hands over her mouth, was shaking her head slowly and sobbing. John went up over a swell, disappeared, then reappeared farther off.

"Should I go?" Brad asked again.

"Don't go after him," Meg said quietly. "He's gone."

We rode up a big swell, and I saw John's head again, dark against the dark sea. And then we heard a terrible, gut-twisting scream.

"My God, he's calling me," Meg said and dissolved into tears.

We scanned the black water hoping for another glimpse of him. But Meg was right. John was gone.

U. S. Frigate UNITED STATES under full Sail.

_{from} Thirty Years from Home or
A Voice from the Main Deck
by Samuel Leech

First-hand accounts of sea battles during the Napoleonic era often are written in a formal, cautious style. This description of the October 25, 1812 battle between the HMS Macedonian *and the heavier* USS United States *during the War of 1812 is refreshingly forthright. Samuel Leech (b. 1798; d. 1848), who as a very young teenager fought on the* Macedonian, *later wrote a distressingly realistic description of the engagement and its horrors.*

At Plymouth we heard some vague rumors of a declaration of war against America. More than this, we could not learn, since the utmost care was taken to prevent our being fully informed. The reason of this secrecy was, probably, because we had several Americans in our crew, most of whom were pressed men, as before stated. These men, had they been certain that war had broken out, would have given themselves up as prisoners of war, and claimed exemption from that unjust service, which compelled them to act with the enemies of their country. This was a privilege which the magnanimity of our officers ought to have offered them. They had already perpetrated a grievous wrong upon them in impressing them; it was adding cruelty to injustice to compel their service in a war against their own nation. But the difficulty with naval officers is, that they do not treat with a sailor as with a *man*. They know what is fitting between each other as officers; but they treat their crews on another principle; they are apt to look at them as pieces of living mechanism, born to serve, to obey their orders, and administer to their wishes without complaint. This is alike a bad morality and a bad philosophy. There is often more real manhood in the forecastle than in the wardroom; and until the common sailor is treated *as a man*, until every feeling of human nature is conceded to him in naval discipline—perfect, rational subordination will never be attained in ships of war, or in merchant vessels. It is needless to tell of the intellectual degradation of the mass of seamen. "A man's a man for a' that;" and it is this very system of discipline, this treating them as automatons, which keeps them degraded. When will human nature put more confidence in itself?

Leaving Plymouth, we next anchored, for a brief space, at Torbay, a small port in the British Channel. We were ordered thence to convoy a huge East India merchant vessel, much larger than our frigate and having five hundred troops on board, bound to the East Indies with money to pay the troops stationed there. We set sail in a tremendous gale of wind. Both ships stopped two days at Madeira to take in wine and a few other articles. After leaving this island, we kept her company two days more; and then, according to orders, having wished her success, we left her to pursue her voyage, while we returned to finish our cruise.

Though without any positive information, we now felt pretty certain that our government was at war with America. Among other things, our captain appeared more anxious than usual; he was on deck almost all the time; the "look-out" aloft was more rigidly observed; and every little while the cry of "Mast-head there!" arrested our attention.

It is customary in men of war to keep men at the fore and main mastheads, whose duty it is to give notice of every new object that may appear. They are stationed in the royal yards, if they are up, but if not, on the topgallant yards: at night a look-out is kept on the fore yard only.

Thus we passed several days; the captain running up and down and constantly hailing the man at the mast-head: early in the morning he began his charge "to keep a good look-out," and continued to repeat it until night. Indeed, he seemed almost crazy with some pressing anxiety. The men felt there was something anticipated, of which they were ignorant; and had the captain heard all their remarks upon his conduct, he would not have felt very highly flattered. Still, everything went on as usual; the day was spent in the ordinary duties of man-of-war life, and the evening in telling stories of things most rare and wonderful; for your genuine old tar is an adept in spinning yarns, and some of them, in respect to variety and length, might safely aspire to a place beside the great magician of the north, Sir Walter Scott, or any of those prolific heads that now bring forth such abundance of fiction to feed a greedy public, who read as eagerly as our men used to listen. To this yarn-spinning was added the most humorous singing, sometimes dashed with a streak of the pathetic, which I assure my readers was most touching; especially one very plaintive melody, with a chorus beginning with,

"*Now if our ship should be cast away,*
It would be our lot to see old England no more,"

which made rather a melancholy impression on my boyish mind, and gave rise to a sort of presentiment that the *Macedonian* would never return home again; a presentiment which had its fulfilment in a manner totally unexpected to us all. The presence of a shark for several days, with its attendant pilot fish, tended to strengthen this prevalent idea.

The Sabbath came, and it brought with it a stiff breeze. We usually made a sort of holiday of this sacred day. After breakfast it was common to muster the entire crew on the spar deck, dressed as the fancy of the captain might dictate; sometimes in blue jackets and white trowsers, or blue jackets and blue trowsers; at other times in blue jackets, scarlet vests, and blue or white trowsers with our bright anchor buttons glancing in the sun, and our black, glossy hats, ornamented with black ribbons, and with the name of our ship painted on them. After muster, we frequently had church service read by the captain; the rest of the day was devoted to idleness. But we were destined to spend the Sabbath, just introduced to the reader, in a very different manner.

We had scarcely finished breakfast, before the man at the mast-head shouted, "Sail ho!"

The captain rushed upon deck, exclaiming, "Mast-head there!"

"Sir!"

"Where away is the sail?"

The precise answer to this question I do not recollect, but the captain proceeded to ask, "What does she look like?"

"A square-rigged vessel, sir," was the reply of the look-out.

After a few minutes, the captain shouted again, "Mast-head there!"

"Sir!"

"What does she look like?"

"A large ship, sir, standing toward us!"

By this time, most of the crew were on deck, eagerly straining their eyes to obtain a glimpse of the approaching ship and murmuring their opinions to each other on her probable character. Then came the voice of the captain, shouting, "Keep silence, fore and aft!" Silence being secured, he hailed the look-out, who, to his question of "What does she look like?" replied, "A large frigate, bearing down upon us, sir!"

A whisper ran along the crew that the stranger ship was a Yankee frigate. The thought was confirmed by the command of "All hands clear the ship for action, ahoy!" The drum and fife beat to quarters; bulk-heads were knocked away; the guns were released from their confinement; the whole dread paraphernalia of battle was produced; and after the lapse of a few minutes of hurry and confusion, every man and boy was at his post, ready to do his best service for his country, except the band, who, claiming exemption from the affray, safely stowed themselves away in the cable tier. We had only one sick man on the list, and he, at the cry of battle, hurried from his cot, feeble as he was, to take his post of danger. A few of the junior midshipmen were stationed below, on the berth deck, with orders, given in our hearing, to shoot any man who attempted to run from his quarters.

Our men were all in good spirits; though they did not scruple to express the wish that the coming foe was a Frenchman rather than a Yankee. We had been told, by the Americans on board, that frigates in the American service carried more and heavier metal than ours. This, together with our consciousness of superiority over the French at sea, led us to a preference for a French antagonist.

The Americans among our number felt quite disconcerted at the necessity which compelled them to fight against their own country-men. One of them, named John Card, as brave a seaman as ever trod a plank, ventured to present himself to the captain, as a prisoner, frankly declaring his objections to fight. That officer, very ungenerously, ordered him to his quarters, threatening to shoot him if he made the request again. Poor fellow! He obeyed the unjust command and was killed by a shot from his own countrymen. This fact is more disgrace-ful to the captain of the *Macedonian* than even the loss of his ship. It was a gross and a palpable violation of the rights of man.

As the approaching ship showed American colors, all doubt of her character was at an end. "We must fight her," was the conviction of every breast. Every possible arrangement that could insure success was accordingly made. The guns were shotted; the matches lighted; for, although our guns were all furnished with first-rate locks they were also provided with matches, attached by lanyards, in case the lock should miss fire. A lieutenant then passed through the ship, directing the marines and boarders, who were furnished with pikes, cutlasses, and pistols, how to proceed if it should be necessary to board the enemy. He was followed by the captain, who exhorted the men to fidelity and courage, urging upon their consideration the well-known motto of the brave Nelson, "England expects every man to do his duty." In addition to all these preparations on deck, some men were stationed in the tops with small-arms, whose duty it was to attend to trimming the sails and to use their muskets, provided we came to close action. There were oth-ers also below, called sail trimmers, to assist in working the ship should it be necessary to shift her position during the battle.

My station was at the fifth gun on the main deck. It was my duty to supply my gun with powder, a boy being appointed to each gun in the ship on the side we engaged, for this purpose. A woollen screen was placed before the entrance to the magazine, with a hole in it, through which the cartridges were passed to the boys; we received them there, and covering them with our jackets, hurried to our respective guns. These precautions are observed to prevent the powder taking fire before it reaches the gun.

Thus we all stood, awaiting orders, in motionless suspense. At last we fired three guns from the larboard side of the main deck; this was followed by the command, "Cease firing; you are throwing away your shot!"

Then came the order to "wear ship," and prepare to attack the enemy with our starboard guns. Soon after this I heard a firing from some other quarter, which I at first supposed to be a discharge from our quarter deck guns; though it proved to be the roar of the enemy's cannon.

A strange noise, such as I had never heard before, next arrested my attention; it sounded like the tearing of sails, just over our heads. This I soon ascertained to be the wind of the enemy's shot. The firing, after a few minutes' cessation, recommenced. The roaring of cannon could now be heard from all parts of our trembling ship, and, mingling as it did with that of our foes, it made a most hideous noise. By-and-by I heard the shot strike the sides of our ship; the whole scene grew indescribably confused and horrible; it was like some awfully tremendous thunder-storm, whose deafening roar is attended by incessant streaks of lightning, carrying death in every flash and strewing the ground with the victims of its wrath: only, in our case, the scene was rendered more horrible than that, by the presence of torrents of blood which dyed our decks.

Though the recital may be painful, yet, as it will reveal the horrors of war and show at what a fearful price a victory is won or lost, I will present the reader with things as they met my eye during the progress of this dreadful fight. I was busily supplying my gun with powder, when I saw blood suddenly fly from the arm of a man stationed at our gun. I saw nothing strike him; the effect alone was visible; in an instant, the third lieutenant tied his handkerchief round the wounded arm, and sent the groaning wretch below to the surgeon.

The cries of the wounded now rang through all parts of the ship.

These were carried to the cockpit as fast as they fell, while those more fortunate men, who were killed outright, were immediately thrown overboard. As I was stationed but a short distance from the main hatchway, I could catch a glance at all who were carried below. A glance was all I could indulge in, for the boys belonging to the guns next to mine were wounded in the early part of the action, and I had to spring with all my might to keep three or four guns supplied with cartridges. I saw two of these lads fall nearly together. One of them was struck in the leg by a large shot; he had to suffer amputation above the wound. The other had a grape or canister shot sent through his ancle. A stout Yorkshireman lifted him in his arms and hurried him to the cockpit. He had his foot cut off, and was thus made lame for life. Two of the boys stationed on the quarter deck were killed. They were both Portuguese. A man, who saw one of them killed, afterwards told me that his powder caught fire and burnt the flesh almost off his face. In this pitiable situation, the agonized boy lifted up both hands, as if imploring relief, when a passing shot instantly cut him in two.

I was an eye-witness to a sight equally revolting. A man named Aldrich had one of his hands cut off by a shot, and almost at the same moment he received another shot, which tore open his bowels in a terrible manner. As he fell, two or three men caught him in their arms, and, as he could not live, threw him overboard.

One of the officers in my division also fell in my sight. He was a noble-hearted fellow, named Nan Kivell. A grape or canister shot struck him near the heart: exclaiming, "Oh! my God!" he fell, and was carried below, where he shortly after died.

Mr. Hope, our first lieutenant, was also slightly wounded by a grummet, or small iron ring, probably torn from a hammock clew by a shot. He went below, shouting to the men to fight on. Having had his wound dressed, he came up again, shouting to us at the top of his voice, and bidding us fight with all our might. There was not a man in the ship but would have rejoiced had he been in the place of our master's mate, the unfortunate Nan Kivell.

The battle went on. Our men kept cheering with all their might. I cheered with them, though I confess I scarcely knew for what. Certainly there was nothing very inspiriting in the aspect of things where I was stationed. So terrible had been the work of destruction round us, it was termed the slaughter-house. Not only had we had several boys and men killed or wounded, but several of the guns were disabled. The one I belonged to had a piece of the muzzle knocked out; and when the ship rolled, it struck a beam of the upper deck with such force as to become jammed and fixed in that position. A twenty-four-pound shot had also passed through the screen of the magazine, immediately over the orifice through which we passed our powder. The schoolmaster received a death wound. The brave boatswain, who came from the sick bay to the din of battle, was fastening a stopper on a back-stay which had been shot away, when his head was smashed to pieces by a cannon-ball; another man, going to complete the unfinished task, was also struck down. Another of our midshipmen also received a severe wound. The unfortunate ward-room steward, who, the reader will rec-ollect, attempted to cut his throat on a former occasion, was killed. A fellow named John, who, for some petty offence, had been sent on board as a punishment, was carried past me, wounded. I distinctly heard the large blood-drops fall pat, pat, pat, on the deck; his wounds were mortal. Even a poor goat, kept by the officers for her milk, did not escape the general carnage; her hind legs were shot off, and poor Nan was thrown overboard.

Such was the terrible scene, amid which we kept on our shouting and firing. Our men fought like tigers. Some of them pulled off their jackets, others their jackets and vests; while some, still more deter-mined, had taken off their shirts, and, with nothing but a handkerchief tied round the waistbands of their trowsers, fought like heroes. . . . I also observed a boy, named Cooper, stationed at a gun some distance from the magazine. He came to and fro on the full run and appeared to be as "merry as a cricket." The third lieutenant cheered him along, occasionally, by saying, "Well done, my boy, you are worth your weight in gold."

I have often been asked what were my feelings during this fight. I felt pretty much as I suppose every one does at such a time. That men are without thought when they stand amid the dying and the dead is too absurd an idea to be entertained a moment. We all appeared cheerful, but I know that many a serious thought ran through my mind: still, what could we do but keep up a semblance, at least, of animation? To run from our quarters would have been certain death from the hands of our own officers; to give way to gloom, or to show fear, would do no good, and might brand us with the name of cowards, and ensure certain defeat. Our only true philosophy, therefore, was to make the best of our situation by fighting bravely and cheerfully. I thought a great deal, however, of the other world; every groan, every falling man, told me that the next instant I might be before the Judge of all the earth. For this, I felt unprepared; but being without any particular knowledge of religious truth, I satisfied myself by repeating again and again the Lord's prayer and promising that if spared I would be more attentive to religious duties than ever before. This promise I had no doubt, at the time, of keeping; but I have learned since that it is easier to make promises amidst the roar of the battle's thunder, or in the horrors of shipwreck, than to keep them when danger is absent and safety smiles upon our path.

While these thoughts secretly agitated my bosom, the din of battle continued. Grape and canister shot were pouring through our port-holes like leaden rain, carrying death in their trail. The large shot came against the ship's side like iron hail, shaking her to the very keel, or passing through her timbers and scattering terrific splinters, which did a more appalling work than even their own death-giving blows. The reader may form an idea of the effect of grape and canister, when he is told that grape shot is formed by seven or eight balls confined to an iron and tied in a cloth. These balls are scattered by the explosion of the powder. Canister shot is made by filling a powder canister with balls, each as large as two or three musket balls; these also scatter with direful effect when discharged. What then with splinters, cannon balls, grape and canister poured incessantly upon us, the reader may be assured that the work of death went on in a manner which must have been satisfactory even to the King of Terrors himself.

Suddenly, the rattling of the iron hail ceased. We were ordered to cease firing. A profound silence ensued, broken only by the stifled groans of the brave sufferers below. It was soon ascertained that the enemy had shot ahead to repair damages, for she was not so disabled but she could sail without difficulty; while we were so cut up that we lay utterly helpless. Our head braces were shot away; the fore and main top-masts were gone; the mizzen mast hung over the stern, having carried several men over in its fall: we were in the state of a complete wreck.

A council was now held among the officers on the quarter deck. Our condition was perilous in the extreme: victory or escape was alike hopeless. Our ship was disabled; many of our men were killed, and many more wounded. The enemy would without doubt bear down upon us in a few moments, and, as she could now choose her own position, would without doubt rake us fore and aft. Any further resistance was therefore folly. So, in spite of the hot-brained lieutenant, Mr. Hope, who advised them not to strike, but to sink alongside, it was determined to strike our bunting. This was done by the hands of a brave fellow named Watson, whose saddened brow told how severely it pained his lion heart to do it. To me it was a pleasing sight, for I had seen fighting enough for one Sabbath; more than I wished to see again on a week day. His Britannic Majesty's frigate *Macedonian* was now the prize of the American frigate *United States*.

I went below, to see how matters appeared there. The first object I met was a man bearing a limb, which had just been detached from some suffering wretch. Pursuing my way to the ward-room, I necessarily passed through the steerage, which was strewed with the wounded: it was a sad spectacle, made more appalling by the groans and cries which rent the air. Some were groaning, others were swearing most bitterly, a few were praying, while those last arrived were begging most piteously to have their wounds dressed next. The surgeon and his mate were smeared with blood from head to foot: they looked more like butchers than doctors. Having so many patients, they had once shifted their quarters from the cockpit to the steerage; they now removed to the ward-room, and the long table, round which the officers had sat over many a merry feast, was soon covered with the bleeding forms of maimed and mutilated seamen.

While looking round the ward-room, I heard a noise above, occasioned by the arrival of the boats from the conquering frigate. Very soon a lieutenant, I think his name was Nicholson, came into the ward-room and said to the busy surgeon, "How do you do, doctor?"

"I have enough to do," replied he, shaking his head thoughtfully; "you have made wretched work for us!" These officers were not strangers to each other, for . . . the commanders and officers of these two frigates had exchanged visits when we were lying at Norfolk some months before.

I now set to work to render all the aid in my power to the sufferers. Our carpenter, named Reed, had his leg cut off. I helped to carry him to the after ward-room; but he soon breathed out his life there, and then I assisted in throwing his mangled remains overboard. We got out the cots as fast as possible; for most of them were stretched out on the gory deck. One poor fellow, who lay with a broken thigh, begged me to give him water. I gave him some. He looked unutterable gratitude, drank, and died. It was with exceeding difficulty I moved through the steerage, it was so covered with mangled men and so slippery with streams of blood. There was a poor boy there crying as if his heart would break. He had been servant to the bold boatswain, whose head was dashed to pieces. Poor boy! he felt that he had lost a friend. I tried to comfort him by reminding him that he ought to be thankful for having escaped death himself.

Here, also, I met one of my messmates, who showed the utmost joy at seeing me alive, for, he said, he had heard that I was killed. He was looking up his messmates, which he said was always done by sailors. We found two of our mess wounded. One was the Swede, Logholm, who fell overboard . . . and was nearly lost. We held him while the surgeon cut off his leg above the knee. The task was most painful to behold, the surgeon using his knife and saw on human flesh and bones as freely as the butcher at the shambles does on the carcass of the beast! Our other mess-mate suffered still more than the Swede; he was sadly mutilated about the legs and thighs with splinters. Such scenes of suffering as I saw in that ward-room, I hope never to witness again. Could the civilized world behold them as they were, and as they often are, infinitely worse than on that occasion, it seems to me they would forever put down the barbarous practices of war, by universal consent.

Most of our officers and men were taken on board the victor ship. I was left, with a few others, to take care of the wounded. My master, the sailing master, was also among the officers, who continued in their ship. Most of the men who remained were unfit for any service, having broken into the spirit-room and made themselves drunk; some of them broke into the purser's room and helped themselves to clothing; while others, by previous agreement, took possession of their dead messmates' property. For my own part, I was content to help myself to a little of the officers' provisions, which did me more good than could be obtained from rum. What was worse than all, however, was the folly of the sailors in giving spirit to their wounded messmates, since it only served to aggravate their distress.

Among the wounded was a brave fellow named Wells. After the sur-geon had amputated and dressed his arm, he walked about in fine spir-its, as if he had received only a slight injury. Indeed, while under the operation, he manifested a similar heroism—observing to the surgeon, "I have lost my arm in the service of my country; but I don't mind it, doctor, it's the fortune of war." Cheerful and gay as he was, he soon died. His companions gave him rum; he was attacked by fever and died. Thus his messmates actually killed him with kindness.

We had all sorts of dispositions and temperaments among our crew. To me it was a matter of great interest to watch their various manifes-tations. Some who had lost their messmates appeared to care nothing about it, while others were grieving with all the tenderness of women. Of these was the survivor of two seamen who had formerly been sol-diers in the same regiment; he bemoaned the loss of his comrade with expressions of profoundest grief. There were, also, two boatswain's mates, named Adams and Brown, who had been messmates for several years in the same ship. Brown was killed, or so wounded that he died soon after the battle. It was really a touching spectacle to see the rough, hardy features of the brave old sailor streaming with tears, as he picked out the dead body of his friend from among the wounded and gently carried it to the ship's side, saying to the inanimate form he bore, "O Bill, we have sailed together in a number of ships, we have been in many gales and some battles, but this is the worst day I have seen! We must now part!" Here he dropped the body into the deep, and then, a fresh torrent of tears streaming over his weather-beaten face, he added, "I can do no more for you. Farewell! God be with you!" Here was an instance of genuine friendship, worth more than the heartless professions of thousands, who, in the fancied superiority of their elevated position in the social circle, will deign nothing but a silly sneer at this record of a sailor's grief.

from The Caine Mutiny
by Herman Wouk

Herman Wouk (born in 1915) published The
Caine Mutiny *in 1951. The book has retained
its hold on our culture partly through the 1954
movie it inspired. But it still deserves to be
read—not least for this description of a
typhoon off the Phillipines in December, 1944.
With his ship in danger, Captain Queeg refuses
to do what must be done to save it.*

T he TBS message was so muffled by static and the noise of wind
and waves that Willie had to put his ear to the loudspeaker:
*Chain Gang from Sunshine. Discontinue fueling. Execute to follow.
New fleet course 180. Small Boys reorientate screen.*

"What? What was it?" said Queeg at Willie's elbow.

"Discontinuing fueling, sir, and turning south. Execute to follow."

"Getting the hell out, hey? About time."

Maryk, squat and enormous in his life jacket, said, "I don't know
how she'll ride, sir, with her stern to the wind. Quartering seas always
murder us—"

"Any course that takes us out of here is the right course," said
Queeg. He peered out at the ragged waves, rearing and tossing everywhere as high as the ship's mast. The flying spray was like a cloudburst.
A few hundred yards beyond the ship the gray mountains of water
faded into a white misty wall. The spray was beginning to rattle against
the windows, sounding more like hail than water. "Kay, Willie. Call

Paynter and tell him to stand by his engines for some fast action. Steve, I'm going to conn from the radar shack. You stay here."

The TBS scratched and whined. The voice came through gurgling, as though the loudspeaker were under water: *"Small Boys from Sunshine. Execute reorientation. Make best speed."*

"Kay. All engines ahead full. Right standard rudder. Steady on 180," said Queeg, and ran out of the wheelhouse. The *Caine* went plunging downhill into a foaming trough. Stilwell spun the helm, saying, "Christ, this wheel feels loose."

"Rudder's probably clear out of the water," Maryk said. The nose of the ship cut into the sea and came up slowly, shedding thick solid streams. The wheelhouse trembled.

"Rudder is right standard, sir," said Stilwell. "Jesus, she's getting shoved around fast. Heading 010, sir—020—" Like a kite taking the wind, the minesweeper heeled, and swept sharply to the right. Fear tingled in Willie's arms and legs as he was swung against the wet windows. "Heading 035, sir—040—"

Hanging increasingly to starboard, the *Caine* was rising and falling on the waves, blown sidewise, riding more like flotsam again than a ship under control. Spray blew across the forecastle in clouds. Instinctively Willie looked to Maryk, and was deeply relieved to see the exec hanging with both arms to an overhead beam, his back planted against the bulkhead, calmly watching the swift veer of the forecastle across the water.

"Say, Willie!" The captain's voice was angry and shrill through the speaking tube. "Get your goddamn radio technician up here, will you? I can't see anything on this goddamn radar."

Willie roared, "Aye aye, sir," into the speaking tube and passed a call for the technician over the p.a. He was beginning to feel nauseous from the dizzy sidewise slipping of the *Caine* and the queer rise and fall of the slanted deck.

"Mr. Maryk," the helmsman said in a changed tone, "she's stopped coming around—"

"What's your head?"

"Zero nine three."

'We're broadside to. Wind's got her. She'll come slow."

"Still 093, sir," said Stilwell, after a minute of bad wallowing—heavy slow rolls upright and swift sickening drops to starboard. It was hard to tell whether the *Caine* was moving through the water at all, or simply being flung sidewise and forward. The sense of motion came entirely from the sea and the wind; yet the engines were making twenty knots.

"Bring your rudder hard right," said Maryk.

"Hard right, sir Christ—sir, this goddamn wheel *feels like the wheel ropes are broken!* Just sloppy—" The hair of Willie's head prickled to see the looks of fright on the sailors. He felt the same expression forming on his own face.

"Shut your yap, Stilwell, the wheel ropes are okay," said Maryk. "Don't be such a baby. Haven't you ever had the wheel in a sea before—"

"Now God damn it, Steve," came the squeak of Queeg "what the hell's going on out there? Why aren't we coming around?"

Maryk yelled into the speaking tube, 'Wind and sea taking charge, sir. I've got the rudder at hard right—"

"Well, use the engines. *Get* her around. Christ on a crutch, do I have to do everything here? *Where's* that technician? There's nothing but grass on this radar—"

Maryk began to manipulate the engines. A combination of standard speed on the port screw and slow backing on the starboard started swinging the ship's head slowly to the south. "Steady on 180, sir," Stilwell said at last, turning his face to Maryk, his eyes glinting with relief.

The ship was tossing and heeling from side to side. But there was no alarm in the steepest rolls any more, so long as they were even dips both ways. Willie was getting used to the sight of the three rusty stacks lying apparently parallel to the sea, so that between them he saw nothing but foaming water. The whipping of the stacks back and forth like gigantic windshield wipers was no longer a frightening but a pleasant thing. It was the slow, slow dangling rolls to one side that he dreaded.

Queeg came in, mopping at his eyes with a handkerchief. "Damn spray stings. Well, you finally got her around, hey? Guess we're okay now."

"Are we on station, sir?"

'Well, pretty near, I guess. *I* can't tell. Technician says the spray is giving us this sea return that's fogging up the scope. I guess if we're too far out of line Sunshine will give us a growl—"

"Sir, I think maybe we ought to ballast," said the exec. "We're pretty light, sir. Thirty-five per cent on fuel. One reason we don't come around good is that we're riding so high—"

"Well, don't worry, we're not capsizing yet."

"It'll just give us that much more maneuverability, sir—"

"Yes, and contaminate our tanks with a lot of salt water, so we lose suction every fifteen minutes once we refuel. Sunshine has our fuel report. If he thought there was any danger he'd issue ballasting orders."

"I also think we ought to set the depth charges on safe, sir."

"What's the matter, Steve, are you panicky on account of a little bad weather?"

"I'm not panicky, sir—"

"We're still supposed to be an anti-submarine vessel, you know. What the hell good are depth charges set on safe if we pick up a sub in the next five minutes?"

Maryk glanced out of the blurred window at the colossal boiling waves. "Sir, we won't be making any sub runs in this—"

"How do we know?"

"Sir, the *Dietch* in our squadron got caught in a storm in the Aleutians, and got sunk by its own depth charges tearing loose. Blew off the stern. Skipper got a general court—"

"Hell's bells, if your heart is so set on putting the depth charges on safe go ahead. I don't care. Just be damn sure there's somebody standing by to arm them if we pick up a sub—"

"Mr. Maryk," spoke up Stilwell, "the depth charges are on safe, sir."

"They are!" exclaimed Queeg. "Who says so?"

"I—I set 'em myself, sir." The sailor's voice was shaky. He stood with legs spread, clutching the wheel, his eyes on the gyrocompass.

"And who told you to do that?"

"I got standing orders, sir, from Mr. Keefer. When the ship is in danger I set 'em on safe—"

"And who said the ship was in danger, hey?" Queeg swung back and forth, clinging to a window handle, glaring at the helmsman's back.

"Well, sir, on that big roll around seven o'clock, I—I set 'em. The whole fantail was awash. Had to rig a life line—"

"God damn it, Mr. Maryk, why am I never informed of these things? Here I am, steaming around with a lot of dead depth charges—"

Stilwell said, "Sir, I told Mr. Keefer—"

"You speak when you're spoken to, you goddamned imbecile, and not otherwise!" shrieked Queeg. "Mr. Keith, place this man on report for insolence and neglect of duty! He told *Mr. Keefer!* I'll attend to Mr. Keefer! Now Steve, I want you to get another helmsman and keep this stupid idiot's ugly face out of my sight from now on—"

"Captain, pardon me," said the exec hurriedly, "the other helmsmen are still shot from last night. Stilwell's our best man and we need him—"

"*Will you stop this back talk?*" screamed the captain. "Great bloody Christ, is there one officer on this ship who takes orders from me? I said I want—"

Engstrand stumbled into the wallowing wheelhouse and grabbed at Willie to keep from falling. His dungarees ran with water. "Sorry, Mr. Keith. Captain, the barometer—"

"What about the barometer?"

"Twenty-eight ninety-four, sir—twenty-*eight*—"

"Who the hell's been watching the barometer? Why haven't I had a report for a half hour?" Queeg ran out on the wing, steadying himself from hand to hand on the windows, the engine-room telegraph, the doorway.

"Mr. Maryk," the helmsman said hoarsely, "I can't hold her on 180. She's falling off to port—"

"Give her more rudder—"

"I got her at emergency right, sir—heading 172, sir-falling off fast—"

"Why is the rudder emergency right?" Queeg bellowed, lurching in through the doorway. "Who's giving rudder orders here? Is everybody on this bridge going crazy?"

"Captain, she's yawing to port," said Maryk. "Steersman can't hold her at 180—"

"One *six* zero, sir, now," said Stilwell, with a scared look at Maryk. It was the dreaded weather-vane effect, taking charge of the *Caine*. The rudder was not holding, and the ship was skidding sideways at the pleasure of wind and waves. The head was dropping off from south to east.

Queeg grabbed at the helmsman and steadied himself to stare at the compass. He jumped to the telegraph and signaled "Flank Speed" with one handle and "Stop" with the other. The engine-room pointers answered instantly. The deck began to vibrate with the one-sided strain on the engines. "That'll bring her around," said the captain. "What's your head now?"

"Still falling off, sir, 152—148—"

Queeg muttered, "Needs a few seconds to take hold—"

Once again the *Caine* took a sickening cant to starboard and hung there. Waves coming from the port side broke over the ship as though it were a floating log. It wallowed feebly under the tons of water, but did not right itself. It came halfway back to level and sagged further to starboard again. Willie's face was pushed against the window and he saw water no more than inches from his eyes. He could have counted little bubbles of foam. Stilwell, hanging to the wheel, with his feet sliding out from under him, stammered, "Still falling off, sir—heading 123—"

"Captain, we're broaching to," said Maryk, his voice lacking firmness for the first time. "Try backing the starboard engine, sir." The captain seemed not to hear. "Sir, sir, *back the starboard engine.*"

Queeg, clinging to the telegraph with his knees and arms, threw him a frightened glance, his skin greenish, and obediently slid the handle backward. The laboring ship shuddered fearfully; it continued to drift sidewise before the wind, rising and falling on each swell a distance equal to the height of a tall building. "What's your head?" The captain's voice was a muffled croak.

"Steady on 117, sir—"

"Think she'll grab, Steve?" murmured Willie.

"I hope so."

"Oh holy Mother of Christ, make this ship come around!" spoke a queer wailing voice. The tone made Willie shiver. Urban, the little signalman, had dropped to his knees and was hugging the binnacle, his eyes closed, his head thrown back.

"Shut up, Urban," Maryk said sharply. "Get on your feet—"

Stilwell exclaimed, "Sir, heading *120!* Coming right, sir!"

"Good," said Maryk. "Ease your rudder to standard."

Without so much as a glance at the captain, Stilwell obeyed. Willie noticed the omission, for all that he was terror-stricken; and he noticed, too, that Queeg, frozen to the telegraph stand, seemed oblivious.

"Rudder is eased to standard, sir—heading 124, sir—" The *Caine* stood erect slowly and wabbled a little to port before heeling deep to starboard again.

"We're okay," said Maryk. Urban got off his knees and looked around sheepishly.

"Heading 128—129—130—"

"Willie," said the exec, "take a look in the radar shack. See if you can tell where the hell we are in the formation."

"Aye aye, sir." Willie staggered out past the captain to the open wing. The wind immediately smashed him against the bridgehouse, and spray pelted him like small wet stones. He was astounded and peculiarly exhilarated to realize that in the last fifteen minutes the wind had actually become much stronger than before, and would blow him over the side if he exposed himself in a clear space. He laughed aloud, his voice thin against the guttural "Whooeeee!" of the storm. He inched himself to the door of the radar shack, freed the dogs, and tried to pull the door open, but the wind held it tightly shut. He pounded on the wet steel with his knuckles, and kicked at it, and screamed, "Open up! Open up! It's the OOD!" A crack appeared and widened. He darted through, knocking down one of the radarmen who was pushing against the door. It snapped shut as though on a spring.

"What the hell!" exclaimed Willie.

There were perhaps twenty sailors jammed in the tiny space, all in life jackets with waterproof searchlights pinned to them, all with whistles dangling around their necks, all with the same round-eyed bristly white face of fear. "How are we doing, Mr. Keith?" spoke the voice of Meatball from the rear of the crush.

"We're doing fine—"

"We gonna have to abandon ship, sir?" said a filthy-faced fireman.

Willie suddenly realized what was so very strange about the shack beside the crowd. It was brightly lit. Nobody was paying any attention to the dim green slopes of the radars. He let loose a stream of obscenity that surprised him as it came out of his mouth. The sailors shrank a little from him. "Who turned on the lights in here? Who's got the watch?"

"Sir, there's nothing on the scopes but sea return," whined a radarman.

Willie cursed some more, and then said, "Douse the lights. Get your faces against these scopes and keep them there."

"Okay, Mr. Keith," said the radarman, in a friendly, respectful tone, "but it won't do no good." In the gloom Willie quickly saw that the sailor was right. There was no trace of the pips of the other ships, nothing but a blurry peppering and streaking of green all over the scopes. "You see, sir," said the voice of the technician, patiently, "our masthead ain't no higher than the water most of the time, and, anyway, all this spray, why, it's like a solid object sir. These scopes are jammed out—"

"All the same," said Willie, "the watch will be maintained on these radars, and you'll keep trying till you do get something! And all the guys who don't belong in here—well—well, stay here, and keep your faces closed so the watch-standers can do their duty—"

"Sir, are we really okay?"

"Will we have to abandon ship?"

"I was ready to jump on that last roll—"

"Will the ship come through it, Mr. Keith?"

"We're okay," shouted Willie. "We're okay. Don't lose your heads. We'll be back chipping paint in a few hours—"

"I'll chip this rusty old bitch till doomsday if she just rides out this blow," said a voice, and there was a ripple of small laughs.

"I'm staying up here if I get a court-martial for it—"

"Me, too—"

"Hell, there are forty guys over on the lee of the bridge—"

"Mister Keith"—the gutter twang of Meatball again—"honest, does the old man know what the Christ he's doing? That's all we want to know."

"The old man's doing great. You bastards shut up and take it easy. Couple of you help me get this door open."

Wind and spray blasted in through the open crack. Willie pulled himself out and the door clanged. The wind blew him forward into the pilothouse. In the second that elapsed he was drenched as by buckets of water. "Radars are jammed, Steve. Nothing to see until this spray moderates—"

"Very well."

Despite the whining and crashing of the storm, Willie got the impression of silence in the wheelhouse. Queeg hung to the telegraph as before. Stilwell swayed at the wheel. Urban, wedged between the binnacle and the front window, clutched the quartermaster's log as though it were a Bible. Usually there were other sailors in the wheelhouse—telephone talkers, signalmen—but they were avoiding it now as though it were the sickroom of a cancer victim. Maryk stood with both hands clamped to the captain's chair. Willie staggered to the starboard side and glanced out at the wing. A crowd of sailors and officers pressed against the bridgehouse, hanging to each other, their clothes whipping in the wind. Willie saw Keefer, Jorgensen, and nearest him, Harding.

"Willie, are we going to be okay?" Harding said.

The OOD nodded, and fell back into the wheelhouse. He was vexed at not having a flashlight and whistle, like everyone else. "Just my luck to be on watch," he thought. He did not really believe yet that the ship was going to founder, but he resented being at a disadvantage. His own man-overboard gear was in his desk below. He thought of sending the boatswain's mate for it; and was ashamed to issue the order.

The *Caine* yawed shakily back and forth on heading 180 for a couple of minutes. Then suddenly it was flung almost on its beam-ends to port by a swell, a wave and a gust of wind hitting together. Willie reeled, brought up against Stilwell, and grabbed at the wheel spokes.

"Captain," Maryk said, "I still think we ought to ballast—at least the stern tanks, if we're going to steam before the wind."

Willie glanced at Queeg. The captain's face was screwed up as though he were looking at a bright light. He gave no sign of having heard. "I request permission to ballast stern tanks, sir," said the exec.

Queeg's lips moved. "Negative," he said calmly and faintly.

Stilwell twisted the wheel sharply, pulling the spokes out of Willie's hands. The OOD grasped an overhead beam.

"Falling off to *starboard* now. Heading 189—190—191—"

Maryk said, "Captain—hard left rudder?"

"Okay," murmured Queeg.

"Hard left rudder, sir," said Stilwell. "Heading 200—"

The exec stared at the captain for several seconds while the minesweeper careened heavily to port and began its nauseating sideslipping over the swells, the wind flipping it around now in the other direction. "Captain, we'll have to use engines again, she's not answering to the rudder. . . . Sir, how about heading up into the wind? She's going to keep broaching to with this stern wind—"

Queeg pushed the handles of the telegraph. "Fleet course is 180," he said.

"Sir, we have to maneuver for the safety of the ship—"

"Sunshine knows the weather conditions. We've received no orders to maneuver at discretion—" Queeg looked straight ahead, constantly clutching the telegraph amid the gyrations of the wheelhouse.

"Heading 225—falling away fast, sir—"

An unbelievably big gray wave loomed on the port side, high over the bridge. It came smashing down. Water spouted into the wheelhouse from the open wing, flooding to Willie's knees. The water felt surprisingly warm and sticky, like blood. "Sir, we're shipping water on the goddamn *bridge!*" said Maryk shrilly. "We've *got* to come around into the wind!"

"Heading 245, sir." Stilwell's voice was sobbing. "She ain't answering to the engines at all, sir!"

The *Caine* rolled almost completely over on its port side. Everybody in the wheelhouse except Stilwell went sliding across the streaming deck and piled up against the windows. The sea was under their noses, dashing up against the glass. "Mr. Maryk, the light on this gyro just went out!" screamed Stilwell, clinging desperately to the wheel. The wind howled and shrieked in Willie's ears. He lay on his face on the deck, tumbling around in salt water, flailing for a grip at something solid.

"Oh Christ, Christ, Christ, Jesus Christ, save us!" squealed the voice of Urban.

"Reverse your rudder, Stilwell! Hard right! Hard right!" cried the exec harshly.

"Hard right, sir!"

Maryk crawled across the deck, threw himself on the engine-room telegraph, wrested the handles from Queeg's spasmodic grip, and reversed the settings. "Excuse me, Captain—" A horrible coughing rumble came from the stacks. "What's your head?" barked Maryk.

"Two seven five, sir!"

"Hold her at hard right!"

"Aye aye, sir!"

The old minesweeper rolled up a little from the surface of the water.

Willie Keith did not have any idea of what the executive officer was doing, though the maneuver was simple enough. The wind was turning the ship from south to west. Queeg had been trying to fight back to south. Maryk was doing just the opposite, now; seizing on the momentum of the twist to the right and assisting it with all the force of engines and rudder, to try to swing the ship's head completely northward, into the wind and sea. In a calmer moment Willie would easily have understood the logic of the act, but now he had lost his bearings. He sat on the deck, hanging stupidly to a telephone jack-box, with water sloshing around his crotch, and looked to the exec as to a wizard, or an angel of God, to save him with magic passes. He had lost faith in the ship. He was overwhelmingly aware that he sat on a piece of iron in an angry dangerous sea. He could think of nothing but his yearning to be saved. Typhoon, *Caine*, Queeg, sea, Navy, duty, lieutenant's bars, all were forgotten. He was like a wet cat mewing on wreckage.

"Still coming around? What's your head? *Keep calling your head!*" yelled Maryk.

"Coming around hard, sir!" the helmsman screamed as though prodded with a knife. "Heading 310, heading 315, heading 320—"

"Ease your rudder to standard!"

"*Ease* the rudder, sir?"

"Yes, ease her, ease her!"

"Ru-rudder is eased, sir—"

"Very well."

Ease, ease ease—the word penetrated Willie's numb fogged mind. He pulled himself to his feet, and looked around. The *Caine* was riding upright. It rolled to one side, to the other, and back again. Outside the windows there was nothing but solid white spray. The sea was invisible. The forecastle was invisible. "You okay, Willie? I thought you were knocked cold." Maryk, braced on the captain's chair, gave him a brief side glance.

"I'm okay. Wha-what's happening, Steve?"

"Well, this is it. We ride it out for a half hour, we're okay—What's your head?" he called to Stilwell.

"Three two five, sir—coming around slower, now—"

"Well, sure, fighting the wind—she'll come around—we'll steady on 000—"

"Aye aye, sir—"

"We will not," said Queeg.

Willie had lost all awareness of the captain's presence. Maryk had filled his mind as father, leader, and savior. He looked now at the little pale man who stood with arms and legs entwined around the telegraph stand, and had the feeling that Queeg was a stranger. The captain, blinking and shaking his head as though he had just awakened, said, "Come left to 180."

"Sir, we can't ride stern to wind and save this ship," said the exec.

"Left to 180, helmsman."

"Hold it, Stilwell," said Maryk.

"Mr. Maryk, fleet course is 180." The captain's voice was faint, almost whispering. He was looking glassily ahead.

"Captain, we've lost contact with the formation—the radars are blacked out—"

"Well, then, we'll find them—I'm not disobeying orders on account of some bad weather—"

The helmsman said, "Steady on 000—"

Maryk said, "Sir, how do we know what the orders are now? The guide's antennas may be down—ours may be—call up Sunshine and tell him we're in trouble—"

Butting and plunging, the *Caine* was a riding ship again. Willie felt the normal vibration of the engines, the rhythm of seaworthiness in the pitching, coming up from the deck into the bones of his feet. Outside the pilothouse there was only the whitish darkness of the spray and the dismal whine of the wind, going up and down in shivery glissandos.

"We're not in trouble," said Queeg. "Come left to 180."

"Steady as you go!" Maryk said at the same instant. The helmsman looked around from one officer to the other, his eyes popping in panic. "Do as I say!" shouted the executive officer. He turned on the OOD. "Willie, note the time." He strode to the captain's side and saluted. "Captain, I'm sorry, sir, you're a sick man. I am temporarily relieving you of this ship, under Article 184 of *Navy Regulations*."

"I don't know what you're talking about," said Queeg. "Left to 180, helmsmen."

"Mr. Keith, *you're* the OOD here—what the hell should I do?" cried Stilwell.

Willie was looking at the clock. It was fifteen minutes to ten. He was dumfounded to think he had had the deck less than two hours. The import of what was taking place between Maryk and Queeg penetrated his mind slowly. He could not believe it was happening. It was as incredible as his own death.

"Never you mind about Mr. Keith," said Queeg to Stilwell, a slight crankiness entering his voice, fantastically incongruous under the circumstances. It was a tone he might have used to complain of a chewing-gum wrapper on the deck. "I told you to come left. That's an order. Now you come left, and fast—"

"Commander Queeg, you aren't issuing orders on this bridge any more," said Maryk. "I have relieved you, sir. You're on the sick list. I'm taking the responsibility. I know I'll be court-martialed. I've got the conn—"

"You're under arrest, Maryk. Get below to your room," said Queeg. "Left to 180, I say!"

"Christ, Mr. Keith!" exclaimed the helmsman, looking at Willie. Urban had backed into the farthest corner of the wheelhouse. He stared from the exec to Willie, his mouth open. Willie glanced at Queeg, glued to the telegraph, and at Maryk. He felt a surge of immense drunken gladness.

"Steady on 000, Stilwell," he said. "Mr. Maryk has the responsibility. Captain Queeg is sick."

"Call your relief, Mr. Keith," the captain said at the same instant, with something like real anger. "You're under arrest, too."

"You have no power to arrest me, Mr. Queeg," said Willie.

The shocking change of name caused a look of happy surprise to appear on Stilwell's face. He grinned at Queeg with contempt. "Steady on 000, Mr. Maryk," he said, and turned his back to the officers.

Queeg suddenly quit his grasp on the telegraph stand, and stumbled across the heaving wheelhouse to the starboard side. "Mr. Keefer! Mr. Harding! Aren't there *any* officers out there?" he called to the wing.

"Willie, phone Paynter and tell him to ballast all empty tanks on the double," Maryk said.

"Aye aye, sir." Willie seized the telephone and buzzed the fireroom. "Hello, Paynt? Listen, we're going to ballast. Flood all your empty tanks on the double—You're goddamn right it's about time—"

"Mr. Keith, I did *not* issue any orders to ballast," said Queeg. "You call that fireroom right back—"

Maryk stepped to the public-address system. "Now, all officers, report to the bridge. All officers, report to the bridge." He said aside to Willie, "Call Paynter and tell him that word doesn't apply to him."

"Aye aye, sir." Willie pulled the phone from the bracket.

"I said once and I say again," Queeg exclaimed querulously, "both of you are under arrest! Leave the bridge, right now. Your conduct is disgraceful!"

Queeg's protests gave Willie a growing sense of gladness and power. In this shadowy careening wet wheelhouse, in this twilit darkness of midmorning, with a murderous wind shrieking at the windows, he seemed to be living the happiest moment of his life. All fear had left him.

from The Raft

by Robert Trumbull

Pilot Harold F. Dixon and two crewmen—Anthony Pastula and Gene Aldrich—got lost on an anti-submarine patrol over the South Pacific in 1942. Low on fuel, they ditched their plane, then drifted 34 days and more than a thousand miles in an inflatable rubber raft. The trio had no food, water or navigational instruments. New York Times war correspondent Robert Trumbull interviewed Dixon and retold his story in the pilot's voice.

Tony wanted to die on a calm day, but the weather was becoming worse. The winds were variable, and generally high. The sky was overcast much of the time. Squalls were numerous and nasty. This was the beginning of the hurricane we were to learn about later, the most disastrous hurricane remembered in the South Pacific. It was fortunate, perhaps, that we were unable to recognize the signs of what was in store.

When the clouds blackened and the wind rose, the sea grew angry and lashed us viciously. Even with the canvas anchor it was difficult to control the boat. We were continually drenched and often in danger of upsetting. Worst of all, we had little strength left for fighting. The weakness hit us all at once, and left our ravaged bodies full of pain. Our morale, too, was lowest when we needed it most.

The rain came often and mercilessly. The squalls were cold now—miserably cold, and we huddled together to keep warm. We were almost without flesh, it seemed; when we lay down in the bottom of the boat for warmth we were wedged together, and our sharp bones bumped painfully. The only way I could stretch out was to lie in the middle of the boat, the two boys one on each side. Tony's hips would be punching into me on one side, Gene's knees and elbows digging me in the back. We could lie together in this position only a short while until our circulation would be cut off. Then we would have to get up and stretch to make our starved and sluggish blood move again.

Often we would deliberately leave several inches of water in the bottom of the boat, as it was warmer than the air. When we sat up, the swift wind blew needlepoint spray that seemed to penetrate our tender skin. In our dry mouths, our foul-tasting teeth chattered until they ached.

None of us thought very much about talking and carrying on a conversation. We grew away from that toward the last. Things were becoming serious. We could see that our end was approaching, one way or another. We must be saved soon, or we would die.

Tony and I seemed to be able to take it a little better than Gene. He would beg us to talk to him, and then the only thing he was willing to talk about was food. I made a constant effort to be affable and agreeable with both boys, as I knew we were under a constant strain and I felt that it was up to me as leader to do all in my power to maintain good feeling and harmony amongst us, in an effort to ward off the tendency we were all showing, so obviously, to brood over our position. Clearly, our courage was beginning to fail us at this point.

When we had our sip of water in the middle of the day, we tried imagining it was coffee. The tiny drink would buoy our spirits, and we could conjure, in our minds, a good meal to go with it. Sometimes we would go to Gene's house and have a big dinner of his Missouri hickory-smoked ham with all the fixings. Another time we would visit Tony's, where we ate all kinds of Polish food. One of his favorite dishes was what he called "pigeon in a blanket," made by rolling hamburgers in cabbage leaves. It sounded good to us then, and we devoured it in our minds. Again, we would go to my ranch, Calavo, in La Mesa, and stuff ourselves with avocados and oranges.

Despite my own distaste for this self-torturing conversation, I didn't discourage it, for at least it occupied our minds more pleasantly than any other thoughts we had.

After the twenty-eighth day and the last coconut, we realized at last that we were starving. I am convinced that the small amount we ate contributed nothing toward maintaining our strength. The few unpalatable mouthfuls made our suffering worse, if anything, by stimulating the hunger and starting our juices to work against us.

Inevitably, we discussed cannibalism.

One of the boys suggested one day, "Suppose one of us starves to death—of course one of us would go first—what should we do with the body?"

Tony had shown a horror of being buried at sea on a rough day. The warsman knows, when he goes to sea, that he may not see land again. Many of us have seen a comrade's body given to the waves, and we are conscious that the same fate may await us any day. Tony had said that he wouldn't mind meeting Davy Jones on a calm, beautiful day—he'd be perfectly happy to go if the sun were shining and the sea was still.

Tony was the thinnest of us, and I think he had an idea that he would die first. Perhaps, also, he had a horror of being eaten. I think that may have been one of the reasons why he suggested now that we should jump over the side and end it all. When he recalled this later, he said he didn't think he really meant it —and again I believe him.

At any rate, we put the question before the house: If one of us should die, should the others eat his body?

One of the boys suggested that it might be a good idea to eat part of the dead man, anyway. We talked the proposition over at length. Finally we all agreed that the survivors should eat the heart, liver, and other such organs.

Today I don't believe that any of us had a real intention of stooping so. I'm sure I didn't, and I don't think the others did either. But it offered a new source of conversation to us, and we threshed it out thoroughly.

◆ ◆ ◆

I kept my eyes closed most of the time, now, when the sun was out. Days and days of watching the glaring water had strained my eyes until now I could look into the distance for only a few seconds, then things would begin to blur. Afterward they pained me greatly, and finally I reached the point where even at night the reflection of the moon on the water hurt them.

In the fourth week I had noticed that my feet and legs were losing their sense of feeling. This began in the feet and moved upward, a little farther each day, until the partial paralysis reached my hips. Practically all of the time we spent sitting, or lying in the bottom of the boat, which required us to pull up our knees. Eventually I felt as if I had rheumatism. The suffering was intense when I tried to lie down in the tortuous position that the limited space required me to take.

The pounding of the choppy waves beneath the fabric bottom nearly drove me mad. Every night I thought: Tonight I am more tired than I have ever been before, so maybe this time I can sleep. And every night the monotonous, jarring hammer beneath me, coupled with the always unexpected drenching from above, drove me to sit up and wait for more favorable conditions. No more favorable conditions ever developed. As time went on, exhaustion closed around me like a tightening hand. I had to drive myself to think.

Fatigue, and pain of infinite variety, loosed the reins on my temper. When I spoke to one of the boys, and he didn't answer but continued staring straight ahead, I sometimes forgot that he was under the same strain as I, and I raged like a madman. These outbursts never lasted long; I had not the strength. There was never an answering violence in the boys; they had not the energy, or didn't care, or didn't know.

On the twenty-ninth day the old gray albatross returned and began introducing bad luck to us in large doses. At first I was glad to see him, a familiar thing. I wondered where he had been when the storm was at its height. He circled high above the boat, darting now and then to inspect a wave that rose to meet him.

The sea was rough and sullen. The wind had blown contrarily through the night, and I had left the sea anchor out, to hold us back and steady us. Right after sunrise I thought of the anchor first. It was the only means we had of controlling the boat, and after every misadventure I checked to see that it was safe. This morning I found that the drive of the high wind against the boat had pulled the jacket to the surface, where it lay collapsed. I started to pull it in, intending to shake it out and let it go again. Without its drag the small gale was sending us away from our direction, and I felt that every mile counted in our chance to live a little longer.

As I hauled in the anchor, a small fish came into view beneath the surface at the bow. It was the same kind as we had caught before.

Food!

I watched him warily. He swam under the boat.

As I got the anchor aboard, out he came again. He paused right in front of me. If I had had the knife I could have stabbed him. I turned to look for the knife. I fumbled in the tool pocket for several seconds, trying to keep an eye on the fish at the same time. He lay on the surface, resting.

I moved to the side of the boat, but in my weakness I was not quick enough. A flirt of his tail sent him drifting out of reach. I waited, and he held himself still, tantalizingly lifting and falling with the rolling waves. Finally he swung an inch or two closer and I lunged, but got nothing but water in the face for my pains. I lay across the gunwale for a moment, resting. I needed to gather myself to fix the anchor.

As I waited, a great spotted leopard shark, about seven feet long, poked his nose out of the water not six inches from my face. I drew back, startled. If I had had the nerve I could have snatched him by the gills. I hesitated for several seconds, and tried to make myself grab him, but I couldn't. The truth is, I was a little afraid of him. I was conscious of this, and a little disgusted, as he twisted and dived out of view beneath a gray-green wave.

I cursed my timidity. I probably couldn't have held the monster, but I might have hauled him into the boat before I was exhausted, and then he would have been a goner; we could have held him until he suffocated. That would have been a lot of meat, I reflected wearily. He weighed about a hundred pounds, I guessed.

The wind rose higher, and the waves came faster. The swells uncoiled like great green snakes and burst into white at the top, then fell apart with an angry roar. They rolled beneath the light raft and raised us up until we looked into a sickening depth. Then we would spin downward, sometimes missing the break, sometimes whirling in the wild white froth. We shipped water, gallons at a time, and bailed frantically with our hands. We watched the waves like surf-riders, rolling our weight from side to side as the combers tossed the boat like a toy. We learned to shift ourselves adroitly when the crest hit, to keep the raft in balance.

But the sea is cunning. It can bide its time, and spring like a beast. The wind was its ally.

The raft rose slowly as the comber uncoiled beneath us and a little to one side. The wind seemed to pause for breath. We eyed the wave's curling summit.

A wall of green laced with white, translucent as we saw it against the sky, collapsed all over us. Its weight made our ears ring, and filled our nostrils. Coughing and blinded, we fell across the gunwale. The wind, as if it had been waiting, blew a heavy gust that raised the raft and tipped it over.

We were in the sea again, a more fearsome sea than any of us had ever seen. We all had the same thought, I guess: to grab that raft. Once more we were fortunate. We clasped it in our arms, and held with all our strength. With the mad water pulling at my legs, I looked at the boys. Tony was holding on frantically. His eyes were closed, and he was saying a prayer in Polish. Gene's lips were stretched with his effort and showed his teeth clenched.

"Hold on!" I screamed. I don't think I was heard in the howling wind and waves. It didn't matter.

I maneuvered around to the other side, holding my head down as waves dashed against my face. The sea was clubbing me, trying to beat me down. I pulled my head between my shoulders and took the stunning blows as groggy fighters do.

I got my hand beneath the boat and lifted. I felt as if my heart was stopping. I knew I had to do every little thing right, while in this maelstrom, or I'd die.

Again I tricked the wind. It swept beneath, filled the inside, and lifted the raft right side up, slamming its bottom against a slanted wall of sea.

We flung ourselves against the raft again. I somehow scrambled in, and grabbed Tony by both his wrists. I let myself fall to a sitting position, braced my feet, and pulled him in. Between us, then, we rescued Gene. All of us lay and panted, heads down.

Sometime later, maybe hours, I took the inventory. All our spare rags were gone, but the water-catching rags were there. Then—I missed the anchor.

This was a terrible blow. Now we could not control the raft except by rowing, and our last experience with rowing had so weakened us that I knew we would have to give it up except in the last extremity.

Our peril made my mind sharper. I went over our gear in search of anything that might make a suitable sea anchor, but the only likely thing I found was the piece of patching material, of the same fabric as the boat, about twelve inches long by six inches wide. I rigged it on the line, but I found at once that this makeshift would not do. For one thing, it would not sink deep enough; secondly, it was too small.

I tried putting the pliers on the line, also the few steel pieces remaining from the gun, in an arrangement like the tail of a kite. The weighted line held strongly, but it made our boat yaw back and forth in the trough of the sea, so that we shipped great quantities of water every time we hit a comber.

This was our last possibility, and I was determined to make it work.

I left the new anchor out all day, but we had to bail constantly. By sun-down I could see that we would not have strength to keep this up. Soon the water would begin to rise faster than we could sweep it out, and we would founder. Against my will, I did the only thing I could. There was a strong southwest wind blowing us directly opposite to our desires, but I took the anchor in and let the boat drift.

I thought: It's drift or drown.

We watched night fall, without joy. I noted, irrelevantly, that the alba-tross was feeding.

We passed a night of misery in the brewing hurricane. Without an anchor we were at the mercy of the wind, and it blew viciously. Many times we just missed tipping over again, by maneuvering our weight to shift the boat's center of gravity when the mountainous waves knocked us off balance. High combers kept breaking into the boat, half filling it every time. We scooped the water out with our twisted garments, although we thought we would freeze, naked in the cold, slashing rain.

Toward morning the gale slackened, but the sea still boiled. As dawn approached and I was able to see a few feet around, I marveled that we were still afloat among those giant wind-whipped swells. When full day-light came I saw that our world had closed around us. We were in the center of a small circle of agitated green water, under a dome of gray mist. We could not see far in any direction. Everywhere we looked the sea was in frenzied motion, countless white-topped peaks appearing, rolling, and bursting in a gush of foam.

When we stopped shipping water, we sat in the boat with our backs hunched against the rain and wind. We were still drifting to the north-east, making fast time away from where we wished to go.

We said very little to each other. We were hungry and disheartened.

Toward the middle of the morning, we took the jacket, on which I had drawn our chart, and held it over our three heads to give a little pro-tection from the chilling rain.

"Hold it careful, boys," I said. "If we lose this, we don't know where we are."

The canvas chart kept the rain off us a little bit, but our clothes were soaked and clammy, and plastered to our skin. I would have been glad to see the sun again, and wondered if I ever would.

"There's your albatross," Tony said.

I looked up, and saw the old gray bird sailing along above us, his wings spread wide, apparently oblivious to the rain and wind. I watched him for a while until my eyes began to hurt. I lowered my head, relaxing, and my beard scraped the sunburned triangle below my throat.

Something thumped me on the head. I sat still, and felt a heavy weight settling on the top of my skull. It moved slightly, and after a tense moment I realized what had happened.

The albatross had alighted on my head. He was pluming his bedraggled feathers there.

I sat very still, figuring what to do. The boys hadn't seen him yet. I considered whether to make a grab for him myself, or let one of the others try.

The chart's being over my head rather complicated matters. There was a chance that as I grabbed for the albatross my hand would become entangled in the canvas.

I studied the situation carefully, and decided to chance it.

Silently, I slid my right hand outward, gauged my aim as best I could since I was unable to see my quarry, and snatched quickly.

The albatross must have been squatting down as I reached for him, because my hand struck him in the breast. The blow knocked him backward into the water.

He floundered for an instant, righted himself indignantly, and rose above the water with a flap of his mighty wings. He flew away, high, then circled back as if to reconnoiter us.

"Jeez, you almost got him, though," Tony said.

I was feeling very glum, and bitter at my failure in this heaven-sent opportunity to obtain food that we all needed so badly. I was sorry I had not let one of the boys try to grab the bird. They could have seen him, whereas I could not.

"Well, I'm afraid he's gone," I said disconsolately.

"Cheer up, chief, it was a good try," Tony said.

"Wonder if we can't find a little more room in here?" Gene asked.

"Any change would help," Tony said. "I'm getting pretty stiff."

I myself was sore all over. We shifted our positions so that two of us sat with our backs against the forward thwart, while the third huddled among our knees.

"We'd be better off in a telephone booth," Tony said. "It'd be dry."

Gene and I mustered a feeble laugh at Tony's witticism. Then we sat silent a few moments as the rain beat on the chart we held over our heads, and the water ran down our necks in cold rivulets.

Tony spoke again.

"That damned albatross is getting familiar again," he said. "Look to starboard, chief."

I turned quietly, and there was our friend, sitting right alongside me in the water. He was feeding.

"Oh, God, one more chance," I said softly, not in supplication but in gratitude.

The huge bird drifted to within three feet of the boat, and ducked his head under the water. He held his beak and eyes submerged for all of ten seconds. It was as if he were inviting me to grab him.

I thought: If he keeps his head down that long, I'll wait until he does it again, and give myself more time.

I sat still until he came up for air. He looked about him in the water, but didn't move his body. He seemed to find what he wanted, and jabbed his bill back into the water.

Without waiting longer than it took to gather my muscles for the effort, I dived over the side, my hands outstretched to grab the bird.

But I never finished the dive. My feet, instead of driving me forward, pushed the boat behind me. The next thing I knew, I was lying full length, face down. The whole front of me smarted from the smash against the water.

In my surprise and disappointment I couldn't think but I instinctively dropped my feet and spread my arms to keep myself afloat. My long body was being lifted by the choppy waves, and the boat was already several feet away. As I lunged for the raft I couldn't help looking for the albatross, who had escaped me for the second time in a way that was humiliating, and worse. The bird was fluttering away—taking his time about it, too—and I swear that if birds can laugh, the gray albatross was hooting at me.

Tony grabbed me by an arm, and I was quickly in the boat.

"Where's the chart?" I demanded immediately.

"It went over the side with you, chief."

I turned, but instantly I abandoned whatever idea I might have had of diving to retrieve the chart. In that sea, it was gone.

We were now without a single article of any use to us, except our anchor line, one water rag (badly tattered), a pair of pliers, and the pocketknife. We were without protection of any kind against the weather, except the sparse clothing on our backs.

I decided to strip off the useless oar pocket to make a covering for our heads. This I did. The piece of fabric thus obtained was almost square, twenty inches long by sixteen inches wide. It served us better than nothing.

It rained steadily all morning. Shortly after noon we hit a heavy squall, with high winds and a terrifying sea, and we tipped over again.

How we got back into the raft against the waves I don't know. When we did, we found that all our gear was gone—knife, pliers, our newly obtained head covering, the unsuccessful sea anchor, and our last rag. Now we had nothing to protect ourselves, nothing for bailing, nothing for catching food.

Our courage almost failed. This had been a day of horrible disaster.

Tony Pastula, bless his game soul, spoke up at last.

"Well, fellows," he said wryly, "it has all happened now, it looks like. What do you say we shake hands all around and start all over again?"

Gene and I instantly agreed. Crouching in the wobbling rubber tub, with the wind blowing icy rain at us in fire-hose gusts, we exchanged handshakes and declared to each other that this would be a new beginning.

Evening of the thirty-second day we got a shift of wind to the north. Night fell ominously. The sky was dark and threatening; the sea turned from gray to black. As we tumbled along uneasily, our way was lit by long, jagged streaks of lightning, each flash followed by a rolling thunder clap like cannon fire. The air was heavy and stirred sluggishly in the fitful breeze. The waves had lost their frenzy, but still rose high in powerful surges of slowly expanding force.

In the weird twilight, the sky was an awesome spectacle foreboding ill. I called it to the attention of the boys.

There were several layers of clouds, and each layer seemed to be traveling in a different direction. This was beyond the experience of any of us, and we could not imagine what it portended.

"Whatever it means," Tony said, speaking for us all, "it don't mean nothing good."

In my twenty-two years in the navy I had never seen a sky or sea like this; and I didn't like the look of things a bit.

"Better rest while we can," I advised the boys. "Any minute we'll have to bail."

We lay down in the bottom of the raft. The spray that broke on us was cold, and we squeezed ourselves together to keep the warmth of our bodies.

It rained often during the night. Each time we got up to bail and wring out our clothes again.

Tonight we talked more than usual, trying to cheer each other. We all realized, I think, that our spirits occasionally dropped near the danger point of lowness, and it became a game to see who could do the most to lift us out of our despondency. We made little jokes, forced and desperate.

We didn't mind the bailing. Our hips and shoulders were so numb and sore from lying wedged in the bottom of the raft that we actually welcomed the opportunity to get up and move our stiffened muscles. We suffered from lack of circulation. We had so little flesh that our veins were drawn across our bones. When we sat up, our blood would move, but this exposed us to the wind and spray. We chilled easily, so that after a moment we would be forced to lie down again in search of warmth.

Thus we passed the night. It seemed a long time until daylight came.

With morning, we saw that the sky was almost solidly overcast. We waited in vain for the sun to come out and warm us. Everything was gray, except our yellow raft. Its giddy color on the muttering, gloomy sea accentuated its incongruity.

The wind now had shifted to the northeast again, and was driving us along at a lively clip. This was more to our desire, but we couldn't be sure where we were, and couldn't have done anything about it if we had known. The only chart we had was in my head.

About eleven o'clock in the morning we hit a shower, heavy and as cold as ice water. The raft held water over our ankles when it ended.

We had lost the last of our rags in the last tip-over, so we took off all our clothes, mopped the bottom of the boat and wrung over the side, repeating until the raft was dry.

As we finished this tiresome chore the sun appeared, for the first time that day. In our chilled condition the rays felt good.

"Let's take a sun bath before we put our clothes on," I suggested.

The boys assented readily, and we lay against the sides to rest, for we were tired as well as cold. We stretched our clothes across the thwarts to dry.

After a while Tony spoke up nervously.

"Don't you think we'd better put on our clothes?"

I wasn't looking forward to it. They were damp.

"Well, it's pretty rough, you know," Tony argued. "The boat's liable to go over on us again."

The wind had risen and the waves were coming to a boil. The raft was bobbling like an orange rind.

I hesitated for a few seconds, and was just about to agree with Tony when a big comber caught us.

We were lifted high, the raft on such a slant that we had to grab the sides and thwarts to keep from falling out. As we started to slide down the long, sheer trough of the wave, the breaking crest gave us an extra push upward on one side. The wind caught beneath the rounded air chamber. There was a wild scramble of arms and legs, mad grasping, and a confusion of shouts.

"The clothes! The clothes!" I yelled frantically as I went through the air. The scornful wind snatched the words, and a great wave engulfed me.

My head was out of the water again, and somehow my hand was on the raft. Gene, it appeared, had never let go, and was hanging on desperately. Tony had fallen almost on us. I grabbed him by an arm.

The waves were flinging us about, pulling at our legs as if with hands. The raft was upside down.

Never letting go our handholds, we grouped ourselves together and at an unspoken signal heaved the raft upward, trying to keep our grasp on the upended gunwale at the same time. A comber thundered down and almost tore it from our grip.

Quickly, before the next wave came, we pushed upward again. The light raft went over this time, and I worked my way to the opposite side to hold it down while the boys climbed in.

For a few minutes we rested, panting, each with an arm locked across a thwart in case we tipped again. The blood was pounding in my temples. I couldn't breathe without pain.

My chest and torso ached, and, as I have explained before, I was perpetually half numb from the hips down. With a supreme effort of will I raised my head and rolled my body over so that I faced upward across the raft. The boys were lying still, heads down, twisted, inert, like dead men except for their loud and broken gasps for air.

I noted automatically that our weight was not all on one side, which seemed to be our greatest peril. The raft was riding evenly; although it pitched and swerved in continual jerky motion, the bottom was holding to the water. So I sank my head upon my breast and rested.

How long we lay this way I don't remember. I know that we were not in full possession of our minds. When I myself began to think again, it frightened me to realize how easily I slipped away.

I found myself as if awakened by a noise I half remembered from a dream. The boys were sitting up, revived but not disposed to talk. I tried to straighten on my haunches, and then the situation struck me like a blow.

All our clothes were lost—every thread and stitch, except, ridiculously, a police whistle that hung by a cord around my neck.

Now on this day, our thirty-third in the raft, our position was desperate. Since we had lost even my last inadequate makeshift sea anchor, we had no means whatever of controlling our progress. From now on we would go where the wind sent us, and that might mean that we would float until the rubber boat finally rotted and burst. We had lost all our rags, so had no way of catching drinking water beyond what might lie in the bottom of the raft. We had nothing for bailing except our hands. We had one shoe-paddle left, two wallets which had somehow become wedged in the front of the raft, and my police whistle. I did not see how we could make any use of these.

The worst blow of all was the loss of all our clothes, and the piece of fabric we had been using to shade our heads. From now on we were entirely unprotected against the equatorial sun, and it was midsummer. We knew, too well, what the sun was going to do to us.

We thought we were in the vicinity of islands, but with no charts and no navigation instruments we could not be positive as to our position. As far as we could be sure, we might still be a thousand miles from land. Now we would never know where we were unless we actually sighted an island.

This was the one time during the entire trip that I was truly disheartened. In fact, I was just about ready to give up. I knew that the end of our voyage was very near; we must make an island in a day or two, or die.

Tony shared my gloom. He considered going over the side; it would be a quick death, without the torture that the sun had in store. But he changed his mind.

"We've come this far," he argued, "and by God we'll go on!"

Sitting glumly about the boat, discouraged, the three of us considered all the possibilities.

Loss of our clothes, our only shelter, seemed like a mighty hard blow for us to take at this stage of the game, after we had worked and schemed for so long to save ourselves.

The thought of what we had already gone through—that clinched the argument. We all agreed that neither this nor any other disaster which could overtake us now was sufficient reason for giving up the fight we had been making. Again we shook hands all around, and vowed we'd go on.

It was another night of chilling showers. We huddled together in the bottom of the raft, and talked a great deal to keep up our spirits, pursuing any subject that came into our minds.

After every shower we scooped out most of the water with our hands, and lay down again to keep warm. It took just about all our courage to stay cheerful. We knew that the end of our voyage was coming soon, one way or the other.

We were glad to see daylight in the morning. Although we knew we were going to be badly burned when the sun came overhead, we were anxious to warm ourselves. I tried to keep from thinking about what the sun was going to do to us later in the day. I preferred to let that worry come when it must.

The sun did not emerge from behind the clouds until about 8:30 o'clock in the morning. When it did, I stretched out on the forward thwart to warm myself and rest. Tony lay in the bottom, while Aldrich sat up, watching.

By this time, I thought, the navy must have given us up for dead. I learned later that this was true. I would have preferred another end, but this morning I let the sailor's fatalism have its play. I got to thinking over my past life. I had left home at the age of seventeen, worked my way around the country for a year at various jobs, then joined the navy. My older brother had been in the navy during the First World War, as they call it now.

I envied my older brother. I had been reared in a typical midwestern farm family, and the adventure of going to far places in uniform appealed to me. I tried several times to enlist, but first I was too young, then too thin, to make the grade. As I grew I put on weight, and finally got in at nineteen. I had no idea then of making the navy my career; I just wanted to serve a "hitch" for the experience.

That was twenty-two years ago. The navy had been good to me, and I was glad to die in the service, the warsman's way, if die I must.

I scooped up a bit of the indigo sea in my palm, and drank it. Toward the end I could stand a bit of sea water; my system seemed to be in need of salt. I blamed the sun for this.

I had shed two sets of skin prior to the time we lost our clothes. I was in the process of building a new set now, and the tender underskin was still exposed. Lying there entirely unprotected, I began to smart all over my body. My loins and midriff, which had never been sunburned before in all my life, turned scarlet in a half hour. Before the day was over this part of me looked as if it had been seared with a red-hot iron. The rest of my body, which had been protected somewhat by my rotting clothes, burned almost as severely.

The boys were in the same state. The scalding torture we had felt on our faces, hands, and arms now covered our bodies, every inch. The clouds had rolled away and the sea threw back the glare, so that everywhere we turned there was solid heat. I shifted my position frequently to take all advantage I could of the shade of my own body, and to try to keep from exposing the same area too long, but this did little good. The sun hit us practically all over, all of the time. I felt as if I were on fire. My body will always bear the scars of that cooking.

"Good Lord!" Gene said. "Look at that shark!"

I shaded my aching eyes against the sun, and saw a great black dorsal fin cutting the water a few yards from the boat. It was the largest shark I had ever seen.

He came close to the surface, and I whistled soundlessly when I made out the size of that sinuous, powerful body. I estimate that he was not less than fifteen feet long, and must have weighed upward of a thousand pounds.

"If he hits the boat, it's goodbye," Gene said.

"Don't attract his attention," I whispered.

He cruised about the boat for about twenty minutes, then went away.

The sun began to hit Tony.

He was lying in the bottom of the raft, the back of his hand lying across his eyes. Suddenly he took his hand away, and sat up, listening. He seemed to be looking far off. He smiled slightly.

"Hey, chief," he said softly. "I hear music."

Humor him, and maybe he'll snap out of it, I thought.

"What kind of music, Tony?" I asked casually.

"Beautiful—like a choir of angels!"

He slid back into the bottom of the raft and closed his eyes again, still smiling.

Although we had divided our days into two-hour watches, I was up and vigilant myself most of the time until my eyes began to fail. Now, because of that and my general physical condition, I was forced to let the man on watch take full responsibility for the boat while I conserved my dwindling energy for my own two-hour shift. Thus I lay on the forward thwart this thirty-fourth morning, turning uneasily under the sun so that my body would burn evenly and I would not suffer unnecessarily from overexposure of any one area more than another. Gene was on watch; Tony was lying in the bottom trying to shade his face—his delirium when he heard the music seemed to have passed.

It was about ten o'clock. The sky was hot and clear as a blue flame. The wind was steady, and the boat was rising and falling slowly on long, gentle swells. The sun was just now approaching the fullness of its anger.

We topped a wave, and in that brief instant while we seemed to hang suspended before the long downward slide began, Gene spoke for the first time since taking the watch.

"Chief," he said, "I see a beautiful field of corn."

I didn't even look up. I thought sadly that the boy's mind had finally gone, and I wished he had taken my advice to cover his head when we first went into the raft.

Without moving, I cast my eyes about the sea, but we were in the trough and I saw only the rumpled carpet of waves. It was possible, I said to myself, that Gene was seeing a mirage: the sun does play tricks on you sometimes. At any rate I was not surprised that Gene was affected. There was nothing I could do for him, so I paid no more attention.

After a few minutes, when we had risen to the next crest, he spoke again insistently: "Sure enough, chief!—I see something green in the distance!"

With this statement, so rationally put in his Missouri drawl, it dawned upon me suddenly that perhaps he did see something. I looked hard, but could still see nothing in the tumbling sea. Tony was looking too, but had not spoken. I tried to stand up, and found I couldn't balance on my cramped and crooked legs. I asked the boys to hold me upright.

We stood, the three of us, in the center of the boat, the boys each with one hand against the side and an arm around my waist, holding me erect with their shoulders while I steadied myself with arms around their necks.

We came to the summit of the next large swell. Sure enough, in the distance I could see something green. As Gene had said, it was beautiful. I instantly recognized it as an island, one of the low, verdant atolls of the far South Sea. I let out a hoarse whoop and turned to Gene, tightening my arm about his neck.

"Boy," I said exultantly, "you have won yourself a dinner!"

Tony took a deep breath, and let it go out noisily, trying to repress his joy.

"Well," he said, "thank God—and it's about time."

We were still far off. The island appeared as a low shelf of green—coconut trees, I guessed, and I was right. Chartless, we had no idea what the island was, whether it was inhabited, or whether it was in friend or enemy's hands.

The wind had risen strongly, making long and prominent streaks on the water, which gave me an excellent gauge of the exact wind direction. I took a bearing on the island, compared it with the wind direction, and found that our course of drift was carrying us about ten degrees to the right of the island.

We realized, of course, that this was our God-given chance for refuge, so, weak as we were, we saw nothing for it but to row. I took the port side of the raft, using our one remaining shoe-paddle. Gene and Tony paddled together on the starboard side, using their hands only.

We turned to with a will, rowing across the wind to make up for the distance by which the wind would cause us to miss the island if we simply drifted. In this manner we were able to make about one knot across the wind while we were being driven about five knots downwind.

It was fortunate indeed that we were able to see the island from such a distance. If we had been much closer when we began to row, the wind would have taken us past it because we would not have been able, by our feeble paddling, to compensate sufficiently for the drift.

We rowed all day, exactly across wind at 90 degrees to our sailing direction. I kept watching the island at intervals. We found it better to row facing the stern of the raft, pushing the water behind the boat with a forward sweep of our arms, so I had to stop rowing occasionally and turn to keep my bearing.

At first we thought there was only one island, but as we approached we saw that there were two, with a wide gap of water between. It was easy to make a choice. We took the nearer island.

By one o'clock our progress was visible. The waves were longer and crested in knifelike ridges that curled and broke in a thunderous gush of white foam. There was danger of our tipping over any time one of these breakers got behind us, but, while they were in front, the spray blowing backward enabled me to judge the wind exactly.

Suddenly Tony let out a screech. His hand flew out of the water and over his head as if jerked by a string. He half turned, holding the hand tenderly.

"Chief, a shark hit my hand," he yelled, his voice shaking slightly.

Gene and I hardly hesitated in our rowing.

"Did it bite you?" I asked.

"No," he said, looking and testing his fingers.

"Then to hell with it," I said. "Let's go on rowing!"

Without another second's hesitation he jabbed his hand back into the water, deep, and we went on rowing.

As we came up on the island, I thought it couldn't possibly be anything but a desert atoll, although it was a lovely green and apparently stuck up pretty well out of the water. When we came within six or eight miles I saw what I thought was a ledge of rocks above the white beach. I figured then that it must be a volcanic island, and we might find shelter in a cavern. This would also mean that the island was marked on the map, and might be visited—by our own or friendly forces, I hoped. There was still the uncertainty that this might be in the Japanese mandate, and if that was so I could see our doom. However, as long as we were determined to get there, I preferred to think that it was uninhabited.

The closer we approached, the better the island looked to me. I could see two or three especially tall trees that towered above the others. We wondered if they might be coconut trees, but that seemed too much to hope. Until I was close enough to identify them honestly as palms, I didn't dare believe they were.

I was sure, at any rate, that there would be lots of birds on the island, which meant eggs and possibly young birds that we could capture. I thought too that there might be mussels, and possibly fish in abundance that we would rig spears to catch.

Aldrich's eyes were still in good condition. As we came in closer, perhaps within three miles of the curving beach, he turned and took a long look. We had seen by this time that the island was not so high as we had thought at first.

"Chief," Gene said, "those aren't rocks on the beach. They're shacks."

I looked again, and again I decided they were rocks.

"Wishful thinking, Gene," I said. "If they were shacks it would mean that the island is inhabited. They still look like rocks to me."

Tony had his revenge.

"Hell with the rocks," he said. "Row!"

The waves were very high, and we could see the island only when we came to a crest; when we dipped to the valley of the waves, the island sank from sight. The buoyant raft rode the roughening sea so easily that it appeared as if the island and not we were rising and falling steeply in an even rhythm, while the raft lay perfectly still.

When we were about a mile from the island I saw from the wind streaks and blowing foam that we were directly upwind, and that the stiff breeze would land us at the center of the beach without assistance.

"Okay, boys," I said. "We can knock off the rowing."

We stopped and turned about, to watch our progress. We were completely exhausted, I know now. We had been rowing all day on will power alone, but we were so intent on reaching this island that we didn't realize our terrible weakness, and rose above it.

"Well," Gene said joyfully, "are they shacks or rocks?"

He was right. They were shacks.

From now on it was just a matter of drifting in the wind. I kept a close eye on the bearings by the wind streaks, to be sure that we hit the beach.

We became conscious of a steady, sullen thunder that seemed to grow in volume. I realized after a moment that it was surf breaking over a barrier reef, and I feared we were in for a little trouble. As we drifted closer I was able to see, and immediately gave the order to square away for a possible tip-over.

I had seen natives bring outrigger canoes over heavy surf in Hawaii, but those breakers were not nearly so murderous as these appeared. The nearer we approached the reef, the larger the breakers looked. I soon saw that our eyes were not deceiving us. These waves were building up characteristically in rows one behind the other, each coming to its turn as leader of the irresistible flow to shore.

The leading wave gained swiftly in height and speed as the wall of coral dammed the powerful tide that pushed against it, and the rushing tons of water found their only outlet upward. When the wave reached the reef it was about thirty feet high. The crest began to curl dangerously, seemed to hesitate the merest fraction of a second, then fell forward over the natural dam. There was a roar like a cannon shot as the mass of water smashed, and a great burst of foam spewed forward in a straight line of boiling white which diminished in size but held its form until it washed high on the beach, far ahead.

These rows of waves were building behind us now. Our only hope was to paddle over the reef ahead of the breaker—that is, in the interval between two waves.

We were fortunate enough to pass over the reef at the one brief instant when the surf was not breaking. We could have been dashed against the rocky bottom, or the ledge itself, if we had been caught in that wild churning of forces when the breaker crashes from its great height. As it was, we did not come out unscathed.

The breaker caught the raft behind. The heavy blow of the rushing foam against the stern sped us up the sloping rear of the smaller, shoreward-speeding wave ahead. Instead of sliding down its front, we shot straight out into the air.

The raft turned a complete flip-flop. When we saw it next it was speeding landward like a chip before the surf. The three of us were in the water.

I can remember spinning head over heels three or four times, and raking along the floor of the sea. Whether it was sand or rock I don't know, but afterward I discovered that a patch of skin about six inches in diameter had been scraped from the center of my back. Gene and Tony, I learned, were going through exactly the same thing. Tony said this was the first time he had ever had his eyes open underwater.

"Everything was green and pretty," he said.

After a threshing by the water that left me only half conscious, I found myself sitting on a flat ledge of coral rock. The raft, I saw, was upside down again and was heading for the beach about a hundred yards away from me. Gene and I were close together, and we still had about three hundred yards to go to reach solid ground. Tony was about fifty yards behind us.

None of us was able to stand. I tried to raise myself on my feet, but couldn't get my balance. Then I found that the current was skidding me along on my bottom. Gene, even with me and to my right, also let himself drift and we kept abreast.

I heard a call for help, and looked back. It was Tony. Being unable to swim, he thought he was going to drown. When I waved and yelled, he realized he was out of danger, and thenceforth scooted along like Gene and me. I imagine things had happened so fast that when Tony got into shallow water he didn't realize it, and possibly he was hollering as a nervous reaction from the terrific beating his shrunken body had taken in the surf.

We caught the boat at the very edge of the beach, and grabbed the anchor line. Crawling on all fours, we dragged ourselves from the last persistent clutch of the sea, and somehow hauled the raft behind us.

We tried to stand upon our feet, but couldn't. We were terribly dizzy from exhaustion; the whole world seemed to be spinning around us. We lay on the beach together, faintly conscious of the broken coral that was cutting our flaming, sunburned flesh as our bodies jerked in the effort to breathe.

When I was able to look about, the sun was low.

A short distance away several rotting piles had been driven into the sand, evidently placed there by someone for tying up boats. The three of us took hold of the anchor line, dragging the raft with one hand while with the other we pulled ourselves painfully, inch by inch, over the jagged coral to the row of wooden stakes. I felt each of these ancient poles, selecting the one that was most solid. We tied the boat to that.

There were several thatched huts a few yards from where we lay.

Grasping one of the pilings with both hands, I pulled myself to my knees.

"Boys," I said, "you know there may be Japs here waiting for us."

They raised their heads and nodded.

I looked at each one closely. They were gazing steadily into my eyes. Tony gestured toward the police whistle, still on a cord about my neck.

"If we have to scatter," he suggested calmly, "two blasts on the whistle will be the signal to meet wherever you are."

It was agreed.

We were too weak to try to find food, so we decided to rest for the night in one of the shacks.

I chose three long pieces of driftwood lying about that were best suited to my purpose, and handed one to each.

"If there are Japs on this island," I said, "they'll not see an American sailor crawl. We'll stand, and march, and make them shoot us down, like men-o'-warsmen."

Using the sticks of driftwood as canes to support us, we got on our feet. Three abreast then, myself in the middle, we walked to the nearest hut and went in.

from In Granma's Wake:
Girl Stella's Voyage to Cuba
by Frank Mulville

In 1968, Frank Mulville sailed from England to Cuba in his beloved Girl Stella, a 40-foot gaff-rigged ketch. His crew included his wife Celia Mulville, their young sons Adrian and Patrick, and their friend Dick Morris, who served as mate. Girl Stella left Cuba on March 15, 1969, after a ten-week stay, and the crew decided to visit the Azores on their way home. The decision was a mistake—and more mistakes followed.

A t 15.05 I spied LAND and earned 10 shillings for it. It was Flores in the Azores. Before dark it was abeam. Very high and rocky. Adrian's log   22nd April

The stars came out one by one, the seas began to moderate surprisingly quickly as the wind eased and the next day a bright clear sun made everything blue and white and warm. We matched the decreasing wind with more sail, setting jib, mizzen and finally the mains'l to keep Girl Stella moving at top speed. The cabin and all our wet clothes soon dried out, the boys went back to their morning and afternoon trick at the wheel and in no more than a day we were back in our easy-going routine as if nothing had ever disturbed it. I found by my sights that we had been taken a fair bit to the south but we had made fine progress through the gale. We were eight days out from Bermuda and well over half way to the Azores. The passage was going well—ten days on from the Azores should see us in the English Channel.

Being to the southward of our course had put the Azores almost in line between us and home. 'Of course we'll go in,' Patrick said, 'it will be nice to get a run ashore in a brand new island.' I was doubtful. 'Wouldn't it be better to go straight on home?' Celia and Adrian agreed. 'Let's get home,' Adrian said, 'we'll be late for school—and anyway I want to see the dog.' Dick, if anything, seemed to be in favour of seeing the Azores. 'I must say I'd like to see the whaling boats,' he said. The argument kept us amused for days. 'Look here Daddy.' Patrick said, 'You can't go right past these lovely islands and not go in. That's extremism— it's just eccentric. When will we ever get a chance to see the Azores again? Haven't you seen enough sea? This is just crazy.' In the end I compromised. If we just went in to Flores, the most northerly of the islands, and stayed for a short time, two days at the outside, it wouldn't waste much time or take us far out of our way. We studied the Pilot book. Flores had a harbour of sorts although it didn't say much about it. It was a whaling island—the last place in the world, I believe, where whales are still hunted with pulling boats using hand harpoons. If the whaling boats used the island there was no reason why we should not and the port of Santa Cruz was on the lee side and should be well sheltered. 'After all,' Patrick said, 'Sir Richard Grenville lay in Flores of the Azores, why shouldn't we?' 'All right—we'll go into Flores. But two days only,' I decided. 'We'll fill up with water,' Celia said, 'and get some fresh vegetables.'

It was a bad decision. I knew it was a bad decision because a little voice inside me told me so—a decision dictated not by considerations of careful seamanship and what the Pilot book would call 'A proper regard for the safety of the vessel', but by nothing more tangible than a passing fancy—a set of frail desires. It was trusting to luck instead of careful planning. Once embarked on, it led inexorably on to other decisions, taken one by one and in themselves innocent enough, which built themselves up to produce a misfortune which, to our small world, was a disaster.

The wind worked its way round to the south-west as we got closer to Flores and the glass went down slightly—nothing to worry about, but if it was going to blow a gale from the south-west it would be just as well to be safely tucked away in the lee of a high island. There is no radio beacon on Flores and, unlike any other of our major landfalls of the voyage, I would have to rely completely on my sextant. Flores is not a big island, perhaps half as long as the Isle of Wight, and there was no other island within a hundred and thirty miles of it except Corvo—a very small island immediately to the north-east. I supplemented my sun observations with star sights in the morning and confidently pronounced an E.T.A. 'You'll see it at half past two this afternoon, lying on the port bow and there's ten shillings for the first boy to sight land.' It was Tuesday, April 22nd and we had covered 1,700 miles in thirteen days—an average speed of over five knots; At two o'clock Adrian sighted the island pushing its bulk out of low cloud fine on the port bow.

It took a long time to come up with the southern cape of Flores and it was evening by the time we rounded it and came along the east side of the island towards Santa Cruz—close under great cliffs and mountains that dropped sheer into the Atlantic. White houses high up on the mountainside blinked their lights at us—we could see the gulls wheeling in tight spirals against the sheer rock face and ahead of us the small town of Santa Cruz could just be seen before the sun went behind the mountain and everything was suddenly submerged in darkness. 'What a pity. I thought we'd just get in before dark,' I said to Celia. 'We'll have to hang off till morning—how disappointing,' she said.

We took the sails down off Santa Cruz and just as we were making a neat stow of the mains'l, two bright red leading lights suddenly showed up, one behind the other, showing the way into the harbour. 'Well, what do you think of that?' I said to Dick, 'do you think they switched on the lights specially for us?' 'Perhaps they did. Anyway it must be quite O.K. to go in at night otherwise the leading lights wouldn't be there.' I went below where Celia was. 'They've switched on two beautiful leading lights,' I said, 'I think we'll go in rather than flog about here all night.' 'I think we ought to wait till we can see where we're going,' she said. I consulted Dick again and we overruled her. 'Is everything squared up?—Get the ropes and fenders up and we'll go in,' I said. I knew, deep inside myself, that it was a silly thing to do. The little voice told me so again. 'You're a bloody idiot Mulville,' it said. 'Oh shut your blather— I'm tired—I want a night's sleep.'

When everything was ready to go alongside—the mooring ropes ready, fenders out, side lights lit, boat hook handy, anchor cleared away ready to let go if needed, I put the engine slow ahead and went straight for the leading lights and straight for the black cliff which was all we could see behind them. Soon we could hear the surf pounding against the rocks. 'I don't like it Frank,' Celia said, 'I'm going below.' 'It's not too late to turn back,' the voice said. 'Don't be such a bloody fool.'

'Can you see anything Dick?' I shouted to the fore deck. 'Yes—there's a gap right ahead—starboard a little.' 'Starboard she is.' 'Steady as you go.' 'Steady.' Suddenly we were between the rocks—close on either side. There was no turning now. A swell took us and swept us forward. 'Hard to starboard,' Dick shouted. I spun the wheel, my mouth dry as the bottom of a bird cage. 'There it is—right ahead—put her astern,' Dick shouted.

There was a small stone quay right beside us—a dozen men on it, all shouting at us in Portuguese. The swell was terrific. G. S. was rearing up and down alarmingly. Dick threw a rope, it was made fast and G. S. was pulled in towards the quay. 'We can't lie here,' I shouted to Dick, 'we'll have to get out again.' Just then G. S. grounded on a hard stone bottom. She only touched once, not hard, and I put the engine astern and brought her a few feet along the quay—but it was enough to be unpleasant. 'Anyone speak English?', I shouted. A big man came forward. 'I pilot,' he shouted. 'This harbour no good for you—tide go down—no enough water.' He and two of his friends jumped on board. 'Full astern,' he said. I put the engine astern and opened the throttle. The pilot took the wheel from me. 'Neutral—slow ahead,' he said. We seemed to be surrounded by rocks on all sides and the swell was playing round them, leaping into the air, and crashing down with a noise like a steam train pulling out of a station. The pilot manoeuvred us back and forth—turning G. S. round with great skill as if he had known her ways all his life. 'I don't know how you get in here,' he said, 'no one come in here at night.' 'Then what in Christ's name are the leading lights for?' 'Fishermen,' he said.

It was like the middle of Hampton Court Maze but somehow the pilot got us out, backing and filling and turning until G. S. was clear in the open sea again. The saliva slowly came back to my mouth. 'Give me a drink of water,' I asked Celia whose white face was looking anxiously out of the hatch. 'We take you Porto Piqueran. One mile up coast,' the pilot said, 'You O.K. there.' We motored for a quarter of an hour to the north and then the pilot put G. S.'s head straight for the rocks. 'Don't let him do it,' a voice said. 'Shut up for Christ's sake. I can't tell him his job.'

There were no leading lights here at all—only the black face of the rock. 'No worry,' the pilot said, sensing my apprehension, 'you O.K. here. Quite safe—no swell—I know way.' 'Ça va bien,' one of the other men said, thinking for some reason that I was French and wishing to air his grasp of that language. 'Le Monsieur Pilot—il le connait bien ici.' The pilot was as good as his reputation. He took us straight towards a tower of rock, looming sullenly in the weak light of the stars, then hard to port for a few yards, then to starboard and to port again until suddenly, we were in a small cove—a cleft in the rocks no more than sixty feet across but calm and still. 'Let go anchor. Now we tie you up.'

The pilot and his helpers climbed into our dinghy and ran out ropes to the rocks. They jumped nimbly ashore and fastened every long rope we had in the ship—three on each side. 'Best ropes forward,' the pilot said, 'bad ropes aft. Wind come from west,' he said pointing to the sky where the clouds were racing towards England. 'Always strong wind from west here.' I thought for a moment while they were working on the ropes. 'Pilot,' I said, 'suppose we have to go out quickly. Would it not be better to turn her round, so she's facing the sea?' 'No,' he said, 'strong wind from west—always face strong wind—best ropes forward.' The little person inside me said 'Make him turn her round you weak idiot—this may be a trap.' 'Stop your bloody nagging.'

They tied us up thoroughly, made sure that everything was fast and strong and then they came down to the cabin and we gave them a drink. 'By God—you lucky get out Santa Cruz,' the pilot laughed. 'No ship ever come there at night before. You fine here—you sleep sound.' We put them ashore in the dinghy to a stone quay with a flight of steps hewn out of the rock face and they went off home. 'See you in the morning. You sleep O.K.'

We did sleep sound. G. S. lay as quiet as if she were in Bradwell Creek. The glass was dropping again and it was already blowing a gale from the south-west but Porto Piqueran was quite detached from the gale—the only evidence of wind was the racing clouds far up above and an occasional down draught which would sometimes break away from the body of the gale and find its way like some spent outrider round the mountain and down towards Porto Piqueran where it would hurl the last of its dissipated energy at the top of G. S.'s mast, stirring the burgee forty feet up, making a faint moaning sound and then dissolving into the night. Dick laughed, 'This is a hurricane hole all right—there isn't enough wind in here to lift a tart's skirt.' 'Don't laugh too soon,' the little voice said to me as I went to sleep.

Adrian was up early the next morning. 'I'm going ashore to explore.' 'No—you'll have to wait a bit—we haven't seen the Customs and Immigration yet.' 'Customs and Immigration—in this place? It isn't big enough.' 'Don't you believe it—this is Portugal.' In the daylight we could see the place we found ourselves in. On all sides except one we were surrounded by cliffs of rock about fifty feet high. Ahead the mountain peeped over the top of the cliff and on our right the stone steps where the pilot and his gang had gone ashore led up to a small quay. Astern of us was the sea, a line of vicious rocks spread across the entrance to the cove in a semi-circle, broken only by the narrow and winding channel through which the pilot had brought us.

In the middle of our breakfast there was a shout from the quay and one of the boys ferried our visitors on board in the dinghy. It was the Customs Officer with two policemen. The Customs man was very tall with big, pale eyes, uneven yellow teeth and large floppy ears. His sallow complexion was covered with a stubble left over from his weekly shave on Sunday—it was now Wednesday morning. He was dressed in a long coat—one expected to see a sabre under it but instead there was a revolver in a leather holster. I spoke in Spanish and he in Portuguese—

we managed to understand one another quite well. When he heard we had been to Cuba he sucked his teeth. 'Cuba—Communista?' he said. He mumbled something to his two colleagues and together they searched the ship, spending many minutes poring over the titles of our Spanish books and looking earnestly at the picture of Che in the fo'c'sle. 'Books, books, too many books!' he said. 'We don't like those books in Portugal. You come ashore with me—we visit International Police.'

I gathered all our passports, took Adrian for company and moral support and we all went ashore. There was a long stone ramp leading from the quay up to the top of the cliff where there was a whaling factory with a tall chimney and behind it a cottage. A taxi was waiting and somehow we all piled in and drove a mile to the town of Santa Cruz— a quaint village with clean windswept streets of pastel houses, a small square and a church looking out over the sea. The church had an enormous stone façade, picked out in black and white with imposing bells and a studded door. Behind the façade, the building of the church itself was a modest enough erection.

We first went to the Customs building beside the quay where copious lists and declarations were made out and signed. Adrian and I saw through the window the tiny harbour of Santa Cruz—a stone quay with an ancient steam crane on it, a ramp for hauling out boats and the tortuous entrance between savage rocks which we had somehow negotiated. Next we were taken to the police where our passports were scrutinised. The police wanted to keep our passports until we sailed—a custom in Portugal—but I refused to let them out of my hand and we wrangled and argued for some time before I was allowed to keep them. From the police we went to the Captain of the Port—obviously a very important man in Flores—where there were more papers, more questions and more arguments over passports and finally we went to an office in the square which housed the International Police. This official also wanted to keep our passports—I only resisted his demands with difficulty. 'The wind might change in the night,' I said. 'We might want to go out at a moment's notice. We must have our passports.' We took the taxi back to Porto Piqueran, back on board to finish our breakfast. 'Officials and police seem to outnumber ordinary citizens by about two to one,' I said to Celia, 'and they all have rubber stamps,' added Adrian. We noticed that a policeman had taken up guard duty on the quay.

Later in the morning Celia and I went shopping in Santa Cruz. There wasn't much to be had—a few vegetables, cheese, butter and fresh bread. By the harbour we met our friend the pilot and Carlo who worked on the ferries which take passengers and livestock to and from the ship which calls at the island once every two weeks and is their only link with the rest of the world. There is a French air base on Flores which is supposed to be something to do with the 'Force de Frappe', and a new French hotel where the staff of the base live, surrounded by a new estate of prefabricated bungalows. The pilot told us the French were not very well liked on the island. They kept themselves to themselves, imported all their needs by air and had done nothing to raise the standard of poverty of the island. 'All the young men want to get away from Flores,' the pilot said, 'there is nothing for a young man here except hard work.'

The pilot showed us the Flores whaling boats, stored in a shed near the harbour and fitted out ready for the whaling season which would start on May 1st. The boats and equipment are superb. Long, narrow pulling boats of forty feet and upwards they are manned by ten oars-men using beautifully fashioned sweeps. They have powerful samson posts fore and aft, grooved from surging the rope when a harpooned whale is pulling them at up to eight knots. The harpoons themselves and ancillary staves and spikes, are beautifully made of ash with hand-forged iron tips. The boats stand by at Porto Piqueran and Santa Cruz in the season and look-outs for whales are posted on high points round the islands. When the whales are sighted, the direction and dis-tance of the prey is signalled to the boats far below by a complex sys-tem of rocket and explosive signals. The boats go out in search of a kill—the harpoons are hurled by hand. The whale is then towed back to Porto Piqueran where it is hauled ashore on the steep ramp and heaved up to the factory, various disembowelling operations being done on the way. Blubber is extracted and the export of whale oil is a valuable source of income to the island. The pilot gave each of us a whale's tooth, the size of a large paperweight. There was a small cafe on the quay where we contracted to have dinner—the proprietor said he would find us a lobster—and we invited the pilot to join us.

Flores is a primitive island—a throw back to a past age. They plough with oxen dragging wooden ploughs—the donkey carts have solid wooden wheels and are constructed without nails or screws—the fastenings are all wooden pegs. The peasants work small plots of land which they rent from landlords who live in Portugal. When the weather is fine the fishermen go out for lobster round the rocks and caverns on the east side of the island. Some of the caverns can be followed in under the black cliffs for a quarter of a mile. The island is densely wooded and quite unsophisticated—one village in the north has no road. Waterfalls cascade down to the sea, wild hydrangeas cover the hedges and the small stone walled fields are carpeted with flowers. Along the coasts there are views of wild primitive beauty—the cliffs have formed themselves into fantastic figurations. The sea worries away at the coast line and the great Atlantic waves beat at it with a force which grows up over 2,000 miles of ocean. It is as if the sea considers this lonely island an interloper—an affront to its dignity—and is bent on smashing it out of its path. Even on a calm day on the lee side of the island the sea has a quality of fretfulness as it deliberately washes round the rocks and sucks at the foreshore.

The boys explored the rocks round Porto Piqueran in the afternoon while Dick and I slept and Celia did her washing. In the evening Antonio, the taxi driver who had become a firm friend, came and fetched us to the little café. We were a big party—a crowd of fishermen and longshoremen had become our comrades for an evening's talk. The place had no pretensions but the lobster was incomparable. The wine flowed round the table, bottle following bottle in a steady procedure of consumption. 'How is it in Cuba?' 'Do the people have food—clothing—work?' 'Do they pay rent for their land? Here, we do not own the land—we pay rent—rent to some aristocrat in Portugal who never comes here—has never seen Flores. Here there is nothing—not even schooling after twelve years of age. If we want to send our children to school we must pay for it—the people here have no money to send their children away to school—half of them can't read or write. The officials and the police grow fat but the people are poor.' One of them went to the door and looked out. 'Here the police are swine. There are so many officials and so many laws that a man can't live without breaking them. The police must always be kept fat or there is trouble. Everything we say is taken note of. The priests get stories from the women and soon the police know more about our lives than we know ourselves. Every young man in Flores wants to get away—but it is difficult. You must have a permit and you must have money.' We told them that in Cuba there was work for everyone, schooling for all children and no rents. 'They tell us lies—lies day and night. They say Castro is an anti-Christ and the people are slaves and you come here and tell us that they pay no rent! How can they be slaves if they pay no rent?'

Antonio came for us at eleven, by which time everyone in Flores is asleep, and took us back to Porto Piqueran. We walked down the whale ramp to find *G. S.* lying peacefully at her moorings—gently moving up and down on the easy swell and sometimes lifting one or other of her ropes out of the water. The wind had dropped although it was still overcast. It was very quiet in Porto Piqueran—even the policeman had gone—it was possible to see no human habitation, no lights, no people except ourselves—there was only the slip-slopping of the lazy waves, the occasional wild cry of a gull and the peaceful rustling that a boat makes in a quiet place—like a soft walker through the dead leaves of the forest floor. 'Watch it,' the voice said.

'This is the bay about 1 mile North of Santa Cruz das Flores that we lost "Girl Stella" in. It is an easy thing to do, to lose a boat.'
Patrick's log   *24th April*

Dick and I checked carefully round the deck before we went to bed. There was nothing amiss. The two strongest warps we had were out over the bow, each made fast to a rock. On the starboard side there was a rope from aft to a ring bolt let into the rock by the steps and another to a stone bollard at the corner of the quay. On the port side the longest rope led from aft to a big rock on the south side of the cove and yet another from amidships. It was something of a work of art. 'If you got out your crochet needles you could make us a Balaclava out of this lot,' I had remarked to Celia. In addition to her ropes the anchor was down although I doubted whether it was doing any good as the bottom was hard and it had not been let go far enough out to be effective. Dick had been round in the day checking that the ropes were not chafing against the rocks and had served a couple of them with rope-yarns. 'I reckon she'll do,' I said to Dick and we went to bed.

A boat is always there—you never stop worrying about her whether you are aboard or ashore—she is always a presence in the mind and you're conscious of her at all times. She may be laid up in some safe berth for the winter or hauled out of the water in a yard, but wherever you may be—at home in your virtuous bed or roistering in some gay spot, a chorus girl on each knee and the air thick with flying champagne corks, a part of your consciousness is always reserved. When the wind moans round the eaves of the house it has a special significance and you check off in your mind, one by one, the possible sources of danger. Men lie awake worrying about their bank balances, their waist-lines, their wives, mistresses actual or potential but sailors worry about boats.

A boat is something more than an ingenious arrangement of wood and copper and iron—it has a soul, a personality, eccentricities of behaviour that are endearing. It becomes part of a person, colouring his whole life with a romance that is unknown to those who do not understand a way of life connected with boats. The older a boat becomes the stronger the power. It gains in stature with each new experience—people look at boats with wonder and say 'She's been to the South Seas,' or 'She's just back from the North Cape' and the boat takes on a reputation in excess of that of its owner. *Girl Stella* had become a very real part of our lives— we each of us loved her with a deep respect. Over the expanses of the ocean we had come to know her true worth—an affection for her had ripened into a bond of mutual sympathy and understanding. We had come to know what she would do and what she would not, what pleased her and what caused her discontent. She repaid our understanding handsomely with the generous breadth and scope of her goodwill towards us. We had asked a lot of her and she had never for a moment failed to give us everything she had and more besides.

I slept badly, frequently waking and listening. At two a.m. it began to rain, softly at first and then more heavily so that I could hear the drips coursing off the furled mains'l and drumming on the cabin top. At four a.m. I heard a slight bump and wondered what it was—then I heard it again and I knew what it was. It was the dinghy bumping against the stern. I froze in a cold sweat. If the dinghy was bumping against the stern, the wind must have changed. I got up, put oilskins on over my pyjamas and went on deck. It was cold—the temperature had dropped three or four degrees—it was pelting with rain and a light breeze was blowing from east by north—straight into the cove of Porto Piqueran.

I undid the dinghy, took the painter round the side deck and fastened it off the bow where it streamed out clear. I went back to the cabin, got dressed and called Dick. I tapped the glass and it gave a small convulsion—downwards. 'Dick—the wind's changed. We'll have to get out of here quick. The glass is dropping. We can't stay here in an easterly wind.' Dick got up and put his head out of the hatch. The rain was pouring down and it was as black as a cow's inside. I believe he thought I was over-nervous—exaggerating. 'We can't do much in this,' he said, 'if we did manage to get her untied and turned round—we'd never get her out through that channel in this blackness. All we can do is wait till morning and then have another look at it.' He went back to bed and was soon snoring peacefully.

The little voice said 'Get him up—start work—now.' 'Shut up—he's right—you can't see your hand in front of you—how the hell can we go to sea in this?' I walked round the deck. There was more swell now and G. S. was beginning to buck up and down—snatching at her ropes so that sometimes the after ones came right out of the water. The forward ropes—the strong nylon warps—were quite slack.

I went down to the cabin, sat at the table and tried to read. The volume of Cuban poetry that Pablo had given Celia in Habana was open. I turned it to Pablo's own verse.

> 'The compass of the Universe may falter,
> Warping spheres that never see their day bring
> > forth planets.
> And tools and grain and words riddled with
> > indolence
> Come to rest in some indifferent corner.
> Do not reach your brain over what seems alien
> Or pass so many sleepless nights.
> Leave off torturing the laws of chance—they also
> > play their part.
> Here no juniper is growing, no sycamore, no
> > cassia,
> Here is the growth of stone
> According us its dominions—its avid dominions.'

I made myself a cup of coffee and sat with the mug warming my hands and the steam wreathing round my face. It all seemed relevant. 'Come to rest in some indifferent corner', and 'The growth of stone—according us its avid dominions' and 'Leave off torturing the laws of chance'. 'That's just what you're doing—torturing the laws of chance,' the little voice said.

I went on deck again. The wind was beginning to increase, a heavy swell was now running and small white waves were beginning to overlay it. The rain had increased and was now slanting with the wind and driving into the cove. *Girl Stella* was beginning to pitch and jerk at the two stern ropes with alarming force. Very slowly and reluctantly it was beginning to get light. I went below and shook Dick. 'Come on—not a minute to waste—it's beginning to get light.' I tapped the glass again and again it dropped.

It seemed an age before Dick was dressed in his oilskins and on deck. 'First we'll get the anchor up. It's doing no good there and it will only hamper us. Then we'll let go the head lines—leave them in the water—they'll drift to leeward and we'll come back for them later. Then we'll go astern on the engine and let her swing round on one of the stern lines.' We set to work. It was a relief to have ended the dreadful inactivity of the last two hours. As the anchor began to come up, Celia woke and put her head out through the hatch. 'What's happening?' 'We're going to get out of here—look at the weather—we're turning her round. Better get the boys up.' In minutes the boys were up on deck in their oilskins and Celia was dressed.

The anchor came home easily and I started the engine. We cast off the head lines and prepared another line which would take the strain after we had turned, passing it round the bow so that we could fasten it to the stem line to starboard, which would then become the head line to port. Now the wind was howling with real ferocity—increasing every minute. The swell had become dangerous and was slapping against G. S.'s blunt stern and sending little columns of spray into the mizzen shrouds. I moved the dinghy painter from the bow to the stern and the boat lay alongside, leaping up and down and banging against the top sides.

We were almost ready when there was a twang like someone plucking a violin string. I looked up and saw that the stern line on which we were relying, had received one jerk too many. It had snapped in the middle and the inboard end was flying back towards the boat like a piece of elastic. G. S. immediately began to move towards the rocks on her port side. I jumped into the cockpit, slammed the engine into reverse, gave her full throttle, and put the rudder hard to starboard. She began to pick up. 'Let go the port stern line,' I yelled to Dick. He began to throw the rope off the cleat. 'Throw it well clear—she'll come.' The engine vibrated and thundered—the spray over the stern drove in our faces—the wind battered our senses but she was coming astern. 'Good old girl,' I muttered, 'we'll get you out.'

Then the engine stopped—suddenly and irrevocably—the bare end of the broken line wound a dozen times round the propeller. 'Now you're in trouble,' the little voice said.

G. S. began to drift inexorably towards the rocks—there was nothing to stop her—no ropes on the starboard side and no engine. 'Fenders, over here, quick,' I shouted to the boys and Celia. 'Fend her off as best you can. I'll go over with another rope,' I shouted to Dick. There was one more rope long enough to reach the shore, still in the fo'c'sle locker. The top of the locker was covered with toys and books belonging to the boys and with Patrick's accordion. I threw them off in a pile on the floor and brought the bare end up through the fo'c'sle hatch. 'Celia,' I shouted, 'pay it out to me as I go in the dinghy.' As I got over the side into the *Starling* I felt G. S. strike the rocks—surprisingly gently, I thought. Perhaps it was a smooth ledge and they would be able to cushion her with fenders until we got another rope out. I rowed desperately towards the shore, the end of the rope wound round the after thwart of the dinghy. The swell was washing violently against the stone steps. I could see the ring-bolt but I couldn't reach it—as soon as the dinghy got in close it would surge up on a swell, strike the slippery surface of the steps and plunge back. I took my trousers and my shirt off, plunged into the sea with the end of the rope, upsetting the dinghy as I jumped out of it, and tried to clamber up the steps. But there was nothing to grasp and three times the weight of the rope pulled me back. With a last effort I managed to roll myself over onto the steps, reach up and keep my balance until I was able to grasp the ring. 'All fast,' I shouted to Celia. I swam back on board and clambered up over the bobstay. It was bitterly cold.

Dick and I took the rope to the winch and began to heave. The strain came on the rope and her head began to come round clear of the rocks but she had moved ahead slightly and the rocks under her stern had shifted their position to right aft, under the turn of the bilge, and begun to do real damage. They were too far below the water-line for the fenders to be of any use. Then she stopped coming. The rope was tight but something was preventing her from moving forward. Dick went aft to look. 'She's all tied up aft,' he reported, 'every bloody rope in the place is tied up round the propeller and they're all bar tight.' I looked over the stern. It was daylight now and I could see a tangle of ropes bunched up round the propeller. 'I'll cut them free.'

Dick gave me his razor sharp knife and I jumped over the side again. I dived and saw that at least two ropes had somehow got themselves into the tangle—I managed to cut one and came up for breath. *G. S.'s* stern was just above me, the swells lifting it and allowing it to settle back on the rock with all the force of her great weight. I could hear the rock cutting into her skin—the unmistakable cracking sound of timbers shattering under blows of irresistible force. I knew then that she was done for.

I dived and cut the other rope, swam round to the bob-stay with difficulty in the heavy swell and dragged myself on board. Dick and I wound furiously on the winch—she moved a little further and then as the swells came more on her beam, she lifted and crashed down with an awe-inspiring crunch. She would move no more. As I went aft Celia was working the hand pump and Patrick jumped into the engine room and switched on the electric pump. Adrian came up out of the saloon and I heard him say to Celia in a quiet voice, 'Mummy, I don't wish to alarm you but the cabin's full of water.' 'It's all over,' I said to Celia, 'everybody get into life jackets. We'll have to swim for it.'

Celia and I went below. The water was knee-deep on the cabin floor and was rising as we watched. She was still bumping and every time she hit the rock we could hear the heavy frames splitting, the timbers crumbling. I looked at Celia. Her face was grey, her hair hanging in rat tails, and she had an expression of unimpeded sadness. We stood for a moment among the ruin. The ingredients of our lives were swilling backwards and forwards across the cabin floor, soon to be swallowed by the sea. Books given to us by the Cubans, their pages open and eager, as if they would convert the ocean to revolution, Adrian's recorder, clothes, an orange, the cribbage board, the kettle, a pair of chart rulers, rolls of film, my hat, Celia's glasses case—objects which had somehow jumped out of their context to give mocking offence. The ordered symmetry of our lives was torn apart and scattered—haphazard and suddenly meaningless.

I could see in Celia's face that she had reached the end of a long journey. *Girl Stella* was a precious thing to her—something that was being thrown away in front of her eyes. The years of struggle with the sea were coming to an end—the pinnacles of achievement, the harrowing crises, the light-hearted joys and the endless discomforts had slowly spiralled upwards as we had progressed from adventure to adventure. Now they had reached an explosive zenith and for her there could be no going on. I knew in that moment that she would never come sailing with me again. I had at last betrayed her trust—forfeited her confidence in me. Before, we had always come through—snatched victory out of disaster—but now she was facing a fundamental confrontation of truth. I put my hand in hers—pleading for a glance of sympathy. It was cold and clammy with sweat.

Celia passed the life jackets up the hatch to Dick and then she gathered a plastic bag and put in it the log books—the ship's, the children's and her own—and a few oddments. I found myself unable to think—I was almost insensible with cold. I grabbed my wallet and a book of traveller's cheques, the last of our money, and stuffed them into the bag. I took one last look—the clock and the barometer shining on the bulkhead, the cabin stove, its doors swung open and the water ebbing and flowing through the grate, the lamp swinging unevenly with a stunted motion, and floating lazily across the floor, G. S.'s document box, *Girl Stella*—Penzance, scrolled on the lid.

On deck the boys were calmly putting on their life jackets. I bent down to help Patrick with the lacings. 'This is the end, Daddy,' he said quietly, 'the end of *Girl Stella*—poor, poor G. S.' Now she had settled deep in the water and her motion had suddenly become sickening. She had lost her liveliness and when she rolled to the swell it was with a slow, tired lurch. Her stability, the quick sense of recovery, the responsiveness that she always had, was gone. 'Quick. She may turn turtle—we must get off. I'll go first, then boys, then you Celia and Dick last. Grab the rope and pull yourselves along it. I'll help you up the steps.'

I jumped into the sea, found the rope and shouted back 'Come on Pad—jump.' Patrick hesitated for a moment and then his body came flying through the air and he bobbed up, gasping with cold beside me—then Adrian, then Celia. We pulled ourselves hand over hand along the rope. Now the swell was much heavier and there were vicious seas breaking in the cove. It was much more difficult to get on to the steps. The ring-bolt was high up out of the water and it was necessary to let go of the rope and swim the last few yards to the steps. My puny strength was of no consequence in the swell—like a piece of floating stick I was swept back and forth across the rock face, the small aperture of the steps flashing past as I was carried first one way and then the other. Then, more by some quirk of the swell than by my own efforts, I was dumped heavily on the bottom step and was able to scramble to my feet. I grabbed Patrick by one arm and heaved him up, then Adrian came surging past and I was able to grasp the back of his life jacket and pull him on the bottom step. Celia was more difficult. She was all but paralysed by the cold—she was heavy and slippery and there seemed to be nothing of her that I could grip. Then she managed to get her body half on to the step and with Patrick helping me we pulled and rolled and tugged until she finally got herself clear and struggled to her feet. 'Up you go—quick before the sea snatches you back again.'

Dick had not come. I looked up and saw that G. S. had moved ahead and was now lying athwart a towering rock pillar. I saw that he had been below and had brought up the two sextants and placed them on a narrow ledge of rock which he could reach. G. S. was now low in the water and sinking fast 'Dick,' I shouted, 'come out of it—now.' If she sank before he came he would be denied the rope and I doubted whether he would be able to swim through the broken water without its help. He took a last and reluctant look round and then he jumped and we watched him working along the rope, hand over hand, until I was able to grasp his arm and he scrambled up the steps.

We stood in a dejected, shivering group on the little stone quay and watched G. S. work out this last moment of her span of life. A thing of grace and beauty—agile, sure-footed, tender in her responses to our demands at the same time she was a block of solid assurance. We had always felt safe in her—we always knew that she would do whatever was asked of her. She was our home—she gave us a dignity which we would otherwise have been without.

She had come to her end not by any misdeed of hers—not through any wilfulness or delinquency—but by misuse—a sheer disregard of the elements of seamanship. I felt the dead weight of my responsibility settle heavily on my shoulders. It was a score against me that could never be wiped clean—nothing that I could ever do would relieve me of the knowledge that I had destroyed a thing of beauty.

The Whale Hunters
by Sebastian Junger

Sebastian Junger's readers know that he is a painstaking reporter and a careful writer. This piece, which appeared in Outside *in 1995, is about an old man and the sea; the man uses a wooden sailboat to hunt humpback whales. Like Junger's 1997 book,* The Perfect Storm, *the piece is an elegy of sorts—an unsentimental lament for something lost.*

The last living harpooner wakes to the sound of wind. It has been blowing for two weeks now, whipping up a big ugly sea, ruining any chance of putting out in the boat. On this strong, steady wind, the northeast trades, European slave ships rode to the New World bringing 15 million Africans across the Atlantic. One of their descendants now creeps through his house in the predawn gloom, wishing the wind would stop.

The man's name is Athneal Ollivierre. He is six feet tall, 74 years old, as straight and strong as a dock piling. His hair rises in an ash-gray column, and a thin wedge of mustache suggests a French officer in the First World War. On his left leg, there's the scar of a rope burn that went right down to the bone. His eyes, bloodshot from age and the glare of the sun, focus on a point just above my shoulder and about 500 miles distant. In the corner of his living room rests a 20-pound throwing iron with a cinnamon-wood shaft.

Ollivierre makes his way outside to watch the coming of the day.

The shutters are banging. It's the dry season; one rainfall and the hills will be so covered with poui flowers that it will look like it just snowed. Shirts hang out to dry on the bushes in front of his house, and a pair of humpback jawbones forms a gateway beyond which sprawls the rest of his world: seven square miles of volcanic island that drop steeply into a turquoise sea. This is Bequia, one of 32 islands that make up the southern Caribbean nation of St. Vincent and the Grenadines. Friendship Bay curves off to the east, and a new airport, bulldozed across the reefs, juts off to the west. More and more tourists and cruise ships have been coming to Bequia, the planes buzzing low, the gleaming boats anchoring almost nightly in the bay, but at the moment that matters very little to Ollivierre: He's barefoot in the tropical grass, squinting across the water at a small disturbance in the channel. Through binoculars it turns out to be a wooden skiff running hard across the channel for the island of Mustique. It emerges, disappears, emerges again behind a huge green swell.

"Bequia men, they brave," he says, shaking his head. He speaks in a patois that sounds like French spoken with an Irish brogue. "They brave too much."

Ollivierre hunts humpback whales from a 27-foot wooden sailboat called the *Why Ask*. As far as he's concerned, his harpooning days are over, but he's keeping at it long enough to train a younger man, 43-year-old Arnold Hazell, to do it. Otherwise the tradition, and the last remnant of the old Yankee whaling industry, will die with him. When they go out in pursuit of a whale, Ollivierre and his five-man crew row through the surf of Friendship Bay and then erect a sail that lets them slip up on whales undetected. Ollivierre stands in the bow of his boat and hurls a harpoon into the flank of an animal that's 500 times as heavy as he is. He has been knocked unconscious, dragged under, maimed, stunned, and nearly drowned. When he succeeds in taking a whale, schools on Bequia are let out, businesses are closed, and a good portion of the 4,800 islanders descends on the whaling station to watch and help butcher, clean, and salt the whale.

"It's the only thing that bring joy to Bequia people," says Ollivierre, a widower whose only son has no interest in whaling. "Nobody don't be in their homes when I harpoon a whale. I retired a few years ago, but the island was lackin of the whale, and so I go back. Now I'm training Hazell. When I finish with whalin, I finish with the sea."

When a whale is caught, it's towed by motorboat to a deserted cay called Petit Nevis and winched onto the beach; the winch is a rusty old hand-powered thing bolted to the bedrock. Butchering a 40-ton animal is hard, bloody work—work that has been condemned by environmentalists around the world—and the whalers offer armloads of fresh meat to anyone who will help them. Some of the meat is cooked right there on the beach (it tastes like rare roast beef) and the rest is kept for later. The huge jawbones are sold to tourists for around a thousand dollars, and the meat and blubber are divided up equally among the crew. Each man sells or gives his share away as he sees fit—"Who sell, sell; who give, give," as Ollivierre says. The meat goes for $2 a pound in Port Elizabeth.

If there is a species that exemplifies the word *whale* in the popular mind, it's probably the humpbacks that Ollivierre hunts. These are the whales that breach for whale-watching boats and sing for marine biologists. Though nearly 90 percent of the humpback population has been destroyed in the last hundred years, at least half of the remaining 11,000 humpbacks spend the summer at their feeding grounds in the North Atlantic and then migrate south in December. They pass the winter mating, calving, and raising their young in the warm Caribbean waters, and when the newborns are strong enough—they grow a hundred pounds a day—the whales journey back north.

It is by permission of the International Whaling Commission based in Cambridge, England, that Ollivierre may take two humpbacks a year. In 1986 a worldwide moratorium was imposed on all commercial whaling, but it allowed "aboriginal people to harvest whales in perpetuity, at levels appropriate to their cultural and nutritional requirements." A handful of others whale—in Greenland, Alaska, and Siberia—but Ollivierre is the only one who still uses a sailboat and a hand-thrown harpoon. These techniques were learned aboard Yankee whaling ships a hundred years ago and brought back to Bequia without changing so much as an oarlock or clevis pin.

"You came and put a piece of your history here, and it's still here today," says Herman Belmar, a local historian who lives around the corner from Ollivierre. Belmar is a quiet, articulate man whose passion is whaling history. He is trying to establish a whaling museum on the island. "Take the guys from Melville's *Moby Dick* and put them in Athneal's boat, and they'd know exactly what to do."

One day at dawn I drive over to meet Ollivierre. His house is a small, whitewashed, wood-and-concrete affair on the side of a hill, surrounded by a hedge. Except for the whalebone arch, it's indistinguishable from any other house on the island. I let myself through a little wooden gate and walk across his front yard, past an outboard motor and a vertebra the size of a bar stool. It's mid-February, whaling season, and Ollivierre is seated on a bench looking out across the channel. I stick out my hand; he takes it without meeting my eye.

By Bequia standards, Ollivierre is a famous man. Many people have stood before him asking for his story, but still I'm a little surprised by his reaction. Not a word, not a smile—just the trancelike gaze of someone trying to make out a tiny speck on the horizon. I stand there uncomfortably for a few minutes and finally ask what turns out to be the right question: "Could I see your collection?"

If you wander around Port Elizabeth for any length of time, a taxi driver will inevitably make you the offer: "Come meet the real harpooner! Shake his hand, see his museum!" A museum it's not, but Ollivierre has filled the largest room of his house with bomb guns, scrimshaw, and paintings. The paintings are by a local artist and commemorate some of Ollivierre's wilder exploits—*Athneal done strike de whale*, reads one. As Ollivierre discusses his life, he slowly becomes more animated and finally suggests that I walk up to the hilltop behind his house to meet the rest of the crew.

A path cuts up the hill past another low wood-and-concrete house. Split PVC pipe drains the roof and empties into a big concrete cistern, which is almost dry. (Every drop of drinking water on Bequia must be caught during the rainy season.) At the top of the hill are some wind-bent bushes and a thatch-and-bamboo sunbreak that tilts southward toward the sea. Four men sit beneath it, looking south across the channel. They gnaw on potatoes, pass around binoculars, suck on grass stems, watch the sky get lighter. In the distance is a chain of cays that used to be the rim of a huge volcano, and seven miles away is the island of Mustique. When the wind permits, the whalers sail over there to look out for humpbacks.

"Hello. Athneal sent me," I offer a little awkwardly.

The men glance around—there's been some bad press about whaling, even the threat of a tourist boycott, and everyone knows this is a delicate topic. An old man with binoculars motions me over. "We can tell whatever you want," he says, "but we can't do anything without Dan, de cop'm."

After Ollivierre, Dan Hazell, who bears some distant relation to Arnold Hazell, is the senior member of the crew. He's the captain, responsible for maneuvering the boat according to Ollivierre's orders. A young man named Eustace Kydd says he'll round up Dan and a couple of others and meet me at a bar in Paget Farm. Paget Farm is a settlement by the airport where the whalers live: ramshackle houses, dories pulled up on rocks, men drinking rum in the shade. Most of the men on the island make their living net-fishing. They go out before dawn and one crewman strings the nets along the ocean bottom—30 feet down with just two lungfuls of air, but it's a living. Later, the crew hauls in the catch, hoping to find snapper, kingfish, and bonita caught up in the twine.

I nod and walk back down the hill. Ollivierre is still in his yard, glassing the channel and talking to a young neighborhood man who has dropped by. They give me a glance and keep talking. The wind has dropped; the sun is thundering impossibly fast out of the equatorial sea.

Unfortunately for Ollivierre, the antiquity of his methods has not exempted him from controversy. First of all, he has been known to take mother-calf pairs, a practice banned by the IWC. In addition, Japan started giving St. Vincent and several neighboring islands tens of millions of dollars in economic aid after the imposition of an international moratorium on whaling in 1986. The aid was ostensibly to develop local fisheries, but American environmental groups charged that Japan was simply buying votes on the IWC. The suspicions were well founded: St. Vincent, Dominica, and Grenada have received substantial amounts of money from Japan, and all have voted in accordance with Japan's whaling interests over and over again.

Things came to a head last year when the IWC introduced a proposal to create an enormous whale sanctuary around Antarctica. The sanctuary would offer shelter to whales as the worldwide moratorium was phased out in keeping with growing whale populations. The Massachusetts-based International Wildlife Coalition, headed by Dan Morast, threatened to organize a tourist boycott against any country that voiced opposition to the proposal, and in the end only Japan voted against it. St. Vincent, Dominica, and Grenada abstained from the vote, and the South Seas Sanctuary was passed.

But the controversy over Bequia is more emotional than a vote. Ollivierre has become the focal point for dozens of environmental lobbyists, for whom everything he does is drenched in symbolism. First there was Ollivierre's flip-flop: In 1990 he announced his retirement, but a year later he was back at it, sitting on his hilltop, looking out for whales. It was a move that angered environmentalists who thought they'd seen the last of whaling on Bequia. The reaction was compounded by Ollivierre's efforts to sell the island of Petit Nevis, the tiny whaling station that has belonged to his family for three generations; a Japanese businessman's offer of $5 million was an outrage. Of course Ollivierre's personal impact on the humpback population is negligible. Morast's point seems to be more conceptual: that the land sale is just another form of bribery to encourage the St. Vincent representative on the IWC to vote for whaling.

And contrary to Morast's view, Ollivierre would love to retire. His joints ache, his vision is clouded, he's an old man. Harpooning is dangerous and apprentices are hard to come by. Several years ago he trained his nephew, Anson Ollivierre, to harpoon, but Anson branched out on his own before even bloodying his hands. Now he's building his own whaleboat, and Ollivierre fears Anson will get his whole crew killed. So this year Ollivierre tried again, taking on Arnold Hazell. Hazell's great-grandfather crewed for Ollivierre's great-grandfather, and now, a hundred years later, the relationship continues. Since there are no whales to practice on, Hazell just hangs out at Ollivierre's house, listens to the old stories, soaks up the lore.

When Hazell has killed his first whale, Ollivierre will retire. And the antiwhaling community will have a new face upon which to hang its villain's mask.

A short time after meeting with Ollivierre and his crew, I drive down to Paget Farm. On the way I pass a new fish market, paid for by the Japanese government as part of a $6 million aid package. According to the Japanese, it's a no-strings-attached token of affection for the Bequia fishermen. Past the market I turn onto a narrow cement road that grinds up a desperately steep hillside. At one end of the road is the sky; at the other end is the sea. The appointed bar is a one-story cement building halfway up the hill. I park, chock the wheels, and wander inside. It's as clean and simple inside as out: a rough wooden counter, a half-dozen chairs, no tables, a big fan. The walls are a turquoise color that fills the room with cool coral-reef light. A *Save The Whales* poster hangs in tatters on one wall, and a monumental woman opens soft drinks behind the counter. Five men are ranged at the far end of the room. They are dressed in T-shirts and baggy pants, and one has a knife in his hand. Captain Dan, too shy to speak, just looks out the window into the midday heat. Arnold Hazell greets me with a smile.

"In Bequia we don't have much opportunity like you in de States," he begins. "We grew up on de sea an live from de sea. Even if we don't cotch a whale for de next ten years, it will be good just to be whalin. Just to keep de heritage up. Japanese an Norwegians—they killin whales by the thousands, an those people could afford to do something else. They have oil, they have big industry, they have a better reason to stop." He pauses. "You know, we can put the boat out, we can talk to you, you can take snaps, but it a whole day's work for us. We need something back."

Luckily, I've been told about this ahead of time. It's a tourist economy—the sunshine, the water, the beaches, it's all for sale—and the whalers see no reason why they should be any different. A young man in dreadlocks steps in quietly and leans against the bar. He listens with vague amusement; he's heard this all before.

"A few years ago a French crew come here," says Eustace. "They come to make a film. They offer us thousands of dollars; they prepared to pay that. But we say no because we know they makin so much more on the film. Why should we work an they make all the money?"

After this statement, negotiations proceed slowly. Some careful wording, a few ambiguous phrases, and finally an agreement is reached: We'll meet at Friendship Bay tomorrow before dawn. "And," says Captain Dan, his eyes never wavering from the horizon, "you'll see the *Why Ask* fly."

In the distant past, most of the Caribbean islands were inhabited by the peace-loving Arawak people. Very little is known about them, because most were killed, and the rest were driven from the islands, by the Caribs, whose name comes from the Arawak word for "cannibal." Unfortunately for the Caribs, Columbus discovered their bloody little paradise within years of their ascendancy, and 200 years later most of them were gone as well. Bequia—dry, tiny, and poor—was one of their last hideouts, and when the French finally settled here, they found people of mixed Carib-African ancestry hiding in the hills. The Africans, as it turned out, had swum ashore from a wrecked slave ship, the *Palmira*, in 1675.

France ceded Bequia to Britain in 1763, and inevitably the Black Caribs, as they were called, were put to work on the local sugar and cotton plantations. Only free labor could coax a profit from such poor soil, and when the British abolished slavery in 1838, Bequia's economy fell apart. The local elite fled, and islanders reverted to farming and fishing—and eventually whaling—to survive.

The first Bequian to kill a whale was Bill Wallace, a white landowner's son who went to sea at age 15 and returned 20 years later with a New England bride and an armful of harpoons. As a child on Bequia he'd watched humpbacks spouting offshore during the winter months, and he didn't see why boats couldn't put out from the beach to kill them. Crews could keep lookout from the hilltops and then man their boats when they saw a spout. He recruited the strongest young men he could find and established the first whaling station on Friendship Bay in 1875.

There was nothing benevolent in Wallace; he was a tough old salt who was essentially out for his own gain. He'd lost his father shortly before leaving the island and had grown up in an industry that was considered brutal even by the brutal standard of the times. Whaling crews were at sea for three or four years at a stretch, under conditions that would have made prisoners of war balk. Captains had absolute authority over their men, and some were known to demonstrate it by occasionally whipping one to death. The crews themselves were no blessing, often largely composed of criminals, drunks, and fresh-faced kids just off the farm. It's easy to guess whose habits, after four years at sea, rubbed off on whom.

The only thing that kept such an enterprise together was the unspeakable danger that these men faced and the financial rewards of making it through alive. The largest whales in the world—blue whales—weigh 190 tons and measure up to 100 feet long. They have hearts as big as oil drums; the males have penises nine feet long. When scared, the first thing they do is thrash the water with their flukes. Enraged whales have been known to rush headlong at three-masted ships and sink them; the chase boats that put out after whales were light, fast, and no more than 30 feet long.

Harpooned whales often bolted at such speed that the rope would catch fire as it ran out through the chocks. A coil in the line could yank a man's arm off or pull him overboard. Sometimes the whale would sound and then come up through the bottom of the boat at full speed. A slack line was always a bad sign; the men could do little but peer anxiously into the depths and try to see from what angle their death would come. Inexperienced whalers were known to jump right out of the boat at the first sight of a whale. Others, intoxicated by terror, whaled until they grew old or were killed.

Four in the morning, the air soft as silk. I'm speeding along the dark roads in a rented jeep, slowing down just enough to survive the speed bumps. The northern part of Bequia is almost completely uninhabited, steep, scrub-choked valleys running up to cliffs of black volcanic rock. Shark Bay, Park Bay, Brute Point, Bullet. Between the headlands are white-sand beaches backed by cow pastures and coconut groves. Land crabs rustle through the dead vegetation, and enormous spiders spindle up tree trunks. The road passes a smoldering garbage dump, climbs the island's central ridge, and then curves into Port Elizabeth. The only signs of life at this hour are a few dockworkers loading a rusted interisland cargo ship under floodlights. The road claws up a hill and then crests the ridge above Lowerbay—Lowby, as it's called—and starts down toward Friendship.

A dry wind is blowing through the darkness, and the surf against Semples Cay and St. Hilaire Point can be heard a mile away. I pull off the road near Ollivierre's house and feel my way down a steep set of cement stairs to the water's edge. The surf smashes white against the outer reefs; everything else is the blue-black of the tropics just before dawn. The whalers arrive ten minutes later, as promised, moving single-file down the beach. They stow their gear without a word and put their shoulders to the gunwales of the *Why Ask*; she rolls heavily over four cinnamon-wood logs and slips into the sea. The wind has abated enough to sail to the preferred lookout on Mustique; otherwise we'd have to make do with the hill above Ollivierre's.

Within minutes they're under way: Captain Dan at the tiller, Ollivierre up front, and Biddy Adams, Eustace, Arnold Hazell, and Kingsley Stowe amidships. They pull at the 18-foot oars, plunging into the surf. Once clear of the reef they step the mast, cinch the shrouds, becket the sprit and boom. They scramble to work within the awkward confines of the boat as Ollivierre barks orders from the bow.

The *Why Ask* is heartbreakingly graceful under sail, as much a creature of the sea as the animals she's designed to kill. She was built on the beach with the horizon as a level and Ollivierre's memory as a plan. Boatwrights have used such phrases as "lightly borne" and "sweet-sheared and buoyant" to describe whaleboats of the last century, and they apply equally to the *Why Ask*.

The boat quickly makes the crossing to Mustique, where the crew spends half the day on a hilltop overlooking the channel. With an older whaler named Harold Corea stationed above Ollivierre's house with a walkie-talkie, they have doubled the sweep of ocean they can observe. In addition they often get tips from fishermen, pilots, or people who just happen to look out their window at the right moment. These people are always rewarded with whale meat if the chase is successful.

In the early days, between 1880 and 1920, there were nine shore-whaling stations throughout the Grenadines, including six on Bequia, and together they surveyed hundreds of square miles of ocean. They'd catch perhaps 15 whales in a good year, a tremendous boon to the local economy. In 1920, 20 percent of the adult male population of Bequia was employed in the whaling industry.

Five years later all that changed; a Norwegian factory ship set up operation off Grenada and annihilated the humpback population within a year and a half. Almost no whales were caught by islanders between 1925 and 1948, and none at all were caught for eight years after that. The whaling stations folded one by one, and by the 1950s only the Ollivierre family was left. Today the humpback population has recovered slightly—the IWC now considers the species "vulnerable" rather than "endangered"—but sightings off Bequia are still rare. Last year the crew put out after a whale only once; so far this season they have yet to see a spout.

The boat returns from Mustique in the afternoon with nothing to report. The crew shrugs it off: Waiting is as much a part of whaling as throwing the harpoon.

On those lucky occasions when Ollivierre spots a whale from Mustique, he fixes its position in his mind, sails to the spot, and waits. If there's no wind, the crew is at the oars, pulling hard against oarlocks that have been lined with fabric to keep them quiet. Humpbacks generally dive for ten or 15 minutes and then come up for air; each time they do, Ollivierre works the boat in closer. The harpoon, protected by a wooden sheath, rests in a scooped-out section of the foredeck called the clumsy cleat; when the harpoon is removed, it fits the curve of Ollivierre's thigh perfectly.

The harpoon is heavy and brutally simple. A thick cinnamon-wood shaft has been dressed with an ax and pounded into the socket of a throwing iron. The head itself is made of brass and has been ground down to the edge of a skinning knife; it is mounted on a pivot and secured by a thin wooden shear pin driven through a hole. Upon impaling the whale, the pin breaks, allowing the head to toggle open at 90 degrees, catching deep in the flesh of the whale. It's a design that hasn't changed in 150 years. The harpoon is attached to a nine-fathom nylon tether, which in turn is tied—"bent," as Ollivierre says—to the manila mainline, which is 150 fathoms long. The line passes through a notch in the bow, runs the length of the boat, takes two wraps around the loggerhead, and is coiled carefully into a wooden tub. The loggerhead is a hefty wooden block that provides enough friction to keep the whale from running out the entire tub of rope. When a whale is pulling the line, Eustace scoops seawater over the side and fills the tub—otherwise the friction will set the loggerhead on fire. Meanwhile, Ollivierre takes his position in the bow, delivering orders to Captain Dan in a low, harsh voice. Above all they must stay clear of the tail: It's powerful enough to launch a humpback clear out of the water and could obliterate the boat in a second. Ollivierre's leg is braced against the clumsy cleat, and the other men are wide-eyed at the gunwales, the rank smell of whale-vapor in their faces. The harpoon has been rid of its sheath, and Ollivierre holds it aloft as if his body has been drawn like a bow, right hand cupping the butt end, left hand supporting it like some kind of offering. You don't throw a harpoon; you drive it, unloading it downward with all your weight and strength the moment before your boat beaches itself—"wood to black-skin"—atop the whale.

"De whale make no sound at all when you hit it. It just lash de tail and it gone," says Ollivierre. "Dan let go of everything an put his two hands on de rope. De whale have to take de rope from him; he have to hold it down."

A struck whale gives a few good thrashes with its tail and then tries to flee. It is a moment of consummate chaos: the line screaming out through the bow chock, the crew trying to lower the mast, the helmsman bending the line around the smoking loggerhead. Some men freeze, and others achieve ultimate clarity. "After we harpoon it, that frightness, that cowardness go from me," says Harold Corea, who at 63 is one of the oldest members of the crew. "It all go away; I become brave, I get brave."

Brave or not, things can go very wrong. Around 1970—Ollivierre doesn't remember exactly when—a whale smacked the boat with a fluke, staving in the side and knocking Ollivierre out cold. When he came to, he realized that the rope had grabbed him and turned his leg into a loggerhead. It sawed down to bone in an instant, cauterizing the arteries as it went, and nearly ripped his hand in half. Ollivierre refused to cut the rope because he didn't want the whale to get away, but finally the barnacle-encrusted fluke severed it for him. The boat returned to shore, and Ollivierre walked up the beach unassisted, his tibia showing and his foot as heavy as cement. Two men on the beach fainted at the sight.

There is no such thing as an uneventful whale hunt; by definition it's either a disaster or almost one. As soon as the harpoon is fast in the whale, the crew drops the mast and Dan tightens up on the loggerhead to force the whale to tow the boat through the water, foredeck awash, men crammed into the stern, a 20-knot wake spreading out behind. Too much speed and the boat will go under; too much slack and the whale will run out the line. (There is one account of a blue whale that towed a 90-foot twin-screw chaser boat, its engines going full-bore astern, for 50 miles before tiring.) Every time the whale lets up, the crewmen put their hands on the line and start hauling it back in. The idea is to get close enough for Ollivierre to use either a hand lance or a 45-pound bomb gun, whose design dates back to the 1870s. It fires a shotgun shell screwed to a six-inch brass tube filled with powder that's ignited by a ten-second fuse. Ollivierre packs his own explosives and uses them with tremendous discretion.

The alternative to the gun is a light lance with a rounded head that doesn't catch inside the whale; standing in the bow, Ollivierre thrusts again and again until he finds the heart. "De whole thing is dangerous, but de going in and de killing of it is de most dangerous," he says. He's been known to leap onto the back of the whale and sit with his legs wrapped around the harpoon, stabbing. Sometimes the whale sounds, and Ollivierre goes down with it; if it goes too deep, he lets go and the crew pulls him back to the boat. When his lance has found the heart, dark arterial blood spouts out the blowhole. The huge animal stops thrashing, and its long white flippers splay outward. Two men go over the side with a rope and harpoon the head to tie up the mouth; otherwise water will fill the innards and the whale will sink.

As dangerous as it is, only one Bequian has ever lost his life in a whaleboat: a harpooner named Dixon Durham, who was beheaded by a whale's flukes in 1885. So cleanly was he slapped from the boat that no one else on board was even touched. The closest Ollivierre has come to being Bequia's second statistic was in 1992, when the line caught on a midship thwart and pulled his boat under. He and his crew were miles from Bequia, and no one was following them; Ollivierre knew that, without the boat, they would all drown. He grabbed the bow and was carried down into the quiet green depths. Equipment was rising up all around him: oars, ropes, wooden tubs. He hung on to the bow and clawed desperately for the knife at his belt. By some miracle the rope broke, and the whole mess—boat, harpoons, and harpooner—floated back up into the world.

Ollivierre found his VHF radio floating among the wreckage and called for help. Several days later, some fishermen in Guyana heard a terrible slapping on the mudflats outside their village and went to investigate. They found Ollivierre's whale stranded on the beach, beating the world with her flippers as she died.

The next day, Ollivierre, Hazell, and Corea are back up at the lookout, keeping an eye on the sea. Corea, who was partially crippled by an ocean wave at age 19, is one of the last of the old whalers. Hazell is the future of Bequia whaling, if there is such a thing. They sit on the hilltop all morning without seeing a sign. No one knows where the whales are. A late migration? A different route? Are there just no more whales?

After a couple of hours Ollivierre is ready to call it quits for the day. If anyone sees a spout, they can just run over to his house and tell him. More than anything he just seems weary—he's whaled for 37 years and fished up until a few years ago. Enough is enough. He says good-bye and walks slowly down the hill. Corea watches him go and scours the channel one more time.

Hazell squats on a rock in the shade with half his life still ahead of him. He is neither old nor young, a man caught between worlds, between generations. Down the hill is a scarred old man who's trying to teach him everything he knows; across the ocean is a council of nations playing tug-of-war with a 27-foot sailboat. Hazell would try to reconcile the two, if it were possible, but it's not. And so he's left with one simple task: to imagine what it will be like to face his first whale.

A long winter swell will be running. The sunlight will catch the spray like diamonds. He'll be in the bow with his thigh against the foredeck and the harpoon held high. The past and the future will fall away, until there are no politics, no boycotts, no journalists. There will be just one man with an ancient weapon and his heart in his throat.

from Ice Bird
by David Lewis

New Zealand has produced at least one adventurer better-known than David Lewis: That would be Sir Edmund Hillary, first to climb Everest. But Lewis is no less intrepid. His attempt to circumnavigate the Antarctic continent was almost too audacious: His small yacht twice rolled completely over in the huge seas of the southern ocean. When the yacht was dismasted 3,500 miles from help, it seemed unlikely that Lewis would survive the voyage.

ce Bird continued to make steady, if unspectacular, progress eastward, keeping generally about 61°S. A progression of gales—north-west with heavy snow and falling glass, as the warm front of the depression rolled over us—would be succeeded abruptly after eight to twelve hours by the cold front, with its falling temperatures, clearing sky and rising glass—an intensified south-west gale. The resulting jumble of cross seas kept the ocean's face in a state of furious confusion even without the rogue seas which, every now and then, reared up and dashed right across the line of the prevailing swells. I kept the yacht running with the wind on one or the other quarter, nearly down-wind. Usually she carried only the storm jib, sometimes the storm tri-sail as well. The mainsail had been put to bed somewhere in the mid-fifties and remained furled ever since.

One of the most awkward operations that had to be carried out in the brief intervals between gales was filling the petrol tank. Balancing a four-gallon plastic can on a deck rolling at a 30° angle was not easy, but at least it had the advantage that the considerable spillage was soon washed overboard. This was more than could be said when I performed the chore of topping up lamps and stove with kerosene. Inevitably a good deal of kerosene spilled over as the yacht lurched and wallowed and this made of the cabin floor a skating rink on which I slithered helplessly.

The fresh water in the tank let into the keel froze. Fortunately I had a supply of plastic cans to fall back upon. The drop in sea temperature was because we were now south of the Antarctic Convergence. Fogs, due to relatively warm north-west winds blowing over a colder sea, became more frequent and persistent than ever. Heavy snow showers became the norm.

Navigation was far from easy. A quick sight of the sun emerging from cloud cover; a dubious horizon as the sloop, rolling her gunwales under, lifted on a crest; numb fingers feverishly manipulating the sextant. To balance things a little, radio time signals were being received very clearly. Not so radio transmissions. An attempt to keep a schedule with Sydney on the 22nd, not unexpectedly, failed.

Evening, 26 November, the worst gale so far, a raging 10 knot, force ten north-wester that drove long lines of foam scudding down the faces of enormous waves and literally whipped away their crests. Each time a breaker burst against *Ice Bird* everything loose in the cabin went flying and I was forever thankful for the steel plates protecting her windows. The bilge water appeared to defy gravity by distributing itself everywhere. It surged violently uphill and whizzed round the hull.

I kept *Ice Bird* under snow-plastered storm jib, running off before the sea at about 20° from a dead down-wind run, so that she moved diagonally across the faces of those huge waves at a slight angle. During the night the gale backed to the south-west and the glass began to rise. It must eventually blow itself out, but when? I was shocked with the scene that full daylight revealed; scared, then gradually fascinated; though still terrified on looking out through the dome. It seemed as if the yacht's stern could never lift to each wave that reared up behind us. But rise it did; each time with a sensation like being whisked up in a lift. The yacht was being steered by the wind vane, assisted from inside the cabin by occasional tugs at the tiller lines. 'She's bloody near airborne,' I wrote, and added that she was running incredibly smoothly. But was this in spite of, or because of, my tactics? Were they the right ones?

This last is a perennial query in storms. Vito Dumas, the heroic Argentine farmer who in 1944 circumnavigated alone through the roaring forties in a yacht the same size as *Ice Bird*, never took in his jib. He did the same as I was doing now. Bernard Moitessier, after his memorable non-stop voyage from Tahiti to Spain, had also suggested the tactics I was adopting—running before gales at an angle under headsail, the sail being necessary to give control and maneuverability.

Dumas and Moitessier had been two of the successful ones, but so many had come to grief in the Southern Ocean. I recalled reading in Captain W. H. S. Jones's book, *The Cape Horn Breed*, that out of 130 commercial sailing vessels leaving European ports for the Pacific coast of America in May, June and July 1905, four were known to have been wrecked and *fifty-three* were still missing in Cape Horn waters in November—four to six months later.

The 37-foot Australian ketch *Pandora*, the very first yacht ever to round Cape Horn—this was in 1911—was capsized and dismasted off the Falkland Islands. She was towed into port by a whaler. The Smeaton's big British *Tzu Hang* was pitchpoled and dismasted on her first attempt to round the formidable Cape; on her second gallant try she was rolled and lost both masts. She succeeded the third time. Only the previous year the 34-foot *Damien*, crewed by two young Frenchmen, was thrice capsized off South Georgia, the first time righting herself only after a considerable interval. Again the mast was a casualty.

Yet here I was, traversing even stormier waters than they. No wonder I was scared. The gale seemed to be bearing out what I had somewhat wryly termed Lewis's law—for every point the wind increases your boat shrinks and becomes one foot shorter. This great truth has been my own discovery. I was brought back from my musings about other voyagers by bilge water surging up over the 'permafrost' that coated the inside of the hull these days, as an exploding crest threw the yacht over on her beam ends. She righted herself, water streaming off her decks. So far there had been no damage. But there was very little respite. This 26–27 November gale was barely over before, on the night of the 27th, the barometer started dropping again.

These repeated gales were at last seriously beginning to get me down. Gradually my morale was being sapped and increasing physical exhaustion was taking its toll. My whole body was battered and bruised and I was suffering from lack of sleep. Increasingly I dwelt on my in many ways disastrous personal life; what a mess I had made of things. I could hardly remember when my storm clothes had last been removed; standing in squelching boots had become habitual but was hardly comfortable. To make matters worse, my left hip, damaged in a skiing accident the previous winter, ached intolerably. I no longer day-dreamed about the voyage and its outcome—I had already dreamed and was now living it.

Instead, present reality became illusory. In my exhausted state the wild irregular seas that were tossing us around like a cork were only half apprehended. I jotted down in the log that everything was an effort; there were constant mistakes of every kind in my sight workings; I could no longer grasp simple concepts. Twice, I recorded with scientific detachment that I heard ill-defined imaginary shouts. I drifted out of reality altogether . . .

A girl companion and I are ploughing through the long fragrant grass of autumn towards the Ginandera Falls. Green scarlet lorikeets flash by in streaks of vivid colour. We push our way through some heavy scrub, then go stumbling thigh-deep over slippery stones across the icy Murimbidgee. A tangle of deadfall, tall gums and casuarinas, then a grassy glade under lichen-covered rock walls and ahead the leaping cascade. Imperceptibly the scene changes to the coast. A water-lily covered secret lake behind the sandhills. The same girl, Susie and Vicky, naked and laughing in the hot sunshine, splashing up into the shallows.

Such are my memories, false and nostalgic though they be, of 27

November, the last day of my great adventure; such was my mental condition on the eve of disaster.

On the 28th the bottom fell out of the glass. How true, even if unintended, were the words of the poet MacNiece.

> The glass is falling hour by hour, the glass will fall for ever,
> But if you break the bloody glass you won't hold up the weather.

Nothing I or any other man might do could control the barometer. The pointer moved right off the scale and continued downwards to about twenty-eight inches or 950mb during the night. This time it was for real. Long before the barometer had reached this point it was apparent that something altogether new had burst upon us—a storm of hurricane intensity. This was the home of the unthinkable 105-foot waves the Russians had recorded, I recalled with dread. A breaker half as tall, falling upon *Ice Bird*, would pound her flat and burst her asunder.

The waves increased in height with unbelievable rapidity. Nothing in my previous experience had prepared me for this. Yet I had known the full fury of North Atlantic autumn gales when homeward bound in 25-foot *Cardinal Vertue* from Newfoundland to the Shetlands in 1960 (coincidentally, the Shetlands straddle the 60th *north* parallel).

Barry and I had weathered Coral Sea cyclone 'Becky' in *Isbjorn*, only partially sheltered by an inadequate island. Severe gales off Iceland, Magellan Strait and the Cape of Good Hope had been ridden out by *Rehu Moana*—the most seaworthy catamaran built so far—in the course of her Iceland voyage and her circumnavigation.

But this storm was something altogether new. By evening the estimated wind speed was over sixty knots; the seas were conservatively forty feet high and growing taller—great hollow rollers, whose wind-torn crests thundered over and broke with awful violence. The air was thick with driving spray.

Ice Bird was running down wind on the starboard gybe (the wind on the starboard quarter), with storm jib sheeted flat as before. Once again

I adjusted the wind-vane to hold the yacht steering at a small angle to a dead run, and laid out the tiller lines where they could be grasped instantaneously to assist the vane. This strategy had served me well in the gale just past, as it had Dumas and Moitessier. But would it be effective against this fearful storm? Had any other precautions been neglected? The Beaufort inflatable life raft's retaining straps had been reinforced by a criss-cross of extra lashings across the cockpit. Everything movable, I thought, was securely battened down; the washboards were snugly in place in the companionway; the hatches were all secured. No, I could not think of anything else that could usefully be done.

Came a roar, as of an approaching express train. Higher yet tilted the stern; *Ice Bird* picked up speed and hurtled forward surfing on her nose, then slewed violently to starboard, totally unresponsive to my hauling at the tiller lines with all my strength. A moment later the tottering breaker exploded right over us, smashing the yacht down on to her port side. The galley shelves tore loose from their fastenings and crashed down in a cascade of jars, mugs, frying pan and splintered wood. I have no recollection of where I myself was flung—presumably backwards on to the port bunk. I only recall clawing my way up the companionway and staring aft through the dome.

The invaluable self-steering vane had disappeared and I found, when I scrambled out on deck, that its vital gearing was shattered beyond repair—stainless steel shafts twisted and cog wheels and worm gear gone altogether. The stout canvas dodger round the cockpit was hanging in tatters. The jib was torn, though I am not sure whether it had split right across from luff to clew then or later. My recollections are too confused and most of that day's log entries were subsequently destroyed.

I do know that I lowered the sail, slackening the halyard, hauling down the jib and securing it, repeatedly unseated from the jerking foredeck, half blinded by stinging spray and sleet, having to turn away my head to gulp for the air being sucked past me by the screaming wind. Then lying on my stomach and grasping handholds like a rock climber, I inched my way back to the companionway and thankfully pulled the hatch to after me.

I crouched forward on the edge of the starboard bunk doing my best to persuade *Ice Bird* to run off before the wind under bare poles. She answered the helm, at best erratically, possibly because she was virtually becalmed in the deep canyons between the waves; so that more often than not the little yacht wallowed broadside on, port beam to the sea, while I struggled with the tiller lines, trying vainly to achieve steerage way and control.

And still the wind kept on increasing. It rose until, for the first time in all my years of seagoing, I heard the awful high scream of force thirteen hurricane winds rising beyond 70 knots.

The remains of the already-shredded canvas dodger streamed out horizontally, flogging with so intense a vibration that the outlines blurred. Then the two stainless steel wires supporting the dodger parted and in a flash it was gone. The whole sea was white now. Sheets of foam, acres in extent, were continually being churned anew by fresh cataracts. These are not seas, I thought: they are the Snowy Mountains of Australia—and they are rolling right over me. I was very much afraid.

Some time later—I had no idea how long—my terror receded into some remote corner of my mind. I must have shrunk from a reality I could no longer face into a world of happier memories, for I began living in the past again, just as I had in my exhaustion in the gale two days earlier. It is hard to explain the sensation. I did not move over from a present world into an illusory one but temporarily inhabited both at once and was fully aware of doing so, without feeling this to be in any way strange or alarming. My handling of the tiller was quite automatic.

Mounts Kosciusko, Townsend, the broken crest of Jagungal; sculptured summits, sweeping snow slopes streaked with naked rock; all this mighty snow panorama rolled past like a cinema film. It was moving because those snow mountains were simultaneously the too-fearful-to-contemplate watery mountains of paralysing reality.

I am watching, as from afar, four of us gliding down off the snow-plumed divide, four dots in a vast whiteness. Then I am striving for balance under the weight of my pack, skis rattling a bone-shaking tattoo over a serration of ice ridges. We ski to a rest under a snow cornice overlooking the headwaters of the Snowy River, where we tunnel a snow cave to shelter us for the night—a survival exercise in preparation for my present venture.

But why are those snow mountains rolling onward? Where are they going? I have drifted away even further from the present and my tired brain baulks at the effort of solving the conundrum.

The picture blurs. I am leading a party up this same Kosciusko during the winter lately past, something like three months ago, amid the same rounded shoulders and rolling summits—literally rolling. My little Susie, refusing help with her pack, prods gamely up the endless snow slope, eyes suffused with tears of tiredness. We halt to rest. Almost at once, with the resilience of child-hood, Susie is away—laughing, her tears forgotten, the swish of her skis answering the song of the keen mountain wind.

The intolerable present became too intrusive to be ignored; the past faded into the background. Veritable cascades of white water were now thundering past on either side, more like breakers monstrously enlarged to perhaps forty-five feet, crashing down on a surf beach. Sooner or later one must burst fairly over us. What then?

I wedged myself more securely on the lee bunk, clutching the tiller lines, my stomach hollow with fear. The short sub-Antarctic night was over: it was now about 2 a.m.

My heart stopped. My whole world reared up, plucked by an irre-sistible force, to spin through giddy darkness, then to smash down into daylight again. Daylight, I saw with horror, as I pushed aside the cabin table that had come down on my head (the ceiling insulation was scored deeply where it had struck the deck head) . . . daylight was streaming through the now gaping opening where the forehatch had been! Water slopped about my knees. The remains of the Tilley lamp hung askew above my head. The stove remained upside down, wedged in its twisted gymballs.

Ice Bird had been rolled completely over to starboard through a full 360° and had righted herself thanks to her heavy lead keel—all in about a second. In that one second the snug cabin had become a shambles. What of the really vital structures? Above all, what of the mast?

I splashed forward, the first thought in my mind to close that yawning fore hatchway. My second—oh, God—the mast. I stumbled over rolling cans, felt the parallel rules crunch underfoot and pushed aside the flotsam of clothes, mattresses, sleeping bag, splintered wood fragments and charts (British charts floated better than Chilean, I noted—one up to the Admiralty). Sure enough the lower seven feet of the mast, broken free of the mast step, leaned drunkenly over the starboard bow and the top twenty-nine feet tilted steeply across the ruptured guard wires and far down into the water, pounding and screeching as the hulk wallowed.

The forehatch had been wrenched open by a shroud as the mast fell. Its hinges had sprung, though they were not broken off and its wooden securing batten had snapped. I forced it as nearly closed as I could with the bent hinges and bowsed it down with the block and tackle from the bosun's chair.

Then I stumbled back aft to observe, incredulously, for the first time that eight feet of the starboard side of the raised cabin trunk had been dented in, longitudinally, as if by a steam hammer. A six-inch vertical split between the windows spurted water at every roll (it was noteworthy, and in keeping with the experience of others, that it had been the lee or down-wind side, the side underneath as the boat capsized, that had sustained damage, not the weather side where the wave had struck).

What unimaginable force could have done that to eighth-inch steel? The answer was plain. Water. The breaking crest, which had picked up the seven-ton yacht like a matchbox, would have been hurtling forward at something like fifty miles an hour. When it slammed her over, the impact would have been equivalent to dumping her on to concrete. The underside had given way.

Everything had changed in that moment of capsize on 29 November at 60° 04′S., 135° 35′W., six weeks and 3,600 miles out from Sydney,

2,500 miles from the Antarctic Peninsula. Not only were things changed; everything was probably coming to an end. The proud yacht of a moment before had become a wreck: high adventure had given place to an apparently foredoomed struggle to survive.

I hastily stuffed the nearest floating rag into the gap in the side of the coach roof (later I substituted sealing compound). My Omega wrist watch, kept on Greenwich time for navigation, was providentially still running. In the absence of radio time signals—I correctly assumed that the radios would all be shorted out by salt water—I must rely solely upon it for longitude, estimating its probable error as best I could.

A hurried search for gloves was fruitless. Well, gloves would be no use to me if *Ice Bird* sank. Seizing a bucket (the pump, of course, was useless) I began bailing for life.

The capsize must have occurred soon after first light, or around 2 a.m. Hour after hour I bailed until I was repeating the sequence of operations in a haze of tiredness, mechanically, like an automaton. The glass was beginning to rise, I noted dully, so the cold front must have passed, switching the storm winds to the southwest. This presumption was confirmed when ragged tears began to appear in the driving cloud wrack. Bursts of sunlight momentarily illumined a scene that, even in my then state, I appreciated was of awesome grandeur. The screaming wind had not let up in the slightest. The tormented sea was a sheet of white water that looked like snow. At least I have seen the sun again before I die, I thought.

By about 8:30 a.m. the yacht was empty down to the floorboards. Then *crash!* I picked myself up from the corner where I had been hurled when this second killer wave had knocked *Ice Bird* flat, this time over to starboard, to find her flooded again to almost exactly the same level as before. The carefully salvaged logbook, charts and sleeping bag were once more awash.

When I wearily recommenced bailing I saw that the life raft was gone from the cockpit. I was without thought; conscious only of pain and weariness; actuated only by some obscure instinct for survival. An age passed until suddenly there was no more water to scoop up. Then I was knocking out the bolts securing the floorboard battens and scooping the remaining thirty or so bucketfuls out of the bilge.

Noon. *Ice Bird* was dry again. Habit was strong. With numb hands I picked up a ballpoint pen, opened the sodden logbook and laboriously recorded the incident.

'Gale moderating to force 10–9. Heavy seas breaking against us. Everything soaked and destroyed. Must rest a little.' I finished. I had been bailing continuously for something like ten hours.

The thumping of the mast against the hull soon had me on my feet again. Thank goodness the boat was of steel. Crawling out on deck, I set about knocking out split pins to free the shrouds from the rigging screws that anchored them to the deck. The stainless steel wire rigging, like the mast itself, would have to be sacrificed: there was no way in which I could hoist aboard such a weighty tangle of wreckage nor make use of it if salvage had been possible.

So I pried and levered with a screwdriver, pinched and hammered with pliers at those stubborn split pins. The deck's motion was too violent and I was too tired to hit accurately but I carried on until the sunken mast was held by only two wires, never noticing that I had gashed my left hand deeply in two places, as the wounds neither hurt nor bled.

By 7:30 that evening I could do no more.

'Hands bleeding and very numb,' I wrote in the logbook, incredibly failing to realize what was wrong or to make the slightest attempt to warm my still uncovered fingers—and I a doctor! The numbing effects upon reasoning power of exhaustion and shock were never more apparent. 'Will have a stiff drink and try to sleep. Sleeping bag soaked,' I added in a barely decipherable scrawl. But the rum bottle was nowhere to be found. Smashed to pieces, I assumed and, after some searching,

found another. It was a fortnight before I came upon the original bottle. Driven up through the plywood floor of a locker, it was still intact.

A fitful sleep of utter tiredness followed. In the morning my fingers
were too numb to feel the winder on my wrist watch. My first reaction
was horror. Should the watch stop I had no way of setting it to the correct time again. Result—the ending at one stroke of any possibility of
navigational accuracy and the fading to absolute zero of my already
dim chances. I searched feverishly for my glasses. They misted up as
soon as I put them on. I squeezed out wet toilet paper and wiped them
repeatedly. Now I could *see* the winder turn. This procedure was to be
faithfully repeated night and morning from then on and must never,
on any account, be omitted.

The wider implications of my fingers' numbness came home to me
as I belatedly realized the obvious—that both my hands were frostbitten. From now on I must always keep them covered. The damp
woollen gloves or mitts (I had so far salvaged one of each) I would
reserve for work on deck, using slightly less damp woollen socks when
below. I even learned to write up the log and open cans of corned beef
with the socks on my hands.

The remaining shrouds parted of their own accord about the middle
of the morning and *Ice Bird* floated free of the wreckage. I laboriously
hoisted thirty-five buckets of water out of the companionway and
poured them into the self draining cockpit; later in the day eighteen
buckets more. I tried to force more sealing compound into the split but
had little success. Every single roll of the dismasted yacht put the side
decks under and sent a fresh spurt of water into the cabin.

My first pathetic attempt at rigging some sort of a sail was by cutting
away the remaining fragments of the canvas dodger and wrapping them
round the pulpit forward. It was ineffective. The dry fur coat and fur
trousers that had been stowed carefully away in the forepeak in a waterproof plastic bag I found to be soaked, for the bag had chafed through
unnoticed during the long weeks at sea. Nevertheless, I changed into
them, a procedure which, because of my hands, took over an hour.

The 9 p.m. scribbled entry in the day's log sounds curiously forlorn.

'Blowing up from the west. Both hands fingers frostbitten—attempted to warm them up this p.m. Will now try to run off before the sea.'

And a little later, 'Failed steer. Failed primus. 18 buckets. Estimate watch 4 minutes 33 seconds fast (est. daily gain 6 seconds). Can't be sure if winder turning.'

Depressed by these successive failures, I huddled down in my sleeping bag and pressing my unfeeling hands (which seemed as little part of me as slabs of chilled meat) against my warm body, I dozed the miserable night away.

The first of December. Working in swirling snow, my hands surprisingly well protected by wet woollen gloves, I cleared away the remaining wreckage and set about rigging up a jury mast. The best spar I could find was the surviving spinnaker pole (the other had been broken when the mast had collapsed). It was an aluminium tube ten feet long, far too fragile for the job in hand, as well as being ridiculously short, but I could think of nothing else to use. Shrouds or stays were needed for support and halyards to hoist sails. An old friend, a veteran climbing rope, was sacrificed to make these, supplemented by part of a coil of rope given me by the Stewart Island Fisherman's Cooperative. A deck safety wire was pressed into service as a forestay. I was tired out by the time the task was completed, but at least I was ready to raise the makeshift mast the moment the weather allowed.

I had now time to investigate the motor. Not unexpectedly, it was useless, its electrics brine-soaked. I did succeed, with the expenditure of many waterproof Greenlight matches, in getting one stove burner going erratically and I heated some stew and made coffee over the flaring yellow flame.

'This must be Christmas,' I wrote, with my first flash of humour.

The following day, the third since the capsize, was a landmark, for we got under way. The temperature was $-2°C$ and soft ice—frozen sea water—coated the deck. But between the heavy snow showers it was fine and the wind had at last dropped to a normal breeze. This was the opportunity I had been waiting for. I made fast the jury shrouds, one to each side and one to each quarter at the stern and led the forestay wire from the 'mast head' round the bow anchor warp roller and back aft to where I could reach it. Then, planting one end of the spinnaker pole in the mast step, I pushed the light spar upwards and hauled in on the wire forestay until the pole stood vertical, secured laterally and behind by the rope shrouds. The wire was soon made fast and the shrouds tightened down as far as they would go.

The remaining number two storm jib had next to be dragged up from below. I found by trial and error that two knots in the head of the sail reduced its length to that of the short forestay. It only remained to shackle it to the bow, clip the hanks on to the forestay and reeve a pair of sheets. Finally I crawled along to the foot of the mast, braced my back on it against the rolling, and hauled up the jib.

I dared not think how futile was the gesture. The first sights since the accident had shown the stark ice barriers of the Antarctic Peninsula to be around 2,500 miles off, farther than from New York to Seattle or from England to Siberia. It seemed flouting fate as I sheeted in the pathetic rag of sail on the ten-foot mast (the old mast had measured thirty-six feet) and, at the speed of a good one mile an hour, turned the bow towards grim and distant shelter.

Ice Bird had to be steered by hand (from inside the cabin with the tiller lines) whenever the wind was a following one but she could be left to make good her own rather erratic course in beam winds and, with head winds, she could be persuaded to point ever so slightly to windward. My compass could not function inside the steel hull because of the magnetism, so when steering by hand I had to peer up from my seat on the corner of a bunk through the Perspex dome at the strips of sailcloth I had tied to the backstays to indicate the wind direction. Steering was essentially a matter of keeping these at a constant angle.

Since the most common wind directions were approximately from north-west or south-west, the yacht's natural tendency was to sail sideways to the wind and waves (a characteristic that meant ceaseless rapid rolling—a most vile motion); her preferred direction of advance was frequently towards the south-east or north-east rather than due east and we pursued our way, often as not, in a series of zigzags. Sometimes, the wind being more northerly or southerly, *Ice Bird* could be left to her own devices and would follow roughly the desired course for as long as a day or more. At other times, when the wind was more westerly, I would have to steer by hand for twelve or fourteen hours at a stretch, only letting go of the lines to snatch up a biscuit, slice off a hunk of corned beef or answer the call of nature. Time and again, the need for sleep would overwhelm me and all hope of making progress would have to be abandoned for the time being in favour of my body's imperative demand for rest.

The numbness in my swollen hands was beginning to give way to intense and growing agony, showing that some life at least remained in them. Antibiotics offered the one hope of saving my fingers, else infection would make short work of the damaged and devitalized tissues, so I now began taking double doses of Tetracycline capsules and continued this massive therapy for several weeks. To aggravate matters, my left knee became red and swollen. The same antibiotics might be expected to control this infection too. The hope was happily realized, and the pain and swelling subsided in a few days. The Australian Antarctic medical expert and veteran of the Heard Island expeditions, Dr. Graeme Budd (he himself had been badly frostbitten) had helped me to plan a joint investigation into the effects of prolonged wet cold that I was expected to encounter during the voyage. This scientific study was accumulating far more information than I had bargained for, I thought ruefully.

Whenever I was not otherwise occupied I turned to escapist novels, so that I could forget for a while the surrounding squalor and misery. But to return to the reality of chilly feet squelching in boots that I had no option but to wear day and night—since my clumsy sausage-like fingers were unequal to the task of unlacing them—to damp sleeping bag and aching hands only served to deepen my depression. The violent rolling in the virtual absence of a steadying sail was physically and mentally exhausting too. Then always at the back of my mind was the reality that I still dare not quite face: one mile an hour—and that in favourable conditions. How far to land? I pushed the thought from me.

Then even this dismally slow progress was halted. After the crippled yacht had been crawling eastward for four days, the foot of the little mast broke off in a gale; and a stormy night and day intervened before I could sort out the cat's cradle of rigging tangled around the deck and raise it again.

'Hands always pain,' I wrote.

Assessed soberly, the situation did, indeed, appear hopeless—in the middle of the stormiest ocean on earth with a makeshift mast that kept crumbling away. I silently cursed the unknown busybody who had added a particular statistic to the *National Geographic World Atlas* that I had aboard: 'World's most distant point from land,' he had written. His totally redundant cross on the map lay due north of *Ice Bird*'s position.

It was impossible for me any longer to ignore the facts. 'A shutter has closed between a week ago when I was part of the living and since. Chance [of survival] negligible but effort in spite of pain and discomfort. These last are very great. Must go on striving to survive, as befits a man. Susie and Vicky without a daddy is worst of all.'

Next day, as blinding snow showers driving up from the south ushered in a new gale, I wrote further. 'Surprising no fear at almost certainly having to die, a lot of disappointment though.'

Would all I could offer the children be memories that would soon fade and the austere comfort of the words I had written in the will made before leaving Sydney? 'In the event of my death attempting to storm new frontiers at sea . . . I want Vicky and Susie to know that I expect them always to face life unafraid, with their heads up, and always remembering to laugh. My grown-up children already know this.'

To my own surprise, I realized that the intolerable thought of the little girls left fatherless did even more to keep me striving than did the urge for self-preservation. Also, surprisingly, the expectation of dying in such utter solitude, about as far from human contact as it was possible to be anywhere on earth, did not occasion me any special despondency; since every one of us must ultimately tread this road alone.

A kind of philosophy seemed to have taken shape about this time.

The chances of crossing two and a half thousand miles of Southern Ocean in my leaking, battered boat, with its ludicrous mast were too remote for serious contemplation and the far from welcoming blizzard-swept escarpments that were my destination promised no welcoming havens. I must just live for the day, therefore. The awful effort demanded by the daily struggle was worthwhile in *itself* regardless of its hopelessness; despite its futility this striving would, in some obscure way, not be wasted.

I tried clumsily to express these thoughts in the log. 'Earning membership of humanity—must earn it every day, to be a man.' I proceeded to try for that day's quota by laboriously and painfully emptying out twenty-four bucketfuls of bilge water, clearing the jammed halyard in a snowstorm and hoisting another sail to assist the little jib. This was the storm tri-sail. The head had once again to be knotted so that it could fit the diminutive mast.

If it were not for my hands, how much more I could do, I kept thinking. But even after being outside only long enough to take a sun sight I found myself 'shouting with the pain in my fingers'. The morning of 11 December was relatively calm and I was able to get the stove going, for the first time in five days, to heat up a can of stew and make a lukewarm cup of coffee. I was depressed the greater part of the time, overtired but restless and unable to sleep soundly even when I did have the chance.

By the 12th I had become more obsessed than ever with my terrible hands. Time and again I postponed or put off altogether going on deck to carry out the most urgent and necessary tasks, all for fear of the endless minutes of torture that I knew must inevitably follow. 'Steering by yoke and line from the cabin all afternoon,' I wrote. 'Gashed and frostbitten fingers more painful now. Are they healing? Worry over water [the supply of fresh water aboard was unlikely to prove adequate for reaching land at the present rate of progress], distance, time. Sometimes just get cowardly and whimper a bit in my sleeping bag.'

Then at midnight I concluded the tale of the day's tribulations. 'SW gale, force 8, *lower four inches of jury mast crumbled*. Lowered sail and lay a-hull. Hands stand less cold than ever.'

The grim reality behind these laconic phrases had been my clawing desperately about the deck, as always on hands and knees, smothering the flapping sails with my body until I could secure them with lashings and then tightening down the shrouds to secure the mast, as I had before—only this time even less of it remained. All this was in darkness out of which streamed volleying snow pellets and stinging half-frozen droplets of spray.

I could not know then that *Ice Bird* was on the eve of another new disaster.

from Looking for a Ship
by John McPhee

John McPhee, born in 1931, is known for his thorough reporting and lucid writing on subjects as diverse as basketball and geology. He turned his attention to the merchant marine in Looking for a Ship. *The book described a 42-day run on the* SS Stella Lykes *that was not without incident; pirate attacks and stowaways intruded on the ship's routine. But the ship survived—unlike most that figure in this description of the myriad dangers that beset such vessels.*

Below the bridge deck is the boat deck, and on the boat deck is Captain Washburn's office. Nine a.m. I often sit here in the morning drinking coffee, reading manifests, and listening to him. "My house is your house," he says, and the remark is especially amiable in this eight-deck tower called the house. During the night, a planned avalanche occurred in the office. From seaport to seaport, papers accumulate on the captain's desk. "Paperwork has become the bane of this job," he says. "If a ship doesn't have a good copying machine, it isn't seaworthy. The more ports, the more papers. South American paperwork is worse than the paperwork anywhere else in the world but the Arab countries and Indonesia." Deliberately, he allows the pile on his desk to rise until a deep roll on a Pacific swell throws it to the deck and scatters it from bulkhead to bulkhead. This he interprets as a signal that the time has come to do paperwork. The paper carpet may be an inch deep, but he leaves it where it fell. Bending over, he picks up one sheet. He deals with it: makes an entry, writes a letter—does whatever it requires him to do. Then he bends over and picks up another sheet. This goes on for a few days until, literally, he has cleared his deck.

The roll that set off last night's avalanche was probably close to thirty degrees. In a roll that is about the same, my tape recorder shoots across the office and picks up the captain with Doppler effect. Retrieving it, I ask him, "How many degrees will *Stella* roll?"

"She'll roll as much as she has to. She'd roll fifty degrees if you'd let her—if she was loaded wrong—but normally she'll roll in the twenty-to-thirty-degree range. That's average for ships. It doesn't slow her down or hurt her. She is a deep-sea vessel, built for rough weather. We don't see much rough weather down here. We used to run this coast with the hatches open. That would be suicidal anywhere else. Every day, somewhere someone is getting it from weather. They're running aground. They're hitting each other. They're disappearing without a trace." Once, in a great storm, Terrible Terry Harmon said to Washburn, "Do you know how to pray?" When Washburn nodded, Harmon said, "Then try that. That's the only thing that's going to save us now."

Straightening up with a sheet of paper in his hand, Captain Washburn looks out a window past a lifeboat in its davits and over the blue sea. After a moment, he says, "I love going to sea. I do not love that sea out there. That is not my friend. That is my absolute twenty-four-hour-a-day sworn enemy." He shows me a map of maritime casualties. He also has back issues of the *Mariners Weather Log*, a publication of the National Oceanic and Atmospheric Administration that chronicles marine disasters throughout the world and features among its reported storms a "Monster of the Month." Nautical charts, such as the ones in use in our chartroom, include a surprising number of symbols denoting partially submerged wrecks and completely submerged wrecks. Nearly all the ships that appear on modern charts have been wrecked in the past fifty years. "Here's a handsome ship went down," the captain continues, with a finger on his map. "She just went out and was never heard from again. So it isn't just these little nondescript ships like *In God We Trust* that disappear. Almost every hour of every day someone is getting it. Right now someone is getting it somewhere."

A likely place is a foul sea about eight hundred miles north of Hawaii that is known to merchant seamen as the Graveyard of the North Pacific. "You can pick it up on the shortwave," Washburn says. "You hear, 'SOS. We're taking on water. SOS. We're taking on water.' Then you don't hear the SOS anymore." There are weather-routing services that help merchant ships figure out where to go. Washburn suggests that they are in business not to provide maximum safety or comfort but to shave as close as they dare to vicious weather and thus save time and fuel. He happened to be visiting the home office of one of these services when it had a client in the Graveyard of the North Pacific and was guiding it between two storm systems. He wondered what might happen if the storms coalesced. He asked why such ships did not go past Hawaii on a route that has proved safe for four hundred years. The weather-routers said, "Then who would need *us*?"

When Washburn was a teen-age ordinary seaman, he sailed with a master who had written what Washburn describes as "a big sign inside the logbook":

TAKE CARE OF THE SHIP AND
THE SHIP WILL TAKE CARE OF YOU

The sign now hangs in Washburn's head. In his unending dialogue with the ship, the ship tells him things that its instruments do not. There is no Weatherfax map on the *Stella Lykes*—only the barometer, the barographs, the teletypes from NOAA. The radar can see a storm, but that is like seeing a fist just before it hits you. When a storm is out there, somewhere, beyond the visible sky, the ship will let him know.

"When you get close to a big storm, you can feel it. For some reason, the ship takes on almost a little uncertainty. She's almost like a live thing—like they say animals can sense bad weather coming. Sometimes I almost believe a ship can. I know that doesn't make sense, because she's steel and wood and metal, but she picks up a little uncertainty, probably something that is being transmitted through the water. It's hard to define. It's just a tiny little different motion, a little hesitancy, a little tremble from time to time."

Off Hatteras, things can be really hesitant. A lashed-down crane will pull a pad eye out of the deck. A pad eye is a D ring made of steel two inches thick. "This ship is very strongly built," Washburn says. "She's sturdy and reliable. There's lots of horsepower down there. She will answer the rudder. She will respond. She's a capable and trustworthy ship. You know what she'll do and you know her limitations. They aren't crucial, but you can't expect her to do things where you know she's a little short. You can't suddenly demand that of her and expect to get it. It isn't there. She's American-built. There's good steel in the hull. Those frames are close together. She'll roll on a following sea, but she's got a high-raised fo'c'sle head and a sharp bow. She's built for rough weather. She's built for rough handling. She's built to take seas and fight back. You cannot overpower seas. But she can deal with what's out there. She was built to go to Scandinavia in the middle of winter."

To make the North Europe run in winter is something that many American sailors do everything they can to avoid and others just refuse to do. No matter how straitened they may be and hungry for work, they will pass up the winter North Atlantic. Having grown up near this ocean and knowing no other, I was surprised to learn this. Years ago, when I was a student for a time in Europe and went back and forth on ships in winter, I thought it was normal for the keel to come out of water as the hull prepared to smash the sea. I didn't know anything about load lines—Plimsoll marks—or classification societies. For a ship to thud like a ton of bricks and roll at least forty degrees seemed a basic and expectable standard condition. I had no idea that this ocean in winter was in a category of its own. On various ships on the North Europe run, Captain Washburn has stayed awake for as much as seventy-two hours, catnapping in a chair on the bridge. "You're tacking into weather," he explains. "Winds and seas can become so strong that you can't always go in the direction you want to." For more than four years, he was the skipper of the Ro/Ro *Cygnus* and most of its runs were to North Europe. In the early weeks of 1983, he was trying to make his way north into the English Channel, but the *Cygnus*'s big diesels were overmatched, overwhelmed. Washburn tacked back and forth almost helplessly, and the ship—five hundred and sixty feet, fourteen thousand deadweight tons—was blown sideways into the Bay of Biscay. "We couldn't get out. We ended up near Bilbao."

On the side of a merchant ship is a painted circle, a foot in diameter, with a horizontal line running through it marking the depth to which the ship can be safely loaded in summer. Near it are shorter horizontal lines, more or less like the rungs of a ladder. They indicate the depth to which the ship can be safely loaded in various seasons and places. The highest line, representing the heaviest permissible load, is marked "TF." Tropical fresh. This means that you can go up a river in the tropics to a place like Guayaquil, load yourself down to the TF line, and go back to the ocean, where the density of the water will lift the ship to another line, marked "T." That is as deeply loaded as you are permitted to be in a tropical ocean. These levels, worked out specifically for each ship, "take into consideration the details of length, breadth, depth, structural strength and design, extent of superstructure, sheer, and round of beam," and are collectively called the Plimsoll mark, after Samuel Plimsoll, a member of Parliament who, in the 1870s, wrote the act creating them in order to outlaw the greed-driven excessive loading that was the primary factor in the sinking of ships. When British people call rubber-soled deck and tennis shoes plimsolls, they are referring to him. The United States adopted the Plimsoll mark more than fifty years later. Load lines are set by classification societies, which are private companies that play a checking, testing, and supervisory role in ship construction—services that are optional in the sense that if you don't sign up for them no one will insure your ship. Society initials appear on the hull of a ship as a part of the Plimsoll mark: the American Bureau of Shipping (AB), Lloyd's Register (LR), Bureau Veritas (BV), Germanischer Lloyd (GL), Norske Veritas (NV). Below the summer load line is a line marked "W." It marks the depth to which the ship can be safely loaded in winter. Some distance below that is the lowest line of all. It is marked "WNA." To burden a ship only to that line is to give it the lightest load in the whole Plimsoll series. The WNA line marks the maximum depth to which the ship can be safely loaded in the winter North Atlantic. Andy has remarked about a company that runs to Iceland,"If you get a ship on that line in the winter, you're going to get creamed and you know it." The North Sea, the Cape of Good Hope, Cape Horn, and the Gulf of Alaska are the stormiest waters in the shipping world after the winter North Atlantic.

The great-circle route between North Europe and New York bucks the storms of the upper latitudes. Captain Washburn likes to say that if you were to take two new ships and run one to North Europe via the Azores and the other to North Europe on the great circle, after a year you would have one new ship and one "damaged, beat-up ship." He continues, "If you go south and the weather comes after you, you can go on going south. If you go north and the weather comes after you, you have containers over the side and the crew in the hold chasing loose cargo. You—you are going nowhere."

While Vernon McLaughlin was on the *American Legacy*, her skipper tried to run to the north of a storm and ended up against New-foundland in a Force 12 gale.

"For two days, the ship pounded as it pitched, and rolled forty; you looked out the sides in a trough, and it looked as if you were underwater. There was a great crack in the superstructure in front of the house. Containers were lost over the side. Others were stood against each other like swords when a marine gets married. One that broke open—shoes fell out of it for the rest of the voyage. On other ships, I have seen seamen fall on their knees and pray, they were so afraid."

While Andy was night-mating the Sea-Land Performance in Charleston, Captain Crook told me about a January crossing he had made years before on the great-circle route from the Virginia capes to the Strait of Gibraltar. "We hit the worst sea storm to hit the North

Atlantic ocean in two hundred years," he said. "For fifty-two hours, the captain was on the bridge trying to save the ship. Speeding up in the trough to maintain control, slowing up just before the crest so he wouldn't pound the ship too hard. Waves tore the mast off. The bridge was a hundred and fifteen feet off the water. Waves went over us. The decks were solid ice. Whole tractor-trailers were washed over the side. A forty-five-ton truck-crane was loose on the deck like a battering ram. House trailers on the second deck were completely demolished. I was truly afraid." An ordinary seaman was on lookout on the bridge when the ship lurched and hurled him through the wheelhouse door onto the port-side bridge wing, where he slid on his back across ice and went through the railing. He grabbed the railing, hung on, and dangled above the monstrous sea. Crook went out and pulled him back.

Andy once said to me, "I love being up on the bridge when it's rough. I enjoy being on watch in rough weather. It's so impressive. It's spectacular. Huge seas. Strong winds. At some point, you cross from awe to terror. I haven't been at that point yet—the ultimate storm. It could change my attitude." Andy hasn't seen anything worse than a fifty-five-foot sea breaking over him when he was running coastwise on the *Spray* in the winter North Atlantic. "My height of eye was fifty-two feet off the water, and the water broke over the bridge and hit the radar mast. Water went down stacks into the engine room." Not enough water to change his attitude.

That wave was what the *Mariners Weather Log* calls an ESW, or Extreme Storm Wave—a rogue wave, an overhanging freak wave. Coincidence tends to produce such waves—for example, when the waters of colliding currents are enhanced by tidal effects in the presence of a continental shelf. Often described as "a wall of water," an Extreme Storm Wave will appear in a photograph to be a sheer cliff of much greater height than the ship from which the picture was taken. Captain Washburn calls it "a convex wave." He goes on to say, "You don't get up it before it's down on your foredeck. The center is above sixty feet high. You can't ride over the center. You *can* ride over the edge. A ship has no chance if the wave hits just right. It will break a ship in two in one lick. Because of the trough in front of it, mariners used to say that they fell into a hole in the ocean."

In the winter North Atlantic, the demac David Carter has oftentimes tied himself in his bunk after propping his mattress up and wedging himself against the bulkhead—to avoid getting thrown out and injured by a forty-five- or fifty-degree roll. He got his first ship after nearly everyone aboard had been injured. On one voyage, Carter had a big chair in his cabin that was "bouncing off the bulkhead like a *tennis ball*." In his unusually emphatic, italic way of speaking, he goes on, "Pots won't stay on a *stove*. After a night of no *sleep*, a full day of *work*, you get nothing but a *baloney* sandwich if you're lucky. They soak the tablecloth so nothing will *slide*. I hope you won't get to see that. If you wonder why we *party* and get *drunk* when we're in port, that's why."

On February 11, 1983, a collier called *Marine Electric* went out of the Chesapeake Bay in a winter storm with a million dollars' worth of coal. She was a ship only about ten per cent shorter than the *Stella Lykes* and with the same beam and displacement. Our chief mate, J. Peter Fritz, wished he were aboard her. She was headed for Narragansett Bay, her regular run, and his home is on Narragansett Bay. He grew up there. As a kid, he used to go around on his bike visiting ships. He took photographs aboard the ships, developed and printed them at home, and went back with the pictures to show the crews. They invited him to stay aboard for dinner. ("Some guys liked airplanes. To me it was just the ships.") He watched the shipping card in the Providence *Journal*—the column that reports arrivals and departures. Working on a tug and barge, he learned basic seamanship from the harbormaster of Pawtuxet Cove—knots, splicing, "how to lay around boats the right way." As a Christmas present an aunt gave him a picture book of merchant ships. As a birthday present she gave him the "American Merchant Seamans Manual."

Peter grew up, graduated from the Massachusetts Maritime Academy, and went to sea. It was his calling, and he loved it. He also loved, seriatim, half the young women in Rhode Island. He was a tall, blond warrior out of *The Twilight of the Gods* with an attractively staccato manner of speech. Not even his physical attractions, however, could secure his romantic hatches. "Dear Peter" letters poured in after he left his women and went off for months at sea. Eventually, he married, had a son, and left the Merchant Marine. For several years, he worked for an electronic-alarm company and miserably longed for the ocean. ("I will not admit how much I love this job. The simple life. Having one boss. Not standing still, not being stagnant; the idea of moving, the constant change.") Eventually, he couldn't stand it any longer, and went off to circle the world on the container ship President Harrison. ("I had *the* killer card. I had planned it.") He made more money in eighty-seven days than he could make in a year ashore. After a family conference, he decided to ship out again. Like his lifelong friend Clayton Babineau, he coveted a job that would take him on short runs from his home port. Every ten days, the *Marine Electric* went out of Providence for Hampton Roads, and nine days later she came back. She went right past Peter's house. He night-mated her. His wife, Nancy, said to him, "Hey, wouldn't it be great if you got a job on that one? You could be home with your family." He tried repeatedly, without success. His friend Clay Babineau, sailing as second mate, died of hypothermia that night off Chincoteague in the winter storm. The *Marine Electric* was thirty-nine years old in the bow and stern, younger in the middle, where she had been stretched for bulk cargo. In the language of the Coast Guard's Marine Casualty Report, her forward hatch covers were "wasted, holed, deteriorated, epoxy patched." Winds were gusting at sixty miles an hour, and the crests of waves were forty feet high. As the Marine Electric plowed the sea, water fell through the hatch covers as if they were colanders. By 1 a.m., the bow was sluggish. Green seas began pouring over it. A list developed. The captain notified the Coast Guard that he had decided to abandon ship. The crew of thirty-four was collecting on the starboard boat deck, but before a lifeboat could be lowered the ship capsized, and the men, in their life jackets, were in the frigid water. In two predawn hours, all but three of them died, while their ship went to rest on the bottom, a hundred and twenty feet below, destroyed by what the Coast Guard called "the dynamic effects of the striking sea."

Peter Fritz, who gives the routine lectures on survival suits to the successive crews of the *Stella Lykes*, carries in his wallet a shipping card clipped from the February 13, 1983, Providence *Journal*: "ARRIVING TODAY, MARINE ELECTRIC, 8 P.M."

She is remembered as "a rotten ship." So is the *Panoceanic Faith*, which went out of San Francisco bound for India with a load of fertilizer about six months after Fritz graduated from Massachusetts Maritime. Five of his classmates were aboard, and all of them died, including his friend John McPhee. Getting to know Fritz has not been easy. There have been times when I have felt that he regarded me as a black cat that walked under a ladder and up the gangway, a shipmate in a white sheet, a G.A.C. (Ghost in Addition to Crew). The *Panoceanic Faith* developed a leak, its dampened cargo expanded, its plates cracked. It sank in daytime. "People tried to make it to the life rafts but the cold water got them first."

Plaques at the maritime academies list graduates who have been lost at sea. A schoolmate of Andy Chase was on a ship called Poet that went out of Cape Henlopen in the fall of 1980 with a load of corn. She was never heard from again. Nothing is known. In Captain Washburn's words, "Never found a life jacket, never found a stick."

On the *Spray*, Andy went through one hurricane three times. A thousand-pound piece of steel pipe broke its lashings and "became the proverbial loose cannon." Ten crewmen—five on a side—held on to a line and eventually managed to control it, but they had almost no sleep for two days. The *Spray* once carried forty men. Reduced manning had cut the number to twenty. "Companies are trying to get it down to eleven or twelve by automating most functions," he says. "When everything's going right, four people can run a ship, but all the automation in the world can't handle emergencies like that."

A small ship can be destroyed by icing. Ocean spray freezes and thickens on her decks and superstructure. Freezing rain may add to the accumulation. The amount of ice becomes so heavy that the ship almost disappears within it before the toppling weight rolls her over and sinks her. Ships carry baseball bats. Crewmen club the ice, which can thicken an inch an hour.

To riffle through a stack of the *Mariners Weather Log*—a dozen or so quarterly issues—is to develop a stop-action picture of casualties on the sea, of which there are so many hundreds that the eye skips. The story can be taken up and dropped anywhere, with differing names and the same situation unending. You see the *Arctic Viking* hit an iceberg off Labrador, the *Panbali Kamara* capsize off Sierra Leone, the *Maria Ramos* sink off southern Brazil. A ferry with a thousand passengers hits a freighter with a radioactive cargo and sinks her in a Channel fog. A cargo shifts in high winds and the *Islamar Tercero* goes down with twenty-six, somewhere south of the Canaries. Within a few days of one another, the *Dawn Warbler* goes aground, the *Neyland* goes aground, the *Lubeca* goes aground, the *Transporter II* throws twenty-six containers, and the *Heather Valley*—hit by three waves—sinks off western Scotland. The *Chien Chung* sinks with twenty-one in high seas east of Brazil, and after two ships collide off Argentina suddenly there is one. A tanker runs ashore in Palm Beach, goes right up on the sand. The bow noses into someone's villa and ends up in the swimming pool. The *Nomada*, hit by lightning, sinks off Indonesia. The *Australian Highway* rescues the *Nomada*'s crew. The *Blue Angel*, with a crew of twenty, sinks in the Philippine Sea. The *Golden Pine*, with a shifting cargo of logs (what else?) sinks in the Philippine Sea. A hundred and fifteen people on the *Asunción* drown as she sinks in the South China Sea. The *Glenda* capsizes off Mindanao, and seven of twenty-seven are rescued. The *Sofia* sinks in rough water near Crete, abandoned by her crew. The *Arco Anchorage* grounds in fog. On the *Arco Prudhoe Bay*, bound for Valdez, a spare propeller gets loose on the deck and hurtles around smashing pipes. The *Vennas*, with sixty-nine passengers and crew, sinks in the Celebes Sea. The *Castillo de Salas*, a bulk carrier with a hundred thousand tons of coal, breaks in two in the Bay of Biscay. The container ship *Tuxpan* disappears at noon in the middle of the North Atlantic with twenty-seven Mexicans aboard. A container from *inside* the hold is found on the surface. Apparently, the ship was crushed by a wave. In the same storm in the same sea, a wave hits the *Export Patriot* hard enough to buckle her doors. Water pours into the wheelhouse. The quartermaster is lashed to a bulkhead so that he can steer the ship. In the same storm, the *Balsa 24* capsizes with a crew of nineteen. In the Gulf of Mexico, off the mouth of the Rio Grande, fifteen Mexican shark-fishing vessels sink in one squall. In a fog near the entrance to the Baltic Sea, the Swedish freighter *Syderflord* is cut in two in a collision and sinks in forty seconds. About a hundred miles off South Africa, the *Arctic Career* leaves an oil slick, some scattered debris, and no other clues. The Icelandic freighter *Sudurland* goes down in the Norwegian Sea. The *Cathy Sea Trade*, with twenty-seven, is last heard from off the Canary Islands. Off Portugal, the *Testarossa* sinks with thirty. Off eastern Spain, in the same storm, the cargo shifts on the *Kyretha Star*, and she sinks with eighteen or twenty. The *Tina*, a bulk carrier under the Cypriot flag, vanishes without a trace somewhere in the Sulu Sea. In a fog in the Formosa Strait, the *Quatsino Sound* goes down after colliding with the *Ever Linking*. In the English Channel, the *Herald of Free Enterprise* overturns with a loss of two hundred. The Soviet freighter *Komsomolets Kirgizzii* sinks off New Jersey. In the North Sea, the bridge of the *St. Sunnivar* is smashed by a hundred-foot wave. After a shift of cargo, the Haitian freighter *Aristeo* capsizes off Florida. On the *Queen Elizabeth II*, Captain Lawrence Portet ties himself to a chair on the bridge. Among the eighteen hundred passengers, many bones are broken. Seas approach forty feet. After a series of deep rolls, there are crewmen who admit to fearing she would not come up. Off the Kentish coast with a hundred and thirty-seven thousand tons of crude, the tanker *Skyron*, of Liberian registry, plows a Polish freighter. The tanker bursts into flames. The fire is put out before it can reach the crude. Fifty-seven crewmen abandon two bulk carriers in the Indian Ocean. The *Hybur Trader* loses seventeen containers in a storm off Miami Beach. On the same day, off Fort Lauderdale, a Venezuelan crew of twenty-five abandons the container ship *Alma Llanera*. The *Frio*, out of Miami for Colombia, sinks off Yucatan. In the Gulf of Alaska, the

Stuyvesant spills fifteen thousand barrels of Alaska crude. The *Rolandia* —twenty-seven hundred tons—capsizes off France. The Ro/Ro *Vinca Gordon* capsizes off the Netherlands. The *Vishra Anurag*, a cargo ship under the Indian flag, capsizes off Japan. A Philippine freighter capsizes, too, with forty thousand cases of beer. Somewhere, any time, someone is getting it.

Not every ship that goes down is destroyed by time or nature. Or by collision or navigational error. Crews have been rescued from lifeboats with packed suitcases and box lunches. Say South Africa needs oil desperately as the result of an embargo and is willing to pay at ransom rates. You disguise your supertanker by painting a false name, take it into a South African port to discharge the Persian crude, leave South Africa, open your skin valves to replace the oil with water, pack your suitcase, make your sandwiches, leave the valves open until the ship sinks. If you follow this scenario, you will win no awards for originality. Possibly you will collect insurance payments for the ship, and possibly for the "oil" that went down inside her. You may have to explain why there was no slick.

There is a lot of pentimento on the bows of the *Stella Lykes*. Former names are visible, even in fading light. The ship was built in 1964 and stretched in 1982. When she belonged to Moore-McCormack, she was called the *Mormacargo*. After Moore-McCormack died and United States Lines bought her, she became the *American Argo*. After United States Lines died, Lykes Brothers chartered her from financial receivers. Phil Begin, our chief engineer, has said, "We're operating someone else's ship. It's like a rental car. You don't want to come on here and spend a lot of money for one or two years. You want it to be safe and efficient but no more. You put up with irritations. You can't afford to scrimp and save, though. When you read about ships going down, that's what happens."

In Peter Fritz's letters home he avoids mentioning storms. He doesn't want to worry Nancy. On his long vacations, as he leans back, stretches his legs, and watches the evening news, a remark by a television reporter will sometimes cause him to sit straight up. To Peter it is the sort of remark that underscores the separateness of the American people from their Merchant Marine, and it makes him feel outcast and lonely. After describing the havoc brought by some weather system to the towns and cities of New England—the number of people left dead—the reporter announces that the danger has passed, for "the storm went safely out to sea."

g l o s s a r y

admiral. The commander of a fleet. This title also can apply to the admiral's ship.

aft. At or towards the stern part of a ship.

Antarctic convergence. A boundary in the southern oceans where cold Antarctic surface water flowing north from Antarctica sinks under the warmer, southward flowing sub-Antarctic water.

ballast. Weight carried in a ship to give her stability or to provide a satisfactory trim fore and aft.

Beaufort Scale. A scale used to indicate the force of the wind. It was developed in the 19th century by Sir Francis Beaufort.

bilge. That part of the floors of a ship on either side of the keel which is more horizontal than vertical. The bilge is the lowest part of the ship inside the hull, so water collects there.

binnacle. The wooden housing of a mariner's compass.

boom. A spar, traditionally made of wood, used to extend the foot of a sail.

bow. The foremost end of a vessel.

bowsprit. A spar extending forward from the bow of a ship

bridge. An elevated platform built above the upper deck of a ship from which the ship normally is navigated. The bridge also offers the captain or the officer of the watch a view of activities on deck.

bulkhead. One of the upright partitions that form the cabins in a ship or divide the hold into watertight compartments.

capstan. A cylindrical barrel fitted in larger ships on the forecastle deck and used for heavy lifting work, as when working anchors and cables.

dead reckoning. A system of navigation used to chart the position of a ship without the use of astronomical observation.

dodger. A painted canvas screen erected at chest height around the forward side and wing ends of a ship's bridge as a protection against the weather.

fore. At or towards the bow of a ship.

forecastle. (pronounced fo'c'sle).The space beneath the short, raised deck forward. Forecastle also was the name given to the deckhouse on the upper deck of large sailing ships, where the seamen had their living quarters.

gale. A wind blowing at a speed of between 34 and 47 knots, force 8 to 9 on the Beaufort Scale.

gooseneck. A metal fitting on the inboard end of the boom which allows the boom to swing sideways. The gooseneck is hinged to permit some upward movement.

gybe (or jibe). The action at the moment when the boom of the mainsail swings across as the wind crosses the stern.

halyard. A rope, wire, or tackle used to hoist or lower sails.

hawser. A heavy rope or small cable with a circumference of five inches or more.

heave-to. To bring a ship to a standstill by setting the sails to counteract each other.

jib. A triangular sail set by sailing vessels on the stays of the foremast.

keel. The lowest and principal timber of a wooden ship, or the lowest continuous line of plates of a steel or iron ship, which extends the whole length of the vessel.

knock down. When a small vessel is rolled over with her masts and sails in the water by a sea breaking over her head or by a violent squall.

knot. A nautical measure of speed equivalent to 6,080 feet (about 1.15 miles) per hour.

larboard. The old term for the left-hand side of a ship when facing forward, now known as port.

lee. The sheltered side of the vessel, hence the side away from the wind.

mizen (or mizzen). The third, aftermost mast of a square-rigged sailing ship or three-masted schooner.

painter. A length of small rope in a boat used for securing it to a pier, jetty or ship.

pilot. A coastal navigator taken on board ship for the purpose of conducting her into and out of a port or through a channel or river.

pitchpole. When a vessel is turned stern over bow by heavy seas.

pooped. A ship is pooped when heavy seas break over her stern.

port. The left side of a vessel as viewed from aft.

primus. A type of camp stove.

sea anchor. Anything that will hold a ship's bow to the sea in heavy weather.

sextant. A navigational instrument which measures vertical and horizontal angles at sea.

sheet. A single line used for trimming a sail to the wind.

shrouds. Rigging on a sailing vessel to give a mast lateral support.

spinnaker. A three-cornered lightweight sail, normally set forward of a yacht's mast.

splice the main brace. A traditional expression meaning to serve out an extra portion of rum or grog to a ship's crew.

stanchion. An upright bar or stay used to support a ship's deck, awning, or other elements.

starboard. The right side of a vessel as seen from aft.

stay. A part of the rigging of a sailing vessel which supports a mast from fore and aft.

stern. The back end of a ship.

tender. A small vessel temporarily attached to a larger ship for general harbor duties.

thimble. A metal ring fitted in an eye of a sail to prevent wear.

thwart. The wooden seat where the oarsman sits in a rowboat.

winch. A mechanism used for hoisting or hauling which consists of a horizontal drum (capstan) around which a rope or cable is passed.

acknowledgments

Many people helped make this anthology:

At Thunder's Mouth Press and Avalon Publishing Group:
Neil Ortenberg and Susan Reich offered vital support and expertise;
Dan, Ghadah, and Jeri were also indispensable.

At Balliett & Fitzgerald:
Sue Canavan designed the book, found the artwork to illustrate each
selection and helped pilot the collection to harbor; her good nature is
as impressive as her eye. Tom Dyja and f-stop Fitzgerald generously
shared their time and contacts to land permission for some selections.
Maria Fernandez smoothly managed production, despite many other
pressing demands upon her time. Mike Walters and Aram Song kept
things moving.

At the Thomas Memorial Library in Cape Elizabeth, Maine:
The librarians helped us to find many, many books. Karla Sigel
deserves special thanks.

At the Writing Company:
Meghan Murphy gathered books, permissions and facts. Mark Klimek
helped run things and, together with Nate Hardcastle and Shawneric
Hachey, gracefully took up slack on various projects while I read books.

At various publishers and literary agencies:
Many agents and editors supported this project.

Among friends and family:
Bob Doren and Paul Kelly at the Centerboard Yacht Club in South Portland, Maine, took me sailing. Ellen Brodkey generously helped expedite permissions for some important selections. My sons, Abner Willis and Harper Willis, make my day, daily. Jennifer Willis worked harder on this book than anyone: gathering materials, helping to choose selections, tracking rights, negotiating permissions, issuing contracts and doing everything else that had to be done. I would be astonished at such generosity, but she's always like that.

The book was worth doing just for the pleasure of working with Will Balliett. He's always right, and I always agree with him.

Finally, I am grateful to the writers whose work appears in these pages.

Excerpt from *Shackleton's Boat Journey* by F. A. Worsley. Copyright 1977 by W. W. Norton & Company, Inc. Reprinted by permission of W. W. Norton & Company, Inc. ❖ Excerpt from *Rescue in the Pacific* by Tony Farrington. Copyright 1996 by International Marine/Ragged Mountain Press, a division of The McGraw - Hill Companies. Reprinted by permission of The McGraw-Hill Companies ❖ Excerpt from *Adrift.* by Steven Callahan. Copyright 1986 by Steven Callahan. Reprinted by permission of Houghton Mifflin Co. All rights reserved. ❖ Excerpt from *A World of My Own* by Robin Knox-Johnston. Copyright 1969 by Robin Knox-Johnston. Reprinted by permission of the publishers, W. W. Norton & Company, Inc. ❖ Excerpt from *Desolation Island* by Patrick O'Brian. Copyright 1978 by Patrick O'Brian. Reprinted by permission of W. W. Norton & Company, the publishers, and Harper Collins.❖ Excerpt from *The Breath of Angels* by John Beattie. Edinburgh, UK:Mainstream Publishing Ltd., and Dobbs Ferry, NY: Sheridan House, 1995, 1997. Reprinted with permission. ❖ Excerpt from *Albatross* by Deborah Scaling Kiley and Meg Noonan. Copyright 1994 by Deborah Scaling Kiley. Reprinted by permission of Houghton Mifflin Co. All rights reserved ❖ Excerpt from *The Caine Mutiny* by Herman Wouk. Copyright 1951 by Herman Wouk. Used by permission of Doubleday, a division of Bantam Doubleday Dell Publishing Group, Inc. ❖ Excerpt from *The Raft* by Robert Trumbull. Copyright 1942 by Henry Holt and Company, copyright 1970 by Robert Trumbull. Reprinted by permission of Henry Holt and Company ❖ Excerpt from *In Granma's Wake* by Frank Mulville. Copyright 1970 by Seafarer Books. Reprinted by permission of Seafarer Books. ❖ "The Whale Hunters" by Sebastian Junger. Copyright 1995 by Sebastian Junger. Reprinted by permission of the Stuart Krichevsky Agency and Sebastian Junger. ❖ Excerpt from *Ice Bird* by David Lewis. Copyright 1976 by David Lewis. Reprinted by permission of W. W. Norton & Company, Inc. ❖ Excerpt from *Looking for a Ship* by John McPhee. Copyright 1990 by John McPhee. Reprinted by permission of Farrar, Straus & Giroux, Inc.

We have made every effort to trace copyright holders, but if errors or omissions are brought to our attention we shall be pleased to publish corrections in future editions of this book.

b i b l i o g r a p h y

The excerpts used in this anthology were taken from the editions listed below. In some cases, other editions may be easier to find. Two sources are Armchair Sailor Sea Books in Newport, Rhode Island (800/292-4278; www.seabooks.com) and Robert Hale Co., Inc. in Bellevue, Washington (800/733-5330). Internet sources also may be able to locate these titles.

Beattie, John. *The Breath of Angels*. Dobbs Ferry, N.Y.: Sheridan House, 1997.

Beesley, Lawrence. *The Loss of the S.S. Titanic*. Boston & New York: Houghton Mifflin, 1912.

Callahan, Steven. *Adrift*. New York: Ballantine Books, 1996.

Dana, Richard Henry, Jr. *Two Years Before the Mast*. Boston: Houghton Mifflin, 1911.

Farrington, Tony. *Rescue in the Pacific*. New York: International Marine/ McGraw-Hill, 1996.

Junger, Sebastian. "The Whale Hunters." *Outside* Magazine, October 1995.

Kiley, Deborah Scaling and Noonan, Meg. *Albatross*. New York: Houghton Mifflin, 1994.

Knox-Johnston, Robin. *A World of My Own*. New York: W. W. Norton & Co., 1992.

Leech, Samuel. *Thirty Years from Home or a Voice from the Main Deck*. Boston: Tappen, Whittemore and Mason, 1843.

Lewis, David. *Ice Bird*. New York: W.W. Norton & Co., 1976

McPhee, John. *Looking for a Ship*. New York: Farrar, Straus & Giroux, 1990.

Mulville, Frank. *In Granma's Wake: Girl Stella's Voyage to Cuba*. Suffolk(England): Seafarer Books, 1970.

O'Brian, Patrick. *Desolation Island*. Glasgow: William Collins Sons & Co., 1978.

Trumbull, Robert. *The Raft*. Maryland: Naval Institute Press, 1992.

Worsley, F. A. *Shackleton's Boat Journey*. New York: W.W. Norton & Co., 1977.

Wouk, Herman. *The Caine Mutiny*. New York: Doubleday, 1951.

i l l u s t r a t i o n s

CL 3/00